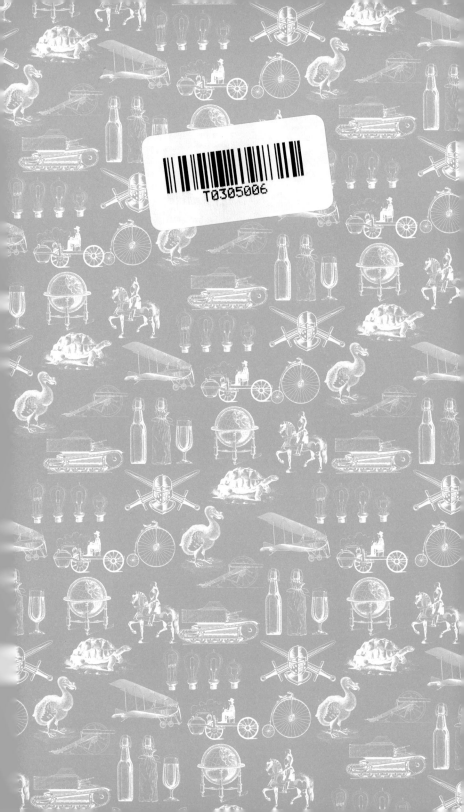

THE HISTORYHIT
MISCELLANY

History Hit makes history more accessible in the digital age. Our podcast *Dan Snow's History Hit* has been broadcasting since 2015, and has over 1,500 episodes. We now have seven regular podcast shows, exploring topics from ancient history to present day. Our online TV channel and app, History Hit TV, is a library of history documentaries and interviews, and we create new and original history documentaries for our subscribers weekly.

You can subscribe to access all of our podcasts and history documentaries at historyhit.com/subscribe.

THE HISTORYHIT

MISCELLANY

of Facts, Figures and Fascinating Finds

Introduction by Dan Snow

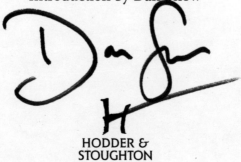

HODDER &
STOUGHTON

INTRODUCTION

Historically promiscuous. That's how I was recently described by a well-known British historian. I think she meant it as a compliment. More than two decades as a television presenter, podcast host and writer have sent me to so many different places and periods. Sometimes for a prolonged stay, like the years I spent writing about the Seven Years' War in North America, at other times just for the duration of a podcast interview as a guest captivates me with stories of the ancient Chinese afterlife, Sumerian poetry, Elvis's health or the Inquisition in Spanish America. I have fallen for them all.

Through it all I have jotted down notes. The surprising, the entertaining, the tragic, the important and the thought-provoking. I stumbled across Roland the Farter, whose particular talent for farting on demand won him the patronage of Henry II. I learned about Enheduanna, high priestess in the city of Ur, daughter of the king, Sargon of Akkad. She wrote beautiful poetry, making her possibly the earliest named author in history. I have amassed a mountain of research, a chaotic mess of different periods and disciplines. In just one week earlier this year I explored Bronze Age passage tombs in the Isles of Scilly, did a session with a traditional shipyard using an adze to shape the sternpost of a wooden ship and finished with an interview with a wartime Mosquito pilot. Every experience yields snippets of history, some given to me by the world's best historians, others gleaned from captions from hundreds of museum visits.

There was something that tickled me about seeing my lists of random facts. Hitler, Tito, Stalin and Freud were all living in Vienna in 1913, not as housemates obviously. In the 18th century, Cock Lane in London was haunted by a well-attested ghost, known as Scratching

Fanny. More Brits were killed in road accidents on blacked-out UK roads for the first six months of the Second World War than were killed in the armed forces. No one in Africa or Eurasia knew what a peanut, tomato or potato was before Christopher Columbus initiated the 'Columbian Food Exchange' by blundering into the Americas.

I never thought my magpie-like collecting of facts and stories would lead to much. But little did I know I was tapping into an ancient literary tradition. Quirky miscellanies with religious reflections, snippets of biblical text, lives of saints and poetry have survived from the early medieval world. They were compiled by hand, shared and added onto with whatever the owner thought worthy. The Nowell Codex is an eccentric, rich blend. It is famous for having the only text of *Beowulf*, but alongside it are a poem inspired by the Old Testament Book of Judith, a biography of one St Christopher and an imagined conversation between Alexander the Great and his tutor, Aristotle. It is one of a handful of miscellanies that together have ensured the survival of Old English poetry.

This miscellany may not prove quite as important, although I suppose there's a chance it will become one of the rare survivors of the cataclysmic 21st and 22nd centuries, a fragment of our culture still pored over 1,500 years hence. But it is certainly inspired by those medieval treasures. It is the product of years of curiosity and collecting. It is also a collaboration by our fantastic team at History Hit. We all contributed the facts, stories, explanations and lists that have enthused us over years of production. We have penned quick explainers of events like the Hundred Years' War or the Iranian Revolution. We have included charts of figures that surprise and provoke, like the number of ships lost by the British to enemy action throughout the Revolutionary and Napoleonic Wars (hint: surprisingly few).

History is everything that has ever happened to anyone who has ever lived. It is a bottomless reservoir of all the bonkers, heroic, awful and weird things we eccentric humans have ever done. We can't help generating extraordinary stories. Lieutenant Hiroo Onoda was a Japanese soldier sent to garrison the Philippines during the Second World War; he was ordered not to surrender, and so he did not – until 1974. One of the greatest ancient Egyptian pharaohs, Hatshepsut, was depicted as a man in physique and dress but was in fact a woman. The planet Pluto was named by an 11-year-old schoolgirl who won the naming competition. Alan Turing would run the 50 miles from Bletchley Park to London if there was an important meeting. Bertha Benz undertook the first long-range car journey in August 1888 to prove her husband's motor car was road-worthy. Colonel Sourd fought all day on horseback at Waterloo, having had his arm amputated without anaesthetic the day before.

Perhaps I find lists of miscellany so fascinating because I simply have a short attention span. Or perhaps after a long day of historical research into a very particular period, a quick list of bizarre trivia assembled from the widest possible span of history is energising, provoking and fun. Like a movie trailer, these miscellanies cherry pick the most engaging bits and fire your determination to see the whole thing. What follows is surprising, shocking, laughable and tragic. Most importantly, like all the best stories, they are true. I would rather curl up with this than a work of fiction.

So dive in. Be promiscuous. Get your head around the fact that for one day only, on 8 September 1944, Bulgaria found itself at war with all four major belligerents of the Second World War in Europe, the USA, USSR, UK and Germany.

And if you're enjoying a quiet moment, and reading this in the corner of a historic hostelry, a pint resting in front of you, remember, since 1872 it's been illegal to be drunk in a pub, so don't get carried away.

Dan Snow

It is an astonishment to be alive, and it behoves you to be astonished.

John Donne

THE COMMONPLACE BOOK

A commonplace book is a kind of historical scrapbook used to compile knowledge. One of the earliest known examples can still be bought from bookshops. The Roman Emperor and Stoic philosopher Marcus Aurelius (r.161–80) kept a collection of private thoughts, sayings he heard and quotations he wanted to remember.

The Enlightenment philosopher John Locke wrote a treatise on commonplace books around the turn of the 18th century, with schemes for indexing and titling, while commonplacing was taught at Oxford University to help student research.

Isaac Newton had a commonplace book handed down to him from his stepfather, and used it extensively as he developed the method of calculus. It is still held by Cambridge University and available to access online in digital format (Newton's Waste Book MS Add. 4004).

Writers such as Robert Burns, Virginia Woolf and Mark Twain all used commonplace books to organise their research and writing ideas. Thomas Jefferson kept both literary and legal commonplace books and Ronald Reagan was a more recent advocate, maintaining traditional headings. These presidential commonplace books have all been published.

FICTIONAL WORKS WITH 100 MILLION SALES

Book	Author	Published
A Tale of Two Cities	Charles Dickens	1859
Le Petit Prince	Antoine de Saint-Exupéry	1943
*Harry Potter and the Philosopher's Stone**	J.K. Rowling	1997
And Then There Were None	Agatha Christie	1939
Dream of the Red Chamber	Cao Xueqin	1791
The Hobbit	J.R.R. Tolkien	1937

*Having sold more than 600 million copies globally, J.K. Rowling's seven-part Harry Potter series is the bestselling book series in history.

QUOTES ABOUT HISTORY

To remain ignorant of history is to remain ever a child.

Cicero

History will be kind to me because I intend to write it.

Winston Churchill

History is a set of lies agreed upon.

Napoleon Bonaparte

We are not makers of history. We are made by history.

Martin Luther King Jr

*Those who do not remember the past are
condemned to repeat it.*

George Santayana

The past changes a little every time we retell it.

Hilary Mantel

History repeats itself, first as tragedy, second as farce.

Karl Marx

We learn from history that we learn nothing from history.

George Bernard Shaw

*I like the dreams of the future better than
the history of the past.*

Thomas Jefferson

Study the past if you would define the future.

Confucius

*The winners write the history, but human history
is a history of constant failure.*

Peter Frankopan

KNOW YOUR STONE AND BRONZE AGE MONUMENTS

The British Isles are rich with monuments that sit outside of recorded history – Stonehenge being the most famous of them all. There are several types of Stone or Bronze Age monument.

MENHIR	STONE CIRCLE	STONE ROW

A solitary standing stone	A circle of standing stones	A row of standing stones

Standing stones, stone circles and rows can be found throughout Britain, with high concentration in southwest England. Despite the prevalence of stone circles, historians are not entirely sure what they are for.

DOLMEN	LONG BARROW	BARROW

A megalithic portal tomb	A long mound, often with many burials	A mound that contains a burial chamber

The highest concentration of Bronze Age remains in Britain is on Dartmoor, South Devon. In the 400 miles^2 of national park, every type of monument above can be found, including 18 stone circles and 75 stone rows.

A dolmen is a large chambered ancient tomb. Megalithic pillar stones hold up a giant capstone. These tombs would have been surrounded by an earthwork, but in many cases these have been weathered away to reveal just the surviving stone structure.

Many dolmens lie on the coast of the Irish Sea in Ireland, Wales and English counties such as Devon and Cornwall. The Brownshill Dolmen in County Carlow, Ireland, is the dolmen with the heaviest capstone in Europe. It weighs 150 tons.

Despite their popularity as a tomb across Northern Europe, Korea has the world's highest concentration of dolmens, with over 35,000 dotted through the peninsula – over 40% of the world's total.

The heaviest dolmen in the world is the Ungok Dolmen in Gochang, South Korea. The capstone weighs in at a monstrous 300 tons. Thousands of men would have been required to shift the huge rock over the tomb.

NOTABLE BRITISH STONE CIRCLES

Arbor Low, Derbyshire : Grey Wethers, Devon : Boscawen-Un, Cornwall : Castlerigg, Cumbria : Stanton Drew, Somerset : Long Meg and Her Daughters, Cumbria : Stonehenge, Wiltshire : Avebury Ring, Wiltshire : Callanish, Isle of Lewis: Rollright Stones, Warwickshire : Duddo Five Stones, Northumberland : Bryn Cader Faner, Gywnedd.

QUITE THE CONFEDERATE COINCIDENCE

On 9 April 1865 General Robert E. Lee surrendered the Confederate Army of Virginia to United States General Ulysses S. Grant. It was the end of the American Civil War, America's bloodiest war to this day.

As he did so he was part of one of history's greatest coincidences. The first pitched battle of the Civil War was at Bull Run in 1861. One of the first shots crashed into a farm-house belonging to Wilmer McLean. He quickly moved his family 120 miles away to the town of Appomattox Court House. Remarkably, it was in this very house that Grant and Lee met and ended the war. He liked to say that the Civil War began in his front yard and ended in his front parlour.

OLDEST KNOWN SHARK ATTACK

The earliest known human victim of a shark attack, referred to as Tsukumo No. 24, lived 3,000 years ago in prehistoric Japan. The victim likely died between 1370 and 1010 BC while fishing or diving for shellfish. No. 24's remains were found in a hunter-gatherer burial site and bore at least 790 deep, often serrated injuries.

The grisly scenario was unveiled after the victim's partial skeleton was analysed. By process of elimination, archaeologists determined that the wounds were most likely caused by a white or tiger shark. The injuries indicate that the victim lost his left hand first while attempting to fend off the shark, followed by the severing of major leg arteries, leading to his rapid death.

While the victim's comrades likely brought his body back to land, his right leg was missing. His detached left leg was buried with his body, possibly placed on his chest. The discovery of No. 24 in 2021 surpassed the previous record of the oldest known shark attack – a 1,000-year-old skeleton of a fisherman on Puerto Rico.

ATTEMPTS ON THE US PRESIDENT

Abraham Lincoln: assassinated – 15 April 1865

James A. Garfield: assassinated – 19 September 1881

William McKinley: assassinated – 6 September 1901

Theodore Roosevelt: shot and injured – 14 October 1912

Franklin D. Roosevelt: unharmed but the mayor of Chicago standing next to him, Anton Cermak, was killed – 15 February 1933

John F. Kennedy: assassinated – 22 November 1963

Ronald Reagan: shot and injured – 30 March, 1981

One UK Prime Minister has been assassinated:
Spencer Perceval – 11 May 1812

ATTEMPTS ON BRITISH MONARCHS

In 1800 **George III** survived two assassination attempts in one day. On the morning of 15 May he was shot in Hyde Park, but the bullet narrowly missed and hit a civil servant, who survived. That evening the king was shot at again at the Theatre Royal in Drury Lane, by a mentally disturbed army veteran, who also missed. George insisted that the play go on.

There were eight attempts on **Queen Victoria's** life. The most serious came in 1850 when Robert Pate struck her on the head with a cane, leaving her with a bad bruise. In 1872 Arthur O'Connor broke into the grounds of Buckingham Palace and raised a gun at her, but was apprehended before firing. The final attempt came in 1882, when Roderick Maclean fired at her carriage near Eton College. Schoolboys beat the shooter before he was taken into custody.

In 1970, a log was placed on an Australian railroad in an attempt to derail the royal train carrying **Queen Elizabeth II**. The incident, known as the 'Lithgow Plot', went without charge. In 1981, a man fired six blanks at the queen as she was riding down The Mall for the Trooping the Colour ceremony. The gunman was charged under the Treason Act of 1842 and sentenced to five years in prison.

The lamps are going out all over Europe,
we shall not see them lit again in our lifetime.

Edward Grey

British Foreign Minister Edward Grey said this on 3 August 1914. It was prescient. Britain declared war on Germany the next day, after Germany did not meet the British deadline to withdraw from neutral Belgium. Britain had entered the First World War, on the side of France and Russia.

Four years of carnage followed, with the loss of over 15 million lives. The map of Europe was redrawn, with the German, Austro-Hungarian, Ottoman and Russian empires all collapsing from the strain. Some twenty years later, Europe was at war again, in an even more destructive conflict than the first.

In the aftermath of World War Two, both Charles de Gaulle and Winston Churchill made reference to a 'Second Thirty Years' War' – the first being the multinational conflict that ravaged central Europe in the first half of the 17th century. While contentious among historians, both conflicts saw appalling destruction and loss of life across a great swathe of Europe, although Russia suffered more deaths in both World Wars than any other combatant nation.

The First World War was originally called 'The Great War', in reference to it being one of Europe's most terrible wars to that point. It later gained the moniker 'World War One' or 'the First World War' due to its relationship to the second. Russia refers to World War Two as 'The Great Patriotic War'.

WORLD WAR TWO LASTED NEARLY 30 YEARS

Stationed on an island in the Philippines, Japanese soldier Hiroo Onoda refused to surrender at World War Two's end. He held out until 9 March 1974, after Japanese explorer Norio Suzuki convinced him to lay down his arms if he could get his commanding officer to visit him.

THE SECOND HUNDRED YEARS' WAR

Of the 126 years between 1689 to 1815 Britain and France were at war for at least 61 of them. It was a giant struggle for global hegemony. The first clash took place in May 1689 in Bantry Bay off the coast of Ireland, the last at the Battle of Waterloo in 1815. Some historians call this protracted period of conflict 'the Second Hundred Years' War'.

SOME 18TH-CENTURY WARS

War of Spanish Succession 1701–15
Ottoman–Venetian War 1714–18
Great Northern War 1720–21
War of Polish Succession 1733–35
Russo-Turkish War 1735–39
The War of Jenkins' Ear 1739–48
First Carnatic War 1744–48
War of Austrian Succession 1740–48
Second Carnatic War 1749–54
Third Carnatic War 1756–63
First Anglo-Mysore War 1767–69
American Revolutionary War 1775–83
Second Anglo-Mysore War 1780–84
Third Anglo-Mysore War 1790–92
French Revolutionary War 1792–1802
Fourth Anglo-Mysore War 1798–99

Along with all of that, the Seven Years' War (1756–63) has also been referred to as the 'first world war' as it was the first global conflict, with over 20 combatant nations.

'It would require a greater philosopher and historian than I am to explain the causes of the famous Seven Years' War . . . indeed, its origin has always appeared to me to be so complicated, and the books written about it so amazingly hard to understand, that I have seldom been much wiser at the end of a chapter than at the beginning, and so shall not trouble my reader with any personal disquisitions concerning the matter.'

William Makepeace Thackeray, *The Luck of Barry Lyndon* (1844)

Luckily he was wrong. The causes of the war that Winston Churchill described as the 'first world war' are reasonably straightforward and not unlike the causes for most wars. Rulers wanted their neighbours' territory. Settlers wanted their neighbours' land.

In Europe, Austria and France were frustrated by the rise of Frederick the Great's Prussia and wanted to reverse his territorial gains. In North America, the Caribbean, Africa and India, the British and the French were in competition for land, influence, slaves and markets. Just as with its more famous namesake, the actual First World War, it was a powder keg waiting for a spark.

That ignition occurred in Pennsylvania when a young British officer, George Washington, ambushed a French scouting force. It triggered a global war. Britain emerged dominant but broke, and high colonial taxation led to the American War of Independence. Washington would feature again, this time leading the fight against the British.

TARRED AND FEATHERED

In rural parts of Scotland and Northern Ireland, a tradition known as 'blackening the bride' was performed in the 18th and 19th centuries. Just before a wedding, friends and family would cover the bride and groom with all sorts of messy substances, such as soot, mud and feathers. This custom was believed to ward off evil spirits and bring good luck to the couple.

WORDS SHAKESPEARE INVENTED

William Shakespeare may have invented as many as 1,700 words. Some, of course, may have already been in use during his time, but it was his deployment of them in his plays that put them into everyday language. But some of the words often attributed to the great bard's invention are:

accommodation : aerial : alligator : arch-villain : bedroom : birth-place : cold-blooded : critic : downstairs : dwindle : engagement : fangled : fitful : foppish : gnarled : gossip : hobnail : hunchbacked : leapfrog : majestic : misquote : never-ending : obscene : premedi-tated : puppy dog : retirement : sanctimonious : shipwrecked : suspi-cious : transcendence : watchdog : zany

---
5 MEDIEVAL ANIMAL TRIALS

1474: In Basel, a rooster was put on trial for laying an egg, feared to contain a cockatrice and to be the work of Satan.

17 August 1487: Jean Rohin, Cardinal Bishop of Autun, ordered all the slugs in his diocese to leave 'and if they do not heed this our command, we excommunicate them with our anathema'.

1494: In Clermont, France, a pig was charged with killing a child in its cradle. Witnesses testified that the pig had entered the house and eaten the infant's face and neck. Found guilty of murder, the pig was hanged.

1510: Rats who destroyed a field of barley were summoned to face trial. Their defence lawyer, Bartholomew Chassenee, argued that attending court would put his clients at risk from local cats and dogs. A reasonable fear of death was a sufficient reason to excuse a human from court. If rats were to be subject to the same laws, surely the same mitigation had to apply? The judge postponed the trial indefinitely.

1516: Officials at Troyes ordered insects who were damaging vines to leave within six days. A counsellor was assigned to the accused, and a prosecutor spoke on behalf of the unhappy residents.

GREEK AND ROMAN GODS

Greek	Deity	Roman
Zeus	King of the . . .	Jupiter
Athena	Reason	Minerva
Aphrodite	Love	Venus
Artemis	Hunt	Diana
Ares	War	Mars
Apollo	Multiple	Phoebus
Demeter	Farming	Ceres
Dionysus	Pleasure	Bacchus
Hades	Underworld	Pluto
Hera	Marriage	Juno
Hermes	Multiple	Mercury
Poseidon	Sea	Neptune

The Romans were famously good at warfare, architecture and engineering, but when it came to the softer cultural side of life more could be desired. The Romans 'adapted' a pantheon of pagan gods from the Greeks, whom they had largely conquered by 146 BC. While Christianity later spread throughout the empire, it was only adopted as the official religion in 380 AD.

Many of the names of Greco-Roman deities have permeated modern culture. All of the planets of the Solar System, other than the one you are currently on, are named after Greek and Roman gods – although only Uranus is Greek, the rest being Roman.

Further afield Apollo is famously the name of the US moon-based space programme. Artemis, Jupiter and Ares are all financial investment managers, Mars is a chocolate bar, Venus is a women's shaving razor and Hermes is both a luxury design house and a postage and logistics company. Greek and Roman gods and goddesses are seemingly all over the place, hidden in plain sight.

Between 264 and 146 BC, the Roman Republic was engaged in a series of wars with another great power for control over the Western Mediterranean: the Carthaginian Empire. These wars were called the Punic Wars; there were three in total. The First Punic War endured for the longest time – between 264 and 241 BC – and was largely fought in and around the island of Sicily. Carthage's ultimate defeat in this war saw them lose control over Sicily, quickly followed by the Romans seizing Corsica and Sardinia.

War erupted between Carthage and Rome a second time in 218 BC, when Hannibal Barca marched his army from Spain, crossed the Alps and invaded Roman Italy. Despite suffering a series of terrible defeats to Hannibal, the Romans ultimately prevailed, defeating Hannibal and the Carthaginians on African soil at the Battle of Zama in 202 BC.

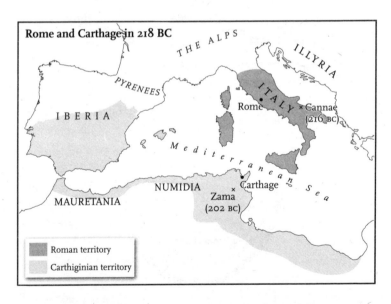

The third and final war between the two hostile powers broke out in 149 BC. By this time Carthage was a shadow of its past imperial self. The Romans invaded Carthaginian territory in present-day Tunisia and besieged Carthage. The war ended with Carthage's capture and destruction in 146 BC.

On 2 August 216 BC the armies of Rome and Carthage met on the plains of southern Italy.

The Roman force was twice the size of the Carthaginians, but the Romans suffered one of their greatest ever defeats, in what was possibly the bloodiest day in the history of warfare.

Outnumbered, the Carthaginian infantry formed into a wedge formation, while the Romans were in straight lines. The Romans moved to attack, but the Carthaginian centre retreated while the flanks advanced. Cavalry battles soon began on both flanks.

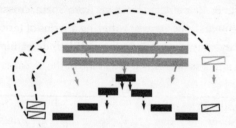

The Carthaginians won the cavalry battle on the west flank. The victorious horsemen then sprinted around the back of the Roman army to attack the engaged cavalry on the other side. In the centre, the huge Roman force advanced into the redeployed reverse wedge of the Carthaginians.

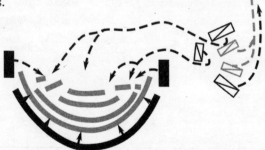

The Carthagian infantry then began to outflank the buckling Roman lines. With the Roman cavalry on both sides routed, the Carthaginians surrounded the confused Romans and began the slaughter. 60,000–80,000 Roman soldiers were estimated to have been killed in a single day.

Elephants were the tanks of the ancient world, and generals found increasingly ingenious ways to armour them so they were very difficult to kill. A large armoured elephant charging at the typical ancient soldier would have been a terrifying sight. Most would never have seen one before, and when it crashed into the line the three-ton animal could easily displace several ranks.

Before his victory at Cannae, Hannibal famously crossed the Alps with war elephants and used them at the start of his war in the Italian peninsula. Elephants are commonly believed to be frightened of mice – although there is scant evidence for this being true. This legend may have its roots in the ancient world, as the Romans deployed pigs to counter the giant beasts. Pliny the Elder reported that 'elephants are scared by the smallest squeal'.

That said, Pliny the Elder's reliability is somewhat debatable. He also wrote of the peculiar Skiapode people, whose single foot could act as a sunshade. Reference to these mythical creatures continued into the Middle Ages.

──────── ROLL OUT THE RED CARPET ────────

The phrase 'red-carpet treatment' comes from the crimson carpet that led passengers to the luxurious 20th Century Limited train on the New York City–Chicago railroad. First launched in 1902, there were only 42 passengers, 5 carriages, a barber shop, gentlemen's club and women's observation car.

──────── ROLAND THE FARTER ────────

The role of a jester in the medieval royal court was to entertain the king. Henry II had a particular fondness for his fool, Roland, who had a special talent for flatulent performance. Each Christmas he performed an act known as 'One jump and whistle and one fart'. Henry was so delighted with Roland's farting that he gave him a manor in Suffolk, with 30 acres of land.

Horses, camels and elephants have all found regular use in military logistics throughout history, along with carrying mounted soldiers quickly into a battle. Beside these stalwarts, there have also been some unusual deployments of animals in combat.

Dragon oxen
Records describing the Siege of Jimo in 279 BC in eastern China tell of a commander frightening and subsequently defeating invaders by dressing up 1,000 oxen as dragons. These were released at the enemy camp in the middle of the night, causing panic among the surprised soldiers.

War dogs
Man's best friend had a variety of roles in World War One. Some combat units had mascots, such as the Boston Terrier 'Sergeant Stubby' who served with the US 102nd Infantry and later became something of a celebrity. Less famous dogs had roles laying telephone wires and carrying messages between the trenches.

Infectious fleas
Japanese aircraft dropped plague infected fleas on Chinese civilians on several occasions during World War Two. These war crimes were perpetrated by the Japanese covert Unit 731, and led to outbreaks of bubonic plague that killed thousands of people.

Explosive rats
In World War Two the British Special Operations Executive filled rat carcasses with explosives, aiming to distribute them in German locomotives and boiler rooms. The first shipment was intercepted by the Germans, and the plan was dropped, but the search for more rats wasted so much German time it was deemed a success.

Dolphin bomb squad
The US Navy created the Marine Mammal Program in the 1960s in which dolphins were trained to locate mines and enemy swimmers. They were deployed in the First and Second Gulf Wars, and the program is still operating.

TYPES OF MEDIEVAL INFANTRY HELMET

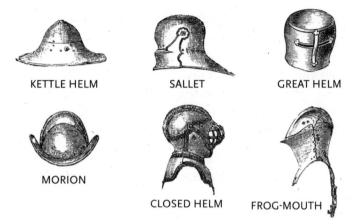

KETTLE HELM   SALLET   GREAT HELM

MORION   CLOSED HELM   FROG-MOUTH

There were many styles of medieval helmet across Europe. Each had the same task of protecting the wearer's head, but each also had advantages and disadvantages.

The more the face was covered, the less the wearer could see, and if the mouth was covered it restricted breathing. Raising the visor to catch your breath and look around could, and did, lead to an arrow in the face.

HELMETS MAKE A COMEBACK

Metal helmets were standard for infantrymen from ancient times through to around 1700, when gunpowder weapons made them all but obsolete. But in World War One, they made a comeback.

Certain aspects of an infantryman's kit made them ill-suited for warfare in 1914. At the war's outset, the British Expeditionary Force wore soft-caps, while the Germans donned the boiled-leather Pickelhaube. The French army even put on bright red trousers during the Battle of the Frontiers. Heavy artillery and shrapnel led to a proliferation of head wounds.

After the destructive power of modern artillery and machine guns was realised, combatants introduced more muted uniforms and steel helmets. The recognisable German steel helmet from both World Wars, the Stahlhelm, was only introduced in 1916.

In 1825, the ruler of Egypt, Muhammad Ali, sent a giraffe to King Charles X of France. She was first transported by camel and then sailing boat to Khartoum, then down the Nile on a barge.

A ship with a hole cut in the deck took her to Marseille, following which she walked 550 miles to Paris, dressed in a coat of yellow taffeta to keep the rain off, along with a pair of boots. When she arrived, 30,000 Parisians turned out to see her. That's one in eight.

NOTORIOUS NICKNAMES

Richard I, King of England, became known as '**Richard the Lionheart**', due to his reputation as a military leader on the Third Crusade. He is one of the few English kings to be better known by his epithet.

John, Richard's brother and king after him, was nicknamed, '**John Lackland**,' by his own father, Henry II, because he was not expected to inherit much land.

Edward Teach, a pirate in the early 18th century, was also known as '**Blackbeard**' for his long, black beard and fearsome reputation.

Robert Burns was born into a farming family and became known as the '**Ploughman Poet**'.

Martha Jane Canary became better known as '**Calamity Jane**'. She acquired the nickname having been involved in gunfights with Native Americans in the 1870s.

Influential Russian peasant **Grigori Rasputin** became known as the '**Mad Monk**', largely after a horror film was released in 1966.

Al Capone, the notorious American gangster of the 1920s, was also known as '**Scarface**' due to the scars on his face from a knife attack.

Erwin Rommel, a World War Two German Field Marshal, was given the nickname der Wüstenfuchs, '**the Desert Fox**', due to his initial success as a tank commander in North Africa.

MEDIEVAL ENGLISH KINGS

Name	Accession	Death	Length
William I	25 Dec 1066	9 Sep 1087	21 years
William II	26 Sep 1087	2 Aug 1100	13 years
Henry I	5 Aug 1100	1 Dec 1135	35 years
Stephen	22 Dec 1135	25 Oct 1154	19 years
Henry II	19 Dec 1154	6 Jul 1189	34 years
Richard I	3 Sep 1189	6 April 1199	10 years
John	27 May 1199	19 Oct 1216	17 years
Henry III	28 Oct 1216	16 Nov 1272	56 years
Edward I	20 Nov 1272	7 Jul 1307	35 years
Edward II	7 Jul 1307	25 Jan 1327	20 years
Edward III	25 Jan 1327	21 Jun 1377	50 years
Richard II	22 Jun 1377	29 Sep 1399	22 years
Henry IV	30 Sep 1399	20 Mar 1413	14 years
Henry V	21 Mar 1413	31 Aug 1422	9 years
Henry VI*	1 Sep 1422	4 Mar 1461*	39 years
Edward IV*	4 Mar 1461	3 Oct 1470*	9 years
Henry VI*	3 Oct 1470	11 April 1471*	6 months
Edward IV*	11 April 1471	9 April 1483	12 years
Edward V	9 April 1483	25 Jun 1483	3 months
Richard III**	26 Jun 1483	22 Aug 1485**	2 years

* Between 1461 and 1471 the crown passed between Henry VI and Edward IV, back again, and back once more, during the tumult of the Wars of the Roses.
** Richard III was killed at the Battle of Bosworth by the forces of Henry Tudor, who was crowned Henry VII, ending nearly 350 years of Plantagenet rule. This is seen as a watershed between the English medieval and early modern periods.

KINGSHIP: A COMPLEX AFFAIR

After the Conquest in 1066, there was still no automatic right of accession to the English throne. This was a hangover from the Anglo-Saxon period in which kings were elected by the Witenagemot (Witan). When a king died, an interregnum followed until the coronation of the next ruler. This allowed space for lawlessness – there is no king's peace without a king – and for interlopers, most notably Henry I and Stephen, the latter's reign being remembered as The Anarchy as he fended off the claim of Henry I's daughter, Empress Matilda. Henry III changed the rules to allow for the automatic succession of his heir in 1272, in part because his son Edward was on crusade.

Four kings were deposed, beginning with Edward II in 1327. There was no mechanism to remove a king, so in Edward's case it was done via Parliament, setting a precedent followed in the subsequent cases of Richard II, Henry VI and Edward IV. Edward V receives a regnal number because he was proclaimed king, but he never underwent a coronation, having been declared illegitimate.

Edward II was presumed murdered in September 1327, but there is some evidence he may have survived much longer. Richard II is similarly thought to have been killed, possibly starved to death, in early 1400, but rumours circulated for many years that he was still alive, possibly in Scotland. Henry VI was killed after Edward IV retook the throne, and the fate of Edward V, as the elder of the Princes in the Tower, remains unknown.

ROYAL KILLJOY

William the Conqueror was the first King of England proven to be coronated at Westminster Abbey. He was crowned on Christmas Day 1066, in line with the customs of the Byzantine and Holy Roman Emperors. Norman guards outside the Abbey mistook a shout of acclamation from the Anglo-Saxon nobility within for a defiant roar. They responded by setting fire to nearby houses, while rioting and looting ensued. Many of the congregation heard the chaos and fled, but the shaken William was still crowned.

THE PRINCES IN THE TOWER

The eldest son of King Edward IV and Elizabeth Woodville, Edward V, was born in sanctuary at Westminster Abbey on 2 November 1470 while his father was in exile in Flanders. Edward IV reclaimed his throne and installed his son as Prince of Wales in 1471. When the king died in 1483, Edward V was proclaimed king. A story then emerged that his parents had married bigamously. Evidence was examined and the charge was considered proven. Edward V and his siblings were declared illegitimate, an absolute bar to becoming king. Edward V and his brother Richard, Duke of York vanished late that summer. Their fates remain a mystery. They may have been murdered, or kept safely. A set of remains in an urn in Westminster Abbey claim to be those of the Princes, but so far, there is no proof that they are genuine.

FORGOTTEN KINGDOMS OF THE BRITISH ISLES

Kingdom	Location	Active
Dál Riata	Eastern Ireland and Western Scotland	500–850
Gwynedd	Snowdonia	400–1216
Dumnonia	Southwest England	500–800
Elmet	West Yorkshire	400–615
Rheged	Northwest England	550–650
The Isles	Isles of Man, Hebrides and Clyde	849–1265

When the Roman Empire retreated from Britain in the early 5th century, it left a power vacuum that saw the establishment of numerous small kingdoms. Eventually, seven kingdoms would emerge in England: Northumbria, Mercia, Wessex, Sussex, Kent, Essex and East Anglia. These became known as the Heptarchy. Scotland would unify. Parts of Wales remained independent until 1283. In England, a gradual process of conquest climaxed in the 10th century. Æthelstan is widely regarded as the first King of the English.

Ken Loach's 1969 film *Kes* is an adaptation of Barry Hines's 1968 novel *A Kestrel for a Knave*. Hines offers in his preface a source for his title of a book aimed at telling the story of a working-class boy's connection to a kestrel he has raised. The quote comes from a structure of hunting birds by social class given in the *Boke of Saint Albans* and another manuscript, Harley MS 2340. The list runs:

> 'An Eagle for an Emperor, a Gyrfalcon for a King; a Peregrine for a Prince, a Saker for a Knight, a Merlin for a Lady; a Goshawk for a Yeoman, a Sparrowhawk for a Priest, a Musket for a Holy water Clerk, a Kestrel for a Knave.'

Rank was of vital importance in the medieval world, and hawking was just one way to display it. A pastime enjoyed predominantly by the elite, it was a form of hunting that women frequently joined in with, typically using a merlin. Many manuscript images show men, women and couples hawking, as well as the odd monkey.

Emperor was the most senior rank of royalty, held in medieval Europe only by the Holy Roman Emperor and the Emperor of Byzantium. Kings came next, followed by princes. The most senior rank of nobility was a duke, followed by a marquess. Next came an earl, or a count in some regions, then barons. The rank of knight was not noble, though noblemen tended to be knights. A lady might be the wife of a nobleman or a knight. Peasants were mostly either freemen, who had some independence, or serfs, who were required to work for others in a form of indentured servitude.

Sumptuary laws, which restricted the right to wear certain colours and materials, also reinforced the class structure. Edward III (r.1327–77) introduced the first of these in England, banning fur for any below the rank of knight or lady. In 1463 and 1483, Edward IV implemented laws to strictly control a range of fabrics and colours. Purple, crimson and royal blue were restricted to royalty. Cloth-of-gold, ermine, sable, satin brocade and velvet were for knights and lords only. Everything about the way a person looked could help you understand their place in society.

CHARACTERS IN GEORGE ORWELL'S
ANIMAL FARM

I am fond of pigs. Dogs look up to us.
Cats look down on us. Pigs treat us as equals.
Winston Churchill

Character	Animal	Historical representation
Mr Jones	Human	Tsarist Regime
Old Major	Boar	Karl Marx
Snowball	Pig	Leon Trotsky
Napoleon	Pig	Joseph Stalin
Squealer	Pig	Propaganda
Boxer	Horse	Workers
Dogs	Dogs	Secret Police

George Orwell's novella about the Russian Revolution, published in August 1945, is a farmyard allegory. After the incompetent Mr Jones is overthrown by the animals, a new regime of intelligent pigs takes over, and a power struggle ensues between Snowball and Napoleon. After Snowball flees into exile, the other animals are gradually forced into oppressive roles. The novella concludes with the famous line, 'All animals are equal, but some are more equal than others.'

THE 8 DE FACTO LEADERS OF
THE USSR IN ORDER

Name	Came to power	Served until
Vladimir Lenin	1917	1924
Joseph Stalin	1924	1953
Georgy Malenkov	Mar 1953	Sep 1955
Nikita Khrushchev	1953	1964
Leonid Brezhnev	1964	1982
Yuri Andropov	1982	1984
Konstantin Chernenko	1984	1985
Mikhail Gorbachev	1985	1991

The Union of Soviet Socialist Republics was officially formed on 30 December 1922, and dissolved 69 years later on 26 December 1991.

Vladimir Lenin was the leader of the Bolsheviks (Communists) before the October 1917 Revolution. Once in power, Lenin set about extricating Russia from the First World War, and then led the Bolsheviks through the Russian Civil War (1917–23). Lenin died in January 1924, leading to a power struggle that Joseph Stalin eventually won. His rival Leon Trotsky was sent into exile, and assassinated in Mexico City in 1940.

Stalin was the longest-serving leader, at 29 years, driving the country with enormous brutality through rapid industrialisation in the 1930s, World War Two and the establishment of the USSR as the superpower adversary of the USA at the beginning of the Cold War.

After Stalin's death, Nikita Khrushchev overcame his rivals and consolidated his position from 'First Secretary of the Communist Party' with 'Chairman of the Council of Ministers' in 1958. He was forcibly removed from his positions in October 1964.

Communist Party power waned in the late 1980s, and Mikhail Gorbachev became President of the USSR, from March 1990 until the state's dissolution almost two years later.

The original story of Atlantis survives from two ancient Greek texts, *Timaeus* and *Critias*, two dialogues written in the early 4th century BC by the Athenian philosopher Plato.

The story centres around a discussion between two Athenians: Timaeus and Critias. The previous day, the famous philosopher Socrates had discussed what he believed an ideal city-state looked like – preserved in Plato's famous *Republic*. Timaeus and Critias had gathered to discuss this ideal city-state; they wanted to know how such a nation would fare in war. They therefore conjured up a scenario. Athens represented the ideal city-state. Its enemy? Atlantis.

In the story, Atlantis was an island nation situated beyond the Straits of Gibraltar in the Atlantic Ocean. Atlantis was incredibly powerful, controlling an empire that stretched as far as the Italian Peninsula. The island nation even had its own divine origin story, founded by Poseidon – god of the sea. Nine thousand years before Timaeus and Critias's time, the mighty forces of Atlantis laid siege to Athens. But the more virtuous Athenians prevailed and defeated their besiegers. The people of Atlantis would descend into further decadence following the failure, with the island nation ultimately sinking into the sea.

That's the original story. Atlantis was created as a literary device to serve as the great nemesis of the ideal city-state, epitomising a once great nation that had declined due to its growing decadence. Before Plato, there is no mention of Atlantis whatsoever. Was Atlantis real? Almost certainly not.

DEN OF INIQUITY

In early 1762, London was gripped by accounts of a ghost called 'Scratching Fanny' who was haunting a lodging on Cock Lane. A press frenzy took off in late January, and crowds gathered at the property, often making Cock Lane impassable. A committee including writer Samuel Johnson concluded the haunting was a fraud.

Born in 1214 and living until 1292, Roger Bacon was a famed thinker who devoured new knowledge reaching Europe from the Muslim Near East. In 1247, he resigned from the University of Paris to devote his time to study, producing his book *Epistola de Secretis Operibus Artis et Naturae*. Bacon is credited with designing a magnifying glass and for producing the first written recipe for gunpowder. Bacon also wrote:

> 'First, by the figurations of art there be made instruments of navigation without men to row them, as great ships to brooke the sea, only with men to steer them, and they shall sail far more swiftly than if they were full of men; also chariots that shall move with unspeakable force without any living creature to stir them. Likewise an instrument may be made to fly withal if one sits in the midst of the instrument, and then do turn an engine, by which the wings, being artificially composed, may beat the air after the manner of a flying bird.'

In the 13th century, Roger Bacon predicted powered ships, cars and aeroplanes. He was also believed to possess a mechanical brass head that could answer any question, like a medieval search engine. Bacon acquired the nickname Doctor Mirabilis – the Admirable Doctor. When we wonder what a medieval person might make of today's technology, Bacon might wonder what took us so long!

ROGER BACON DISCOVERS GUNPOWDER.

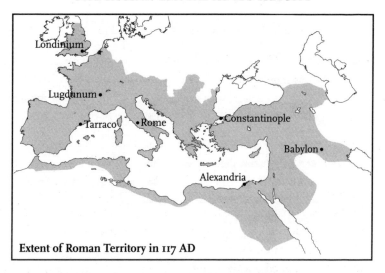

Extent of Roman Territory in 117 AD

The Romans dominated the Mediterranean basin and Western Europe after Julius Caesar's Gallic conquests in the 1st century BC, through to the empire dividing into East and West in the late 3rd century, and the Western empire's eventual collapse in the 5th. The map above was the maximum territorial extent of the empire by the death of the Emperor Trajan, in 117 AD, after he conquered Dacia (modern-day Romania). There were also some vassal states along the northeastern border.

The empire reached this territorial peak during a period known as the 'Pax Romana' or 'Roman Peace', which began in 27 BC, with the reign of Augustus, and ended in 180 AD, upon the death of Marcus Aurelius. There were still wars and conquests in this period, but it was not marked by the civil wars or division that happened in earlier and later periods, particularly from the 3rd century onward.

Walking from the north of England (Hadrian's Wall) to modern-day Baghdad (Babylon) would cover over 3,500 miles by road. This would take six months, so long as you weren't mugged by bandits somewhere along the way. The journey could be sped up by taking a boat where possible. It would take about two weeks or more at sea to cross the entire Mediterranean basin from Spain (Hispania) to Syria.

COMPARATIVE SIZE OF EMPIRES

Empire	Estimated % world	Zenith
British	26	1920
Mongol	18	1270
Russian	17	1895
Qing	15	1790
Spanish	14	1810

At its peak in 117 AD, the Roman Empire covered 3.71% of the world's land surface, making it the foremost power of its time. But the might of Rome pales in comparison with empires that followed it. The provided sizes of empires are estimates, and can also vary between what they claimed and what they actually controlled. Largest of all empires was the British Empire. At its territorial peak in the early 1920s, it covered some 13.7 million square miles.

THE INVASIVE BRITS

According to research, out of the 193 countries that are currently United Nations (UN) member states, Britain invaded or fought conflicts in the territory of 171 countries, which accounts for approximately 90% of the total.

These incursions, which include activities of British pirates, privateers, armed explorers and government-sanctioned expeditions, date back to ancient times, with examples such as the unsuccessful invasion of Gaul (now France) by Clodius Albinus in the 2nd century. However, many of these invasions or conflicts are relatively obscure events, such as British troops taking the Ionian Islands in 1809.

DID THE SUN NEVER SET
ON THE BRITISH EMPIRE?

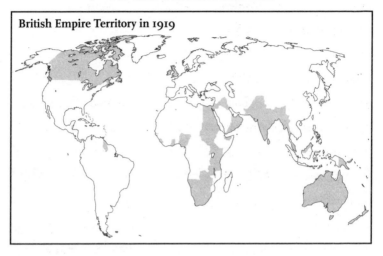

British Empire Territory in 1919

The British Empire was at its largest in 1920, after Britain acquired Germany's East and West African colonies and Samoa through the Treaty of Versailles, following the end of World War One.

At this point, it was true that the sun never set on the British Empire – during a 24-hour day there was never a moment where there wasn't daylight somewhere in Britain's territories. These covered a quarter of the Earth's surface, but included countries that were under protection agreements, rather than being formally under British sovereignty.

The Empire began shrinking almost as soon as it reached its greatest extent as, just two years later in 1922, Ireland and Egypt gained independence. The exertions of World War Two led to its dissolution. By 1967, 20 former colonies were independent nations.

YOUR HOUSE IS YOUR CASTLE

In 1942, Pavlov's House, an apartment building named after its defender, withstood a two-month siege during the Battle of Stalingrad. More Germans died trying to capture it than the casualties they suffered capturing Paris in 1940.

NOTABLE DEFEATS OF THE BRITISH EMPIRE

Battle	Location	Date	War
Monongahela	USA	1755	Seven Years' War
Saratoga	USA	1777	American Revolution
Yorktown	USA	1781	American Revolution
Annagudi	India	1782	Second Anglo-Mysore War
Buenos Aires	Argentina	1806	Napoleonic War
New Orleans	USA	1815	War of 1812
Kabul Retreat	Afghanistan	1842	First Anglo-Afghan War
Isandlwana	South Africa	1879	Anglo-Zulu War
Khartoum	Sudan	1885	Mahdist War
Battle for France	France	1940	World War Two
Singapore	Singapore	1942	World War Two

COMMANDERS' COMPLAINTS

Could I have foreseen what I have, and am like to experience, no consideration upon earth should have induced me to accept this command.

George Washington, first US President, 1775

The Army was and indeed still is, the worst British Army ever sent from England. The General Officers are generally very bad and indeed some of them a disgrace to the service.

Arthur Wellesley, Duke of Wellington, 1810

We are inside a chamber pot, and we shall be shat on.

Auguste-Alexandre Ducrot, French general at Sedan, 1870

The General Staff tells me nothing and never asks my advice... I drink tea, saw wood and go for walks.

Kaiser Wilhelm, 1914

Hernán Cortés's conquest of Mexico was unlikely and surprising. Firstly, he went rogue. The Governor of New Spain, Diego Velázquez de Cuéllar, revoked his expeditionary charter to colonise Mexico, but Cortés left anyway in February 1519.

His expedition was relatively small. He had 600 Spanish infantry, along with 250 indigenous men from the Caribbean acting as servants. He also had a small number of horses and cannons, but his expedition was equipped with muskets and steel armour. The indigenous peoples of Mexico formed their weaponry from obsidian – a form of volcanic glass. Their military capability was pre-Bronze Age.

The Aztecs were not really an empire in the European sense – they did not impose direct rule over a large area. They were an alliance of three powerful city-states in the centre of the Mexican plateau called Tenochtitlan, Tetzcoco and Tlacopan. These had imposed vassal status on other city-states around them, and the total power base was about one-sixth of the land area of modern Mexico. They also didn't call themselves 'Aztecs' – rather they were the 'Mexica'.

As he travelled to Tenochtitlan (one of the most populated cities in the world at the time), Cortés made alliances with indigenous peoples or overcame them in battle, often despite being outnumbered. He would bring them into his growing army, which had over 1,000 natives by the time he arrived in the city in November 1519.

Initially Cortés sought to negotiate with the Aztec Emperor Montezuma, but, after hearing that Spaniards on the coast had been killed by the Aztecs, Cortés took him hostage. Montezuma was killed by his own people on 1 July 1520, or possibly murdered by the Spaniards. Faced by an uprising, Cortés fled Tenochtitlan, losing nearly 900 men and much of his looted treasure.

Cortés returned to Tenochtitlan in May 1521 with a huge number of indigenous allies – likely well over 100,000 – and put the city under siege. The local population was also severely affected by smallpox, carried by the Spanish, who were largely immune. The Emperor Cuitláhuac (Montezuma's brother) died from the disease. The city fell to the Spanish on 13 August 1521.

While a staple of the modern Western diet, potatoes were completely unknown to Europeans before being introduced by the Spanish from the Americas in the late 16th century. Indigenous peoples had domesticated potatoes over the preceding 10,000 years.

Indigenous American people, meanwhile, would have never seen a horse until the Europeans arrived at the turn of the 16th century. Hernán Cortés' 1519 expedition to Mexico took around fifteen horses. How horses then spread across North and South America is something of a mystery, but it is likely some escaped from Mexico City in the 1550s.

Along with the exchange of potatoes and horses, no one from Europe, Africa or Asia had ever tasted a tomato, maize, cassava, chocolate, peanuts, pineapples or a chilli pepper before Christopher Columbus went to the Americas; and no one had ever smoked tobacco.

No American had ever seen a cow, pig, carrot, banana, onion, a loaf of wheat bread or cups of rice or coffee.

American silver paid for European wars and also allowed Europeans to purchase luxury goods from Asia, where silver was scarcer and thus more valuable. While Europeans indulged in Chinese porcelain, silk and tea and fine Indian cottons, China consumed between a half and two-thirds of the silver mined in Mexico and Peru between 1500 and 1800.

A PLAGUE OF SHEEP

In the 1540s, the Mezquital Valley of Mexico featured stands of oak and pine forest and was seen as fit to grow wheat. Within 40 years, Spanish observers recorded an arid region, home to prickly pear cacti and mesquite. What had happened?

Following colonisation by the Spanish, they introduced sheep to graze the land. In fact, sheep were introduced at such a fast pace that they outstripped available resources. Meanwhile the Spanish also deforested the region in pursuit of lumber. Without trees or ground-cover, and with the soil flattened by hoofs, flooding increased and the soil was impoverished. The ecology of the Mezquital Valley of Mexico began to change significantly. What had been fertile, productive land of the local Otomi people became a semi-desert landscape.

HOW TO SPEAK AZTEC

The name 'Aztec' is a 19th-century European creation, deriving from the Mexica's mythical homeland of Aztlan. The Aztecs (or Mexica) spoke Nahuatl (NA-wat), which was the language of the Nahuas (NA-was), who were spread across central Mexico at the time of the Spanish conquest. Classical Nahuatl is closely related to the modern Nahuatl spoken in the valley of Mexico, informing some of the everyday words on this list.

English	Nahuatl	English	Nahuatl
House	Calli	Hello	Pialli
Book	Amoxtli	My name is	Notōcā
Avocado	Ahuacatl	How are you?	Quenin tica?
Tomato	Tomatl	Good	Cualli
Flower	Xochitl	Thank you	Tlazocamahti
Chocolate	Xocolatl	Goodbye	Timo-itazke
Welcome	Ximopanōltih	Let's go	Tiahue

CHEAPER LAWNMOWERS

American President Woodrow Wilson and his wife Edith kept sheep at the White House during World War One to keep the lawn neat and reduce gardening costs. The sheep's wool was also auctioned off to raise money for the Red Cross.

TEOTIHUACAN: AMERICA'S BIGGEST CITY

By the 1st century AD, Rome was probably the biggest city in the world, with upwards of one million inhabitants. In the Americas, the largest city was Teotihuacan, with a population of around 125,000. The huge Pyramid of the Sun and smaller Pyramid of the Moon are the most notable features that remain of the city, which was spread over 11 miles² at its peak in the 5th century. One hundred years later, the city was sacked, and uninhabited by the 8th century.

Teotihuacan lies to the northeast of modern Mexico City. The name would not have been in use during the years it was inhabited, having been coined by the Aztecs in the 1400s. It means 'place of those who have the road of the gods' in the Nahuatl language.

THE FEATHERED SERPENT

Many Mesoamerican cultures revered the Feathered Serpent, and it is present in Olmec, Aztec and Mayan pantheons. At Teotihuacan the third largest pyramid, dating from around 150–200 AD, is dedicated to the god.

For the Aztecs, the Feathered Serpent was known as Quetzalcoatl, and was related to wind, knowledge and the sun, along with being the creator of mankind.

It has been suggested that Montezuma assumed Hernán Cortés to be the return of Quetzalcoatl. However, some historians have disputed the original sources and suggested this was a Spanish-made myth.

EXPLORATIVE POLYNESIANS

The ancient Polynesians were some of the most extraordinary ocean navigators in history. While the Roman Empire dominated the Mediterranean world, groups of pioneering Polynesian voyagers were setting out in their canoes for isolated islands in the world's largest ocean.

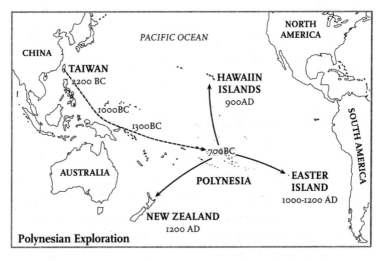

Polynesian Exploration

Did the Polynesians reach South America? This is one of the big questions for scholars of ancient Polynesian exploration. One vegetable might hold the key – the sweet potato. Found across the Polynesian Triangle, the sweet potato originated from South America. This may well be evidence that the Polynesians did reach South America, bringing items such as the sweet potato back with them.

OLL KORRECT

The origin of the phrase 'OK' dates back to a fad for intentionally misspelled abbreviations in 1830s Boston. When witty Bostonians began spelling 'all correct' as 'Oll Korrect', newspapers picked up on the joke. In 1840, US President Martin Van Buren, originally from Kinderhook in New York, adopted the phrase for his re-election campaign and his supporters set up 'Old Kinderhook', or 'OK', clubs across the country. The term may not have saved Van Buren's presidency, but it quickly made the transition from slang to legitimate use.

CAROLINGIAN EMPERORS IN ORDER

Name	Known as	Ruled from	Ruled to
Charles I	Charlemagne	25 Dec 800	28 Jan 814
Louis I	the Pious	11 Sep 813	5 Oct 816
Lothair I		817	29 Sep 855
Louis II	the Younger	844	12 Aug 875
Charles II	the Bald	25 Dec 875	6 Oct 877
Charles III	the Fat	12 Feb 881	11 Nov 887

Charles I, the Great, is better known as Charlemagne. He lived from 747 to 814, ruling as King of the Franks from 768 and as Emperor of the Romans from 25 December 800. His dynasty is called Carolingian, which derives from the Latin for Charles the Great – Carolus Magnus. Charlemagne's father, Pepin the Short, became the family's first ruler in 751 when he became King of the Franks. The Franks ruled much of modern-day France, Germany and the Low Countries. Under Charlemagne's rule, Carolingian authority spread into northern Italy, when he became King of the Lombards in 774.

In 800, Charlemagne was rewarded for helping Pope Leo III against hostile forces in Rome by being crowned Imperator Romanorum – Emperor of the Romans – on Christmas Day. The idea was to resurrect the Roman Empire under a single Emperor. But the eastern Byzantine section, based in Constantinople, also claimed to be the successor of the Roman Empire and became a rival.

Following Charlemagne's death in 814, he was succeeded by his son Louis the Pious. When Louis died in 840 he proclaimed his son Lothair his heir as Emperor. However, Lothair and his brothers Louis and Charles fell into civil war until the Treaty of Verdun in 843 divided the empire between them. Lothair I became King of Middle Francia, a thin strip between modern-day France and Germany that ran into northern Italy. Louis II the German was King of East Francia, a forerunner of modern Germany, and Charles II the Bald was King of West Francia, which laid the foundations for modern-day France.

The phalanx was the most formidable ancient fighting unit in antiquity, before the introduction of the more flexible Roman legionary cohort. Its premise was somewhat simpler – massed ordered rows of men armed with polearms, which allowed several ranks of long spears to be directed at the enemy. From the front, the formation was largely immune from cavalry attack. However, because of its tightly packed formation, it was susceptible to arrow and sling fire.

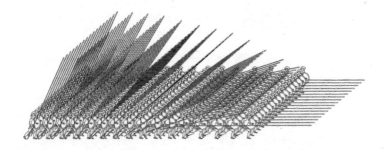

Alexander the Great's father, Philip II of Macedon, perfected the formation through the introduction of the sarissa. Around 6 metres in length, this pike was substantially longer than earlier iterations, and allowed for more ranks of spears to be used. This had a revolutionary impact – by the end of Philip's reign his fragile kingdom controlled much of Greece. His son, Alexander the Great, then took phalanx formations east and conquered the Achaemenid Persian Empire, most famously defeating them at the Battle of Gaugamela in October 331 BC.

HOPLITES

In simplistic terms, a phalanx was a formation, while a hoplite was a soldier. Hoplites were largely free citizens of the Greek city-states, coming from farming or artisan trades to fill the ranks in wartime. They were not commonly professional soldiers, but were able to afford armour and weapons. Phalanx formations of hoplites made up the bulk of the ancient Greek army in the Greco-Persian Wars (499–49 BC).

THE ROMAN LEGION

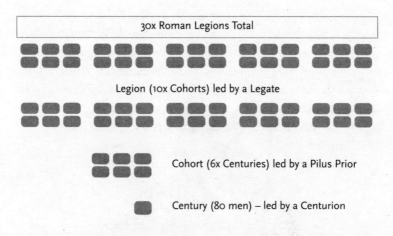

30x Roman Legions Total

Legion (10x Cohorts) led by a Legate

Cohort (6x Centuries) led by a Pilus Prior

Century (80 men) – led by a Centurion

Facing major threats in Gaul and Africa, the Roman army underwent major reforms in 107 BC. These were known as the 'Marian Reforms' after the General and Consul Gaius Marius, who introduced them.

Prior to the Marian Reforms, the Roman army relied on citizen levies, based upon class status, and soldiers had to supply their own equipment, similar to Greek hoplites. Marius introduced the following:

» Opening up the recruitment pool from the lower classes
» Professionalising the army from levies, to a standing army
» Granting Roman citizenship to all soldiers
» Soldiers received land grants and a pension
» The standard unit was changed from a maniple to a cohort
» Army equipment would be supplied by the general

A century was 80 men, a cohort 480 and a legion close to 4,800. Between two and six legions created an army. Unexpectedly, the reforms led to the rise of powerful warlords, such as Julius Caesar, whose infighting caused the demise of the Roman Republic. However, once the Roman Empire was established under Augustus, the legion was crucial to Roman military dominance for centuries.

ROMAN LEGIONARY EQUIPMENT

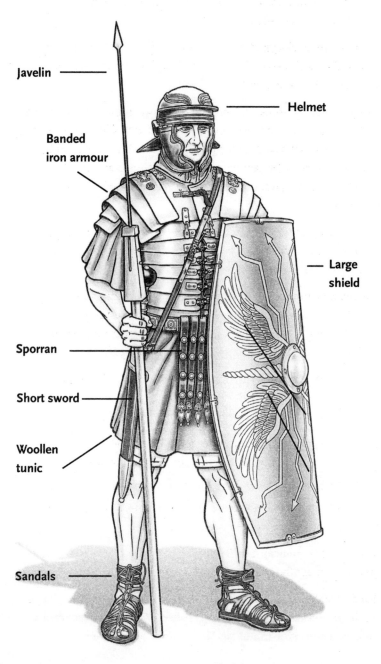

Javelin

Helmet

Banded
iron armour

Large
shield

Sporran

Short sword

Woollen
tunic

Sandals

Helmet (galea): Designed to protect the head from slingshot, spears and swords, complete with a brow plate. The massive backplate served as an elongated neck guard.

Cloak (sagum): Designed to help keep a soldier warm, cloaks could also double as blankets. The cloak itself, and its colour, may have also denoted rank and status.

Javelins (pila): A Roman legionary carried two of these javelins. One of the javelins was more weighted, equipped with a lead or bronze ball attached to the shaft of the pila. This could bend upon hitting a target or the earth, preventing opposing soldiers being able to throw it back. The other javelin style was lighter and did not include this lead weight.

Large shield (scutum): Curved in its shape, the scutum covered a large part of the legionary's body. The iron boss and sharp edges also made it an effective offensive weapon.

Banded iron armour (lorica segmentata): This iconic armour was introduced at the end of the 1st century BC, perhaps in response to when the Romans were fighting spear-wielding Germans. Chain and scaled armour was also used in different periods.

Short sword (gladius): Primarily designed as a stabbing weapon, the gladius had a short, thick blade with a triangular point. The pommels were usually made of bone, wood or even ivory.

Dagger (pugio): A legionary's sidearm. Like the gladius, the tip of the pugio was designed to puncture flesh; the quick widening of the blade was crafted to cause massive haemorrhaging.

Sporran (cingulum): Designed to protect the groin, the cingulum was made of leather with metal plates over the top.

Woollen tunic (tunica): The Romans sometimes also wore trousers (braccae) under the tunic in the colder climates of Northern Europe.

Sandals (caligae): These sturdy leather sandals were designed to let a soldier's feet breathe. In colder climates, the Romans would also wear socks.

When we think of the ancient Romans, tunics and togas are the most commonplace fashion. Trousers, on the other hand, were frowned upon.

According to Edward Gibbon, encircling the legs with bands was 'proof of ill health or effeminacy' in the late Roman Republic. Why? The Mediterranean climate is often more suitable for shorts than trousers, and the Romans saw this in the same way. The standard Greco-Roman fashion was the chiton – a loose-fitting tunic – knee-length for men and generally longer for women.

The Romans also saw trousers as, frankly, barbarian. The Gallic and Germanic tribes to the north had adopted them to combat the colder weather. As Roman territory expanded northward from the time of Julius Caesar, reaching Scotland by the 1st century AD, the military realised trousers could come in handy. Thus some northern soldiers started wearing 'braccae'.

Adoption of their usage in the military is pictured on Trajan's column, unveiled in Rome in 113 AD to depict Emperor Trajan's subjugation of the Dacians. Dacia covered modern-day Romania, so was similarly not as warm as Mediterranean climes.

By the late 4th century, things were going rather badly for the Roman Empire. To counter this decline, Emperor Honorius proposed to ban trousers in the capital. There is probably more sense to this trouser ban than it may first appear. Given trousers were considered military dress, and the Roman state was in a precarious position, banning trousers was a way of distinguishing military personnel from civilians. The logic is similar to the ban on suits of armour being worn in the English Houses of Parliament from 1313.

Additionally, at an uncertain time when barbarian invasion loomed over an empire that had become a melting pot of conquered tribes, perhaps the trouser ban was an effort to re-establish traditional cultural Roman values, setting Romans apart from the trouser-wearing barbarians.

Either way it didn't really work. Rome was sacked by Alaric the Visigoth in 410 AD, for the first time in nearly 800 years.

In the 16th and 17th centuries, facial hair was a sign of manliness. Being clean-shaven indicated effeminacy.

According to the theory of 'humours' that governed the human body, men were 'hot' and 'dry' and women were 'cold' and 'wet'. During puberty, the male body was thought to heat up, pushing out hair into the face as a form of excrement. Beards were a sign that a man was highly virile and fertile – if you can produce hairs you can produce heirs.

A popular beard was the 'peak de bon' – the small pointy beard sported by Sir Francis Drake and Sir Walter Raleigh. Elizabeth I ran her court as if all courtiers were suitors, thus this style became associated with a man wooing a woman. Catholics tended more towards hair removal, so Protestant reformers deliberately grew heavy beards to differentiate themselves.

Later, beards became smaller and thinner. The 'stiletto' was favoured by Charles I and the cavaliers. A 'swallow tail' was more associated with the clergy, whereas a 'square' or 'spade beard' was popular with soldiers, indicating greater masculinity.

Black hair had connotations that a man's body was too hot and aggressive, and their hair had become burnt. This was associated with kingliness, and the Ottomans. Brown hair was seen as the ideal, while red hair denoted deceptiveness (after Judas's red beard), and blond hair was a young man's privilege. Grey hair was inevitably a sign of an older man, symbolising wisdom but also the degeneration of manliness, which was sometimes a cause of derision.

THE SOZZLED PRIME MINISTER

While Winston Churchill's drinking habits have become the stuff of legend, his contemporary, the Liberal Prime Minister Herbert Henry Asquith, outdid him considerably. Asquith became Prime Minister in 1908, leading into a choppy period of British politics of hung parliaments and the First World War. Asquith was well known for his socialising, but particularly his fondness for alcohol. In a time before cameras in Westminster, he was so drunk on occasion that his speeches were noted to be incomprehensible.

In 1911 Asquith appeared on the Government Front Bench 'Very flushed and unsteady in gait' according to Conservative Arthur Lee, and he passed out in proceedings. Winston Churchill wrote to his wife of his embarrassment. By modern standards, Asquith was an alcoholic, and in wartime Cabinet ministers made note of his shaking. He was even labelled 'Squiffy' by other politicians.

By 1916, the Conservatives had withdrawn their support from Asquith's coalition government in favour of David Lloyd George. This led to a Liberal Party schism from which it never recovered, and it has never held power since.

In one of his final speeches in the House of Commons in 1924, Asquith literally drank whisky while speaking.

BAPTISED IN BEER

In early modern Europe and colonial America, a 'groaning ale' would be brewed when a woman became pregnant. The ale would mature over the course of the pregnancy, imbibed by mother and midwife as labour began, and then the remnants of the sterile, 8% liquid washed over the newborn.

SPIRIT PRESERVATION

Rather than bury Nelson's corpse at sea after his death at the Battle of Trafalgar, it was preserved in a cask of brandy stored in the hold of HMS *Victory* for a London burial.

FIRST PINT OF ALE

Beer is one of the oldest drinks in human history and, among beer-drinking cultures, this fortifying refreshment has long joined people in communion. Beer was brewed as far back as the 5th millennium BC in Iran, and we have a receipt for beer from the Sumerian city of Umma, from around 2050 BC. These beers would have tasted more sour, and would have been more nutritious and calorific, than your typical 21st-century pint.

INDUSTRIAL LIBATIONS

One of Britain's preferred beers over the last few centuries is pale ale. Its origins derive from Britain's mid-17th-century coal mines, which produced five times more coal than the rest of the world. When coal was reduced to a purer fuel, coke, brewers experimented with it to malt barley, which resulted in a beer with a unique and enjoyable flavour soon labelled 'pale ale'.

As the Industrial Revolution gained pace it became possible to mass-produce beer. Breweries such as Stratford-le-Bow's Messrs Cook & Co. began milling their grain with steam engines in place of horses. Capable of doing the work of 70 horses (according to one 1810 commentator), steam engines were soon used to pump water, stir mash-tubs, lift casks and transport beer.

The period also saw the growth of pubs. The men yoked together in factories, mills and mines sought diversions in social venues, and the Beerhouse Act of 1830 resulted in a growth of beerhouses. A macho culture developed around these public houses and it wasn't until after the Second World War that social taboos that prevented single women from going to pubs started to break down.

In 1931, Albert Einstein and Charlie Chaplin met at the premiere of the film *City Lights* in Hollywood.

Einstein told him, 'What I most admire about your art, is your universality. You don't say a word, yet the world understands you!'

Chaplin replied, 'True. But your glory is even greater! The whole world admires you, even though they don't understand a word of what you say.'

DID ALEXANDER THE GREAT DIE OF A HANGOVER?

Heavy drinking was nothing unusual for Alexander the Great. Over the course of his reign, we hear of several notorious drinking parties. One infamous banquet saw him hurl a javelin into the chest of one of his best commanders, Cleitus the Black, while he was in a drunken rage. Another drinking bout is linked to the king's early death.

In late May 323 BC, Alexander and his army were in Babylon, preparing for their next campaign. One night, Alexander attended the drinking party of one of his companions – a certain Medius of Larissa. Over the next few days, he developed a fever. His condition worsened as the days went on. Within roughly a week, Alexander's health had deteriorated to such an extent that he was consigned to his bed. Finally, on c.11 June 323 BC, Alexander breathed his last.

The sources highlight Medius's drinking party as this pivotal moment, after which Alexander's health rapidly deteriorated. Some later suggested that a group of his generals had poisoned the king at the party – spiking his wine – but this is unlikely. What's most plausible is that Alexander contracted an illness – typhoid, malaria or pneumonia – that led to his death, at the age of just 32.

Other factors were likely also at play. His many war wounds, his fragile emotional state following the recent death of his best friend Hephaestion and his persistent heavy drinking. So although Alexander almost certainly didn't die, primarily, of a hangover, years of heavy boozing probably played a part in his early death.

THINGS FOUND IN STATUES

Human teeth in the Lord of Patience
An X-ray of a 300-year-old Mexican statue of Jesus, named 'Lord of Patience', found it contained eight human teeth in perfect condition. 'The teeth were probably donated as a token of gratitude,' said head restorer Fanny Unikel upon the 2014 discovery.

Ming era banknote in Chinese sculpture
In 2016, Australian art experts found a rare 650-year-old banknote inside a Chinese wooden sculpture that they were preparing for auction. The note was issued during the Ming Dynasty, and was about the size of an A4 sheet of paper.

Mummified monk in millennium-old Buddha
A 1,000-year-old Chinese Buddha statue was taken to a Dutch hospital for a CT scan in 2017. The scan revealed a mummified monk inside the golden figure with its internal organs missing. The monk was believed to have self-mummified before being encased in the statue.

Everyday letters in wooden Jesus
In 2017, restorers in central Spain found two 240-year-old hand-written notes in the buttocks of a hollowed-out wooden statue of Jesus. The notes were dated from 1777 and depicted daily life in the region at that time. They were signed by chaplain Joaquín Mínguez.

Magazine in Edward Colston's coat-tails
A statue of slave trader Edward Colston was toppled in summer 2020 and tossed into Bristol harbour. When it was retrieved, a copy of a popular 19th-century magazine called *Tit-bits* was found inside the coat-tails, dated 26 October 1895, with the handwritten names of those who had erected the statue.

CHILD PRODIGY

The prolific music maestro Wolfgang Amadeus Mozart was born on 27 January 1756 in Salzburg. He composed his first symphony, Symphony No. 1 in E-flat major, in 1764 when he was just eight years old.

PYRAMIDS, NOT IN EGYPT

Name	Location	Date built	Height
Pyramid of Cestius	Rome, Italy	12 BC	36m
Pyramid of the Sun	Teotihuacan, Mexico	200 AD	65.5m
Tikal Temple IV	Tikal, Guatemala	741 AD	64.6m
El Castillo	Chichen Itza, Mexico	800 AD	30m
Prasat Thom	Koh Ker, Cambodia	921 AD	36m

They're not all in Giza. Egypt has many pyramids outside of the necropolis complex, but further afield Central America has a very large concentration of stepped pyramids, which served more as temples for the Mayan and Aztecs than as places of burial.

The Mesoamerican pyramids were built thousands of years after the Egyptian constructions, with the most famous being finished in the early medieval period.

WATER TANKS

By the end of the first year of World War One, it was clear that traditional cavalry had little place in modern warfare. Middle-ranking British officers proposed to the War Office that they needed a new type of armoured fighting vehicle. Initially the Army rejected the idea, and development was placed in the hands of the Navy.

The name 'Landships' was used for the project, but, in an effort to keep them secret, in 1915 they were labelled 'Water Carriers', because they could be seen as water transports for the front. To give the project more simplicity, they were then named 'tanks'. The British Army first used tanks on the battlefield on 15 September 1916 at Flers–Courcelette (part of the Battle of the Somme).

While some nations occasionally use 'tank' to describe heavily armoured fighting vehicles, many refer to them as 'armour' rather than the British original 'tank'. The German 'Panzer' translates to 'armoured'.

TOUGH LOVE

Letter to young Winston Churchill from his father, 9 August 1893:

> My responsibility for you is over. I shall leave you to depend on yourself giving you merely such assistance as may be necessary to permit of a respectable life. Because I am certain that if you cannot prevent yourself from leading the idle useless unprofitable life that you have had during your schooldays and latter months, you will become a mere social wastrel, one of the hundreds of the public school failures, and you will degenerate into a shabby, unhappy and futile existence. If that is so you will have to bear all the blame for such misfortunes yourself.
>
> Your affectionate father, Randolph SC

THE ROANOKE DISAPPEARANCE

Governor John White founded the Roanoke Colony, in present-day North Carolina, in July 1587 on Roanoke Island. White's granddaughter, Virginia Dare, was born in Roanoke Colony on 18 August 1587, making her the first English child born in the New World.

White left shortly after to return to England. When he came back to the colony in 1590, everyone had disappeared. The only clue was the word 'CROATOAN' etched into a fencepost and 'CRO' on a tree. The word referred to the Croatoan Native American tribe and a nearby island. The disappearance of the settlers has led to various theories and archaeological studies, but no definitive answers have been found. Virginia Dare's fate, along with that of the rest of the settlers, remains a mystery.

MY TOMB IS BIGGER THAN YOURS

The tumulus of King Alyattes at Bin Tepe, Turkey was built around 560 BC. It has a diameter of 360 metres at its base and a height of 61 metres. While not as tall as the Great Pyramid of Khufu at Giza, Egypt, which is twice the height at 139m, the tumulus has a much greater diameter. The Great Pyramid is only a paltry 220 metres at its base.

WHAT IS A VIKING REALLY?

The Viking Age 793–1066 AD was marked by migration, settlement and conquest by Scandinavian peoples across Europe. Viking colonies were founded from Greenland to Ukraine, with significant settlements in eastern England, Normandy and southern Italy.

'Viking' means 'raider' or 'pirate' in Old Norse, and 'the Vikings' would not have called themselves that – there was no 'Kingdom of the Vikings', for instance. The 'Vikings' as a group could be geographically defined as 'Scandinavians'.

THE VIKINGS' TAKE

In the 9th century, Vikings captured some 15% of the West Frankish kingdom's money, a figure enlarged by mighty payoffs such as the 7,000 livres of silver and gold (some 2,500kg) ransomed from Charles the Bald to lift the Siege of Paris in 845 AD. In the 10th century, perhaps as many as 125 million silver dirhams from the Abbasid Caliphate went to Vikings as payment for slaves and furs.

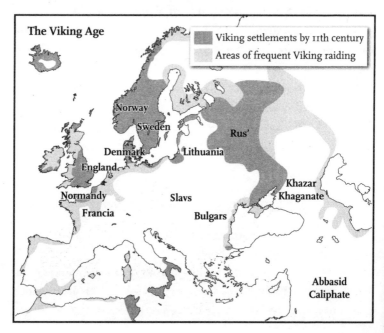

The Viking Age

Viking settlements by 11th century
Areas of frequent Viking raiding

Norway
Sweden
Rus'
Denmark
Lithuania
England
Khazar
Normandy
Slavs
Khaganate
Francia
Bulgars
Abbasid
Caliphate

Vikings have a reputation for raiding and pillaging - hence the name. In Western Europe they ransacked monasteries, besieged cities and occupied parts of England. The Danes and Norwegians were often a violent menace to the Christian kingdoms.

The Swedes had easier access to Eastern Europe across the Baltic Sea, and from there they could reach the great rivers of the Dnieper and Volga. Their narrow, shallow draft boats allowed them to row down these waterways, and they became known as the Rus', which descended from the Old Norse 'those who row.' This word now forms part of the country names of Russia and Belarus.

Eastern Viking activity was less violent than in Western Europe, with the Rus' focusing on trade. They created a river network that stretched from the Baltic down to the Black Sea, reaching as far south as Constantinople and the Abbasid Caliphate, which was a rising power in the Middle East. More Viking archaeological remains have been found in the east than the west.

While these enterprising Vikings traded resources from furs to wine, perhaps their biggest venture was human trafficking. Slaves were taken from Western Europe and brought to Scandinavia, but rarely traded amongst the Christian kingdoms, who had largely abandoned the practice. In the east, slavery was much more common, and the word 'slave' possibly derives from the Slavic people who were taken and traded on slave markets, largely for silver. Islamic silver dirham coins spread throughout the Viking trading network, and have been found in dig sites in England.

VIKING LONGSHIPS

The success of the Vikings can be in part attributed to their ship-building techniques. The longship was a design pioneered in Scandinavia and its success was largely down to its incredible versatility. The hull was made from overlapping planks of timber, nailed together and waterproofed by sealing the joints with animal fat or tar.

They were long and narrow with shallow draughts, which meant they could navigate deep and shallow water. As well as crossing the sea, they could navigate rivers and make beach landings, making them perfect for travelling, attacking and trading. Powered by oars and often a single large woollen sail, probably stiffened with leather strips, some Viking ships are believed to have been capable of speeds of up to 15 knots (17 mph or 28 kmh).

COLD WAR REACHES BOILING POINT

While the world watched the tensions between the Soviet Union and the United States during the Cuban Missile Crisis in October 1962, they didn't know just how close they came to destruction. The US Navy dropped harmless depth charges on a submerged Russian submarine off the coast of Cuba to try and force it to surface.

The crew, believing that World War Three had begun, argued whether they should launch the nuclear torpedo that they had on board, and came close to a unanimous vote to launch. Luckily, Senior Officer Vasili Arkhipov cast the one vote needed to stop the impending destruction.

SHIP LOSSES DURING THE
FRENCH WARS 1793–1815

	British	French	Spanish	Danish	Dutch
Captured	51	279	57	1	93
Wrecked	135	9			
Destroyed	5	99	19	14	4
Mutinied	5				1
Scrapped	7				
Total	203	387	76	15	98

The wars between France and neighbouring powers ravaged Europe for more than two decades. Napoleon's Grande Armée initially was remarkably successful, but he later encountered a number of setbacks, starting with the Peninsular War (1808–14) and the terminal invasion of Russia (1812). The British dominance in the war at sea was also crucial in France's eventual defeat.

The large number of British ships wrecked is evidence that, while its enemies' fleets were blockaded in port, the Royal Navy maintained year-round operations at sea in all weathers.

If the wrecked ships are taken out of the equation the gigantic disparity in losses becomes very clear:

» Britain lost 56 ships to enemy action.
» It inflicted 566 losses on its enemies.
» The French lost the equivalent of one warship a month, for the two-decades-long war.

THE CONTENTIOUS DARK AGES

Perhaps the most contentious naming of a historical period is the 'Dark Ages'. It generally refers to the early medieval period, from the fall of Rome in the 5th century to the end of the Viking Age in the 11th century, but it can also tarnish the entire medieval period up to (roughly) 1500.

Francesco Petrarca (known as Petrarch), an Italian scholar of the 14th century, was the first person to use the term 'Dark Ages'. He was referring to the lack of literature available from the period, compared to the numerous surviving sources from the classical period. The term then gained greater usage during the 18th-century Enlightenment, when many philosophers felt the religious dogma of the medieval period did not sit well within the new 'Age of Reason'.

A 'Dark Age' is also a negative term that refers to a lack of progress, as opposed to a 'Golden Age', which is often used in reference to cultural, economic or military expansion. However, using a pejorative term to describe 1,000 years of European history does not stand up to much scrutiny.

536: THE WORST YEAR IN HISTORY?

The year 536 AD was a very bad year, and the next 25 years were pretty apocalyptic. This period was, quite literally, darker. Starting in 536 AD a series of volcanic eruptions sprayed so much soot into the atmosphere that the temperature of Europe dropped by 2.5 degrees Celsius. This is a drop of halfway to the temperature of the Last Ice Age in one year.

Further volcanic mega eruptions continued over the next decade, causing widespread famine due to lack of sunlight and drops in global temperature. To make matters worse, the Plague of Justinian struck in 541 AD, killing a fifth of the population of Byzantium. That's a dark age.

14TH CENTURY: THE WORST?

The 14th century was a particularly bad period to be alive in Europe. In 1315 the Medieval Warm Period abruptly ended with heavy rainfall, and much of Europe suffered treacherous flooding. The population had been growing quickly in the medieval era, but the bad weather led to widespread food shortages – and the period 1315–17 became known as the 'Great Famine'.

A second widespread catastrophe occurred from 1346, with the sweep of bubonic plague. This was the most fatal pandemic in history, estimated to have caused population drops of 30–50% in Europe. The first phase of the pandemic was over by 1353, but resurgences of the plague were common in the coming decades.

This was marked by further strife. Northern France suffered devastation from English pillaging in the first phase of the Hundred Years' War, which slowed population recovery from the Black Death. The wars continued until the mid-15th century, and it took 200 years for the population to return to its pre-plague level.

By the 1380s, the dramatic drops in population had led to an acute labour shortage, and peasants could charge far more for their labour. Economic disputes and high taxation led to near anarchy, with organised uprisings occurring through Northern Europe. In the Holy Roman Empire between 1336 and 1525, there were at least 60 instances of peasant unrest.

ANIMALS EATEN TO EXTINCTION

Eurasian Aurochs (1627) : Dodo (1681) : Steller's Sea Cow (1768) : Great Auk (1844) : Passenger Pigeon (1914) : Bubal Hartebeest (1954)

The woolly mammoth is commonly thought of as an animal eaten to extinction in the second millennium BC. However, the mammoth was in decline from the end of the Last Ice Age (around 25,000 years ago), and the large mammal had largely disappeared from Europe by 10,000 BC. Isolated populations continued on Arctic islands, but the mammoth was probably the victim of climate change more than human hunting.

PIONEERING FIRSTS

First to . . .	Date	Name
Sail the globe in a boat	Sep 1522	Ferdinand Magellan
Fly in a powered aircraft	17 Dec 1903	The Wright Brothers
Reach the North Pole	21 April 1908	Frederick Cook
Reach the South Pole	14 Dec 1911	Roald Amundsen
Fly solo across the Atlantic	20–21 May 1927	Charles Lindbergh
Break the sound barrier	14 Oct 1947	Chuck Yeager
Climb Mount Everest	29 May 1953	Sir Edmund Hillary
Reach outer space	12 April 1961	Yuri Gagarin
Walk on the moon	20 Jul 1969	Neil Armstrong

Many of the above pioneers worked in teams with crew, although the people named were leaders of the expeditions:

Ferdinand Magellan's circumnavigation of the globe took six ships, with about 270 men. One of these ships completed the voyage. Magellan himself was killed in April 1521 before his expedition returned to Spain.

Frederick Cook's expedition allegedly made it to the North Pole on 21 April 1908, while **Robert Peary's** claimed to have reached it on 6 April 1909. Both arrivals are disputed.

Roald Amundsen's successful expedition to the South Pole was with four other men: **Olav Bjaaland**, **Helmer Hanssen**, **Sverre Hassel** and **Oscar Wisting.**

Sir Edmund Hillary's first summiting of Everest occurred with his team-mate, the Nepali **Tenzing Norgay**.

Pioneers of the Space Race had tens of thousands of people working with them on the projects. **Yuri Gagarin** and **Neil Armstrong's** achievements were the very tip of an iceberg.

FIRST UP EVEREST?

On 29 May 1953 Sir Edmund Hillary, along with Sherpa Tenzing Norgay, became the first to reach the summit of Mount Everest. Or were they?

British mountaineers George Mallory and Andrew 'Sandy' Irvine disappeared during their attempt to climb Everest on 8 June 1924. After setting out from their high camp towards the summit, they were last spotted a few hundred metres below it by a fellow climber.

So did they die on their way up – or on their way down?

Mallory's body was found in 1999, and, although impossible to determine, evidence suggested he had fallen to his death while descending from the summit.

A pair of undamaged sun-goggles were found inside one of his pockets (which Mallory would not have dispensed with if climbing in daylight due to snow-blindness risks), suggesting the summit push had been completed in sunlight and they were making their descent after dark. Mallory was also known to be carrying a photograph of his wife, Ruth, which he vowed to leave on the summit. The photo was not found on his body, even though his wallet and other papers were intact.

Ernest Shackleton's Imperial Trans-Antarctic Expedition departed in 1914 with the aim of crossing Antarctica for the first time. In January 1915, the expedition's ship *Endurance* became trapped in the ice of the Weddell Sea. By October, the ice had snapped her beams and torn off her rudder. On 21 November, she sank.

The stranded crew camped on drifting ice floes for several more months before sailing in small lifeboats to Elephant Island. On 24 April 1916, Shackleton led a smaller crew of five men onboard the 20-foot-long *James Caird* a distance of 800 nautical miles to South Georgia Island. Their mission was to secure the rescue of their companions left behind.

They arrived on 9 May, traversing the island's mountainous interior to reach the Stromness whaling station. Thirty-two miles and thirty-six hours of snow-covered terrain later, they reached the station. Shackleton then picked up three men he had left on the south of the island and set about the rescue of the men at Elephant Island. Initially blocked by ice, Shackleton did not arrive aboard the Chilean steamer *Yelcho* until 30 August 1915. Two years after setting off, all 28 men on *Endurance* were rescued.

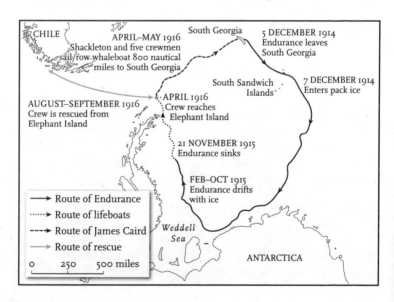

After a hiatus in Arctic and Antarctic exploration following Shackleton's *Endurance* expedition and World War One, it resumed in the 1920s with the increasing use of aircraft and mechanised transportation.

12 May 1926: Airship *Norge* with Roald Amundsen on board flies from Spitsbergen to Alaska non-stop over the North Pole.

December 1928: Hubert Wilkins and Carl Ben Eielson make first successful flight over the Antarctic continent.

1947–8: Finn Ronne proves Antarctica is a single continent after mapping hundreds of thousands of square miles of unexplored territory.

1955–58: Commonwealth Trans-Antarctic Expedition headed by Vivian Fuchs and Edmund Hillary makes first overland crossing of Antarctica.

6 April 1969: Sir Wally Herbert becomes the first person to reach the North Pole on foot (using dog-sleds, supported by airdrops).

2 May 1986: Ann Bancroft becomes the first woman to trek to the North Pole (using dog-sleds).

30 March 1988: Aged 50, Helen Thayer becomes the first woman to trek solo on foot and unsupported to the magnetic North Pole.

17 January 1989: Victoria Murden and Shirley Metz are the first women to reach the South Pole by land (using skis, support of snow-mobiles and resupplies).

February 1993: Sir Ranulph Fiennes and Dr Mike Stroud become the first people to cross the Antarctic continent unsupported.

23 April 1994: Børge Ousland becomes the first person to walk solo and unsupported to the North Pole.

23 January 2012: Felicity Aston becomes the first woman to ski solo across Antarctica.

26 December 2018: Colin O'Brady completes the first solo, unsupported, completely human-powered crossing of Antarctica.

THE TOWER OF LONDON 'ZOO'

The Tower of London's use as a zoo dates back to King John (1199–1216) with records showing payments to lion keepers.

The animal menagerie grew during the reign of Henry III (1216–72), who first received three 'leopards' as a gift from the Holy Roman Emperor Frederick II in 1235. These were probably lions, but referred to as leopards to match the king's heraldry. The lions were joined by a polar bear in 1252 (which was allegedly allowed to hunt and swim in the River Thames) and an African elephant in 1255. The permanent home for the menagerie was built at the western entrance to the Tower during the reign of Edward I (1272–1307). It became known as the 'Lion Tower'.

The menagerie was internationally renowned for the next 600 years, until London Zoo was opened in 1828. The Lion Tower was demolished and the menagerie finally closed in 1835.

THE PIGEON WHO SAVED A BATTALION

Carrier pigeons were commonly used for battlefield communication in World War One.

After initial success in September 1918, the American Meuse-Argonne Offensive stalled. On 2 October, over 500 troops of the 77th Division, under Major Charles Whittlesey, were ordered to attack into the Argonne Forest. Despite capturing high ground, counterattacks saw Whittlesey's men surrounded.

German defences thwarted several carrier pigeon messages. Furthermore, on 4 October, American artillery launched friendly fire on Whittlesey's position. In desperation, another pigeon, Cher Ami, was sent. Despite being shot through the chest and wounding its leg, the pigeon broke through enemy lines and delivered the critical message: 'We are along the road parallel to 276.4. Our own artillery is dropping a barrage directly on us. For heaven's sake stop it.'

The Allied bombardment ceased, facilitating the Lost Battalion's eventual survival – their lives saved thanks to the plucky pigeon. Cher Ami was awarded the prestigious French Croix de Guerre.

STRANGE LAWS

It's been illegal to wear a suit of armour in the UK Parliament since 1313.

Russia in 1698 declared that all citizens (except clergy and peasants) must be clean-shaven.

In Quitman, Georgia, USA, it is illegal to allow chickens to cross the road.

The UK Licensing Act of 1872 makes it illegal to be drunk in a pub.

In Milan, city regulations from Austro-Hungarian times make it a legal requirement to smile at all times.

Châteauneuf-du-Pape, in France, made it illegal to land a flying saucer in the town in 1954.

THE ORIGINS OF VALENTINE'S DAY

The origins of St Valentine's Day as a celebration of love are unclear, but the association was made in the late 15th century. The first recorded Valentine's letter in England was written in 1477 and appears among the Paston Letters, a collection of papers maintained by the Paston family of Norfolk.

OLDEST RESTAURANTS

The restaurant holding the official Guinness World Record for being the 'oldest' is the Casa Botín in Madrid, Spain. While older places exist, it takes top spot because it has operated continuously out of the same 16th-century premises for its entire 300-year history.

Meanwhile, St. Peter Stiftskulinarium, a restaurant within the grounds of St Peter's Abbey in Salzburg, Austria, was first mentioned in 803 AD by Alcuin of York, an English scholar who worked for Charlemagne. It has closed a few times and undergone extensive remodelling over the intervening 1,200 years.

Harold Godwinson exiled his brother Tostig. When Tostig invaded with Harald Hardrada's Viking army, he was killed by his brother's forces at the Battle of Stamford Bridge.

William II never got on with his older brother Robert. He and another brother, Henry, had once dumped a full chamber pot on his head as children. As adults they fought for control of Normandy and England.

Henry I became king after a very unfortunate, certainly not deliberate, accident that saw his big brother William II killed out hunting. Henry continued fighting his older brother Robert and eventually imprisoned him for decades.

Henry II's sons, Henry, Richard the Lionheart, John and Geoffrey fought him and each other. In 1203 John almost certainly had Geoffrey's son killed.

Edward IV had his brother George Duke of Clarence killed. In what may have been the strangest death of the Wars of the Roses, George was reportedly drowned in a vat of malmsey wine.

Charles II's illegitimate sons, the Dukes of Monmouth and Grafton, fought on opposite sides at the Battle of Sedgemoor in July 1685. Monmouth was defeated and executed.

Mary and **Anne** both excluded their little half-brother James 'The Old Pretender' from the throne.

Edward VIII had a little brother John, 11 years younger. He was disabled, and upon his death Edward said he had been 'little more than a regrettable nuisance'.

George VI forbade members of the Royal Family to attend his older brother (the former Edward VIII) the Duke of Windsor's wedding. The Duke regularly called George to yell at him about money and the Duchess's royal status. Meanwhile another brother, the Duke of Kent, said in 1942 that the king and queen were 'inept, ineffectual and inexpert and had no influence in Whitehall, Westminster or anywhere.'

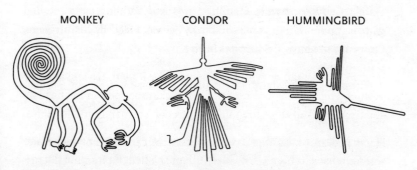

MONKEY   CONDOR   HUMMINGBIRD

The Nazca Lines are some of the world's most extraordinary geoglyphs. Located in the Nazca Desert in southern Peru, there are more than 1,000 'Lines', most of which are simply lines, but some shapes are of animals, plants, trees, hands and geometric designs. They were made by the ancient Nasca culture, who inhabited this area of Peru c. 2,000 years ago. When talking about the ancient culture, Nasca is spelled with an 's'. When talking about the geographic region, it is spelled with a 'z'.

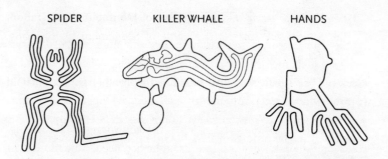

SPIDER   KILLER WHALE   HANDS

There are various speculations on their purpose. One disputed theory is that they related to astronomy and cosmology. They may also have been part of an irrigation system.

Swiss author Erich von Däniken speculated in his 1968 bestseller *Chariots of the Gods?* that the lines were created by visiting aliens. Scientists and archaeologists have declared his ideas absurd, proving that the Nasca would have had the tools to create them.

THE LOST VILLAGE OF IMBER

With its simple church, quaint houses and winding lanes, at first glance Imber looks much like any other rural English village. However, since 1943 Imber has been part of the UK's largest military training area.

Situated on Salisbury Plain, the 94,000-acre site was requisitioned by the War Office in November 1943, on the promise that it would be returned to the residents six months later. Residents were given 47 days' notice to pack up and leave their homes, and the village was then used to train US military troops in street fighting, in preparation for the Allied invasion of Europe. However, despite multiple campaigns in the 80-plus years since, the villagers have never been permitted to return.

Today, access to the village is limited. Since 2009, the annual summer opening of the village has been served by up to 25 vintage and new Routemaster and red double-decker buses, which depart from Warminster and stop at other points on Salisbury Plain including Imber on a regular bus timetable.

ROTTEN BOROUGHS

In the 18th century some parliamentary constituencies had lost so much of their medieval populations that they only had a handful of electors. The voting was also public, so the local landowner could control who went to Parliament. The landowner instructed tenants who to vote for and threatened eviction if they did not comply. These constituencies became known as Pocket or 'Rotten' Boroughs. Each one of them returned two MPs.

Here are some of the most egregious examples:

» Old Sarum, Wiltshire, 7 voters
» Gatton, Surrey, 7 voters
» Newtown, Isle of Wight, 23 voters
» Dunwich, Suffolk, 32 voters
» East Looe, Cornwall, 38 voters

Village	County	Date	Reason
Chysauster	Cornwall	4th–5th century	Unknown
Dunwich	Suffolk	14th century	Coastal Erosion
Northeye	Sussex	14th century	Coastal Erosion
Hundotura	Devon	1350s	Black Death
Upton	Gloucestershire	14th century	Economic
Quarrendon	Buckinghamshire	16th century	Economic
Godwick	Norfolk	16th century	Economic
Wharram Percy	North Yorkshire	16th century	Economic
Hampton Gay	Oxfordshire	19th century	Economic
Tyneham	Dorset	1943	World War Two

There are around 3,000 deserted settlements across Britain. Population decline was often caused by the Black Death, monastery dissolution during the Reformation and economic change during the Industrial Revolution, or a combination of all three. Chysauster was most likely abandoned after the Romans left Britain.

Several villages have also been the victim of flooding or destruction by coastal storms. Dunwich in Suffolk was a thriving medieval trading port, and possibly the biggest town in East Anglia during the Norman period. It was first hit hard by a storm in 1286, with further erosion and flooding coming in 1328, 1347 and 1362.

Similar to the village of Imber, the residents of Tyneham, Dorset, were moved due to military activity during World War Two.

Sputnik 1, 4 Oct 1957: First human-made object (satellite) into space. It transmitted a radio signal back to Earth for three weeks before its batteries ran out, yet orbited Earth for three months.

Sputnik 2, 3 Nov 1957: Carried a dog named Laika, the first animal into orbit. She died of overheating on the craft's fourth orbit.

Luna 1, 2 Jan 1959: First spacecraft to reach the vicinity of Earth's Moon and fly by it. First man-made object to escape Earth's gravity. First data communications to and from outer space.

Sputnik 5, 19 Aug 1960: First animals (two dogs) and a range of plants are returned alive from space.

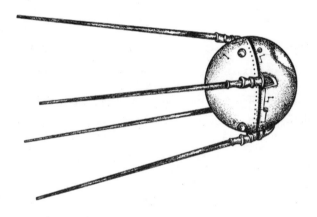

Vostok 1, 12 Apr 1961: First human in space and first to orbit Earth – Yuri Gagarin makes a single orbit around Earth, spending 1 hour and 48 minutes in space.

Vostok 6, 16 Jun 1963: First civilian and first woman in space – Valentina Tereshkova. She spent almost three days in space, orbiting Earth 48 times.

Voskhod 2, 18–19 Mar 1965: First human spacewalk by Alexei Leonov, lasting 12 minutes.

Zond 5, Sep 1968: First spaceship to travel to and circle the moon.

ASTRONAUTS WHO HAVE WALKED ON THE MOON

Name	Date	Mission
Neil Armstrong	20 Jul 1969	Apollo 11
Edwin 'Buzz' Aldrin	20–21 Jul 1969	Apollo 11
Charles 'Pete' Conrad Jr	19–20 Nov 1969	Apollo 12
Alan Bean	19–20 Nov 1969	Apollo 12
Alan Shepard	5–6 Feb 1971	Apollo 14
Edgar Mitchell	5–6 Feb 1971	Apollo 14
David Scott	31 Jul–2 Aug 1971	Apollo 15
James Irwin	31 Jul–2 Aug 1971	Apollo 15
John W. Young	21–23 Apr 1972	Apollo 16
Charles M. Duke	21–23 Apr 1972	Apollo 16
Eugene Cernan	11–14 Dec 1972	Apollo 17
Harrison Schmitt	11–14 Dec 1972	Apollo 17

The Space Race was a component of the Cold War. The two global superpowers – the USSR and USA – competed to achieve milestones in space exploration. The USSR won the initial contest, with both the achievements of Sputnik 1 in 1957 (the first artificial Earth satellite) and Vostok 1 in 1961 (the first spacecraft to carry a human, Yuri Gagarin, into space), causing major concerns in the USA that they were falling behind.

However, the US National Aeronautics and Space Administration (NASA) focused its efforts on landing on the moon through the Apollo Programme and beat the Soviets to this accomplishment. On 20 July 1969, American astronauts Neil Armstrong and Buzz Aldrin became the first humans to set foot on the moon.

The chronicler Gerald of Wales recorded that, in the late 12th century, the grave of King Arthur was 'discovered' by monks at Glastonbury Abbey. Gerald wrote that in Arthur's time, Glastonbury had been known as the Isle of Avalon, which in Old English meant Apple Tree Island. The monks of Glastonbury discovered the grave between two stone pyramids at a depth of 16 feet, matching descriptions in Henry II's research.

Inside the grave was a coffin with a stone cross on which was engraved, 'Here lies buried the famous King Arthur with Guinevere, his second wife, in the isle of Avalon.' The coffin contained two skeletons. One was male, and Gerald wrote that it was of a very tall man, while the other had a lock of golden hair. There was also a sword – King Arthur's sword – Excalibur.

The monks kept the bones as relics and pilgrims flocked to Glastonbury. The discovery came not long after a fire that needed expensive repairs, so the find was timely (and this probably explains how King Arthur's grave was discovered). It also allowed the English to lay permanent claim to a Welsh hero. The bones were lost when Glastonbury Abbey was dissolved by Henry VIII. The stone cross was last recorded in the possession of William Hughes, Chancellor of Wells, in the early 18th century, but then disappeared. The sword that was found was gifted by Richard I, the Lionheart, to Tancred, King of Sicily in 1191. Excalibur was given away.

OLYMPIC GOLD IN. . . WRITING?

From 1912 to 1948, the Olympic Games held competitions in the fine arts. Medals were given for literature, architecture, sculpture, painting and music. The art was required to be inspired by sport. According to the founder of the modern Olympics, Pierre de Frédy, the inclusion of art was necessary because the ancient Greeks used to hold art festivals alongside the games. Before the art events were dropped for the 1952 Olympics in Helsinki, 147 medals had been awarded. Germany was top of the medal table, with seven golds.

— FAMOUS PRISONERS OF THE TOWER OF LONDON —

The first recorded prisoner of the Tower, **Ranulf Flambard**, Bishop of Durham was also the Tower's first escapee. In 1101 he climbed through a window using a rope smuggled to him in a gallon of wine.

Sir William Wallace, the leader of the Scots' resistance during the Scottish Wars of Independence, was imprisoned for a short time before he was executed in 1305.

Anne Boleyn, second wife of Henry VIII of England, was imprisoned on 2 May 1536 on charges of adultery, incest and witchcraft. She was beheaded on 19 May by a French swordsman on Tower Green.

Lady Jane Grey, in July 1553, after ruling for only nine days as queen of England, was kept in the Tower's royal apartments and allowed occasional walks around the castle grounds. She was beheaded on the Tower Green on 12 February 1554.

Sir Walter Raleigh was imprisoned at the Tower in 1603 for 13 years. He lived in the Bloody Tower with his wife and two children, during which he wrote *The History of the World*.

Guy Fawkes was imprisoned in the Tower of London in 1605 for his role in the notorious Gunpowder Plot. He was sentenced to be hanged, drawn and quartered but died of a broken neck while jumping off the scaffold at the gallows in an attempt to escape.

Having flown to Scotland in May 1941 in an attempt to negotiate peace with Britain, **Rudolf Hess**, the deputy leader of the German Nazi Party, was briefly interned at the Tower in May 1941. He was the last state prisoner to be held there.

The last person to be executed in the Tower was **Josef Jakobs**, a Nazi spy, who was shot by a firing squad on 15 August 1941.

The last people to be held in the Tower were **Ronnie and Reggie Kray**, twin brothers who ran an East London crime empire during the 1950s and 1960s. They were imprisoned in 1952 for failing to report for national service.

Political Revolution ....Date

English Civil Wars 1642–1652

American Revolution............. 1765–1791

French Revolution 1789–1799

Haitian Revolution............... 1791–1804

Latin Wars of Independence....... 1808–1833

Greek War of Independence....... 1821–1829

Italian Wars of Independence...... 1848–1866

Russian Revolution and Civil War .. 1917–1923

Revolutions are about power. Who should have it, and how to temper it. Aristocratic factions, enslaved people, workers and intellectuals all rose up at different times and in different places. The English Civil Wars that dogged the mid-17th century were fought over the balance of power between King and Parliament.

The following century's American Revolution was informed by Enlightenment ideals of liberty, which in turn inspired the French Revolution. Yet while Parisian citizens pushed tyrants under guillotines, ex-slave Toussaint L'Ouverture led a successful insurrection against French rule in Haiti.

Spain was weakened by the wars that followed the French Revolution, and could not prevent almost all of its South American colonies proclaiming independence in the following decades. Revolutions also spread to Southern Europe, fought against incumbent monarchies and the Ottoman Empire.

A wave of political upheavals swept through Europe in 1848, becoming also known as the 'Springtime of Nations'. These revolutions stemmed from new feelings of nationalism, the pressures of industrialisation and crop failures. In most European states, the 1848 Revolutions were suppressed.

But where they failed, a new theorist called Karl Marx offered a solution. The ideas outlined in his *Communist Manifesto*, also published in 1848, would influence the leaders of the 1917–23 Russian Revolution as they sought to overthrow their own Tsar.

FRENCH BOURBON MONARCHS

When Henry II of France died in 1599 things were looking okay for the royal House of Valois. He left four sons. But over the next 30 years, three died prematurely and one was assassinated without any surviving sons. After a civil war a distant cousin, Henry of Navarre, succeeded as Henry IV of the House of Bourbon.

He was followed by:

Louis XIII 1610–1643
Louis XIV 1643–1715
Louis XV 1715–1774
Louis XVI 1774–1792

The monarchy was abolished on 21 September 1792 and the First French Republic formed in the French Revolution. Louis XVII was king only to royal supporters from his father's execution at the guillotine in 1793 to his own obscure death in 1795 at the age of ten.

POTATOES

Potatoes contain a rich variety of micronutrients, particularly Vitamin C and Vitamin B6. It is possible to survive solely on potatoes with small amounts of additional proteins provided by milk or fish. They are also hardy and keep well once harvested.

In the mid-1840s, potato blight *Phytophthora infestans* struck the North European potato harvest. The crop failure has led to the decade being known as the 'Hungry Forties' because of the lack of food, and was a catalyst for unrest to spread through Europe in 1848.

The Irish peasantry had become particularly dependent on potatoes and the blight led to famine. Around one million Irish people died and a further million emigrated.

The Iranian Ayatollah Revolution in 1979 (the 'Islamic Revolution') overthrew the Pahlavi dynasty and established an Islamic Republic, led by Iranian Shia Muslim cleric Ayatollah Ruhollah Khomeini.

In 1953 a coup had strengthened the monarchical rule of Iran's Shah Reza Pahlavi. He had aligned Iran with the West, and relied heavily on American support amidst the Cold War. Khomeini had been exiled in 1964 after criticising the Shah's regime and its modernising reforms, which he perceived to be anti-Islamic.

The revolution was sparked by widespread discontent with the Shah's regime, which had become increasingly nepotistic. Power was clustered among a close network of the Shah's friends and relations, and his government was seen as corrupt and oppressive, and backed by Western powers. Economic inequality and rising unemployment also fuelled popular discontent.

Large-scale and increasingly violent protests broke out from January 1978, with workers, students and religious leaders demanding the Shah's resignation. On 16 January, with the unrest intensifying, the Shah left Iran for an 'extended vacation' (never to return), appointing Prime Minister Bakhtiar to run the country in his absence.

Khomeini dramatically returned from exile on 1 February, calling for the establishment of an Islamic republic and the overthrow of the monarchy. The army had little appetite for seizing power and, on 11 February, Khomeini declared himself Iran's new leader. Soon after, Bakhtiar resigned, which formally marked the end.

The Islamic Republic of Iran was established in April 1979 after a national referendum, with a new constitution based on Islamic principles and a return to traditional religious values. The government was led by clerics, with Khomeini as Supreme Leader (until his death in 1989). The new regime implemented strict Islamic laws, including the mandatory wearing of headscarves for women and restrictions on freedom of speech and political dissent. America became hostile to the new government and imposed economic sanctions. The two countries remain at loggerheads as Iran attempts to become a nuclear power.

The sentiments of one of these scribblers have more weight with the multitude than the opinions of the best politicians in the kingdom.

Sir Joseph D'Anvers (1686–1753), MP for Totnes

The Hollanders take care to heighten and aggravate all things by their pamphlets which hint irreverent reflections on the government and endeavour to spirit away the affections of the people and debauch their love to their prince.

William Westby, 1688

The pen is a virgin, the printing press is a whore.

William Cavendish, 17th century

Certainly, whoever has the right to make you absurd has the right to make you unjust.

Voltaire, 1765

The people do not want virtue; but are dupes of pretended patriots, and are misled into the most baneful measures and opinions by the false reports circulated by designing men.

Elbridge Gerry (a future US Vice President), 1787

The man who reads nothing at all is better educated than the man who reads nothing but newspapers.

Thomas Jefferson, 1807

It's humiliating to look back at what we wrote during the war. It was crap. . . We were a propaganda arm of our governments. At the start the censors enforced that, but by the end we were our own censors. We were cheerleaders.

Charles Lynch, World War Two journalist, 1970s

The Six Day War, 1967

The state of Israel was declared on 14 May 1948, the day before the expiration of the British mandate in Palestine. On 15 May, armies of Egypt, Syria, Transjordan and Iraq entered the territory. The ensuing war lasted almost a year, ending in an agreement that left Israel in control of more territory than it had originally been allocated under the United Nations Partition Plan.

In 1956, Egypt nationalised the Suez Canal, which had previously been controlled by British and French interests. Britain and France invaded Egypt with Israeli support, but were later forced to withdraw due to international pressure.

The Palestine Liberation Organization (PLO) was established in 1964, with the goal of creating an independent Palestinian state. The PLO launched a series of attacks on Israel, which further escalated tensions in the region.

In May 1967, the Soviet Union falsely reported to Egypt and Syria that Israel was planning an attack on Syria. This led to an Arab military build-up along Israel's borders, prompting Israel to launch a pre-emptive attack on 5 June 1967. This 'Six-Day War' resulted in a decisive Israeli victory and the annexation of the Sinai Peninsula, the West Bank, the Gaza Strip and the Golan Heights. About one million Arabs were placed under Israel's direct control in the newly captured territories.

Tensions continued and the Arab leaders' consensus of 'three no's' – no recognition, peace or negotiations with the State of Israel – led to further conflict. UN Resolution 242, adopted in November 1967, called for the implementation of the 'land for peace' formula, calling for Israeli withdrawal from territories occupied during the Six-Day War in exchange for peace with its neighbours.

Despite this, Egypt initiated the 'War of Attrition', largely an artillery duel across the Suez Canal, through which the conflict simmered on. On 6 October 1973, Egypt and Syria then launched a surprise attack on Israel on Yom Kippur, the holiest day in the Jewish calendar.

The invasion caught Israel off-guard, and the first few days saw significant Arab advances. Arab countries also enforced an oil embargo, increasing prices fourfold on industrial countries including the USA and others in Western Europe. Nevertheless, Israel eventually achieved a decisive victory. The US, wary of nuclear war, secured a ceasefire after the USSR threatened military intervention.

In September 1978, US President Jimmy Carter invited the Egyptian and Israeli leaders to Camp David to agree a final peace. Israel agreed to return the Sinai Peninsula to Egypt in exchange for a peace treaty in 1979, and withdrew entirely in April 1982. This was the first such treaty between an Arab state and Israel, but the conflict did not end.

After the PLO had launched attacks from Lebanon, Israel invaded the south of the country in June 1982 to stamp them out. The militant organisation Hezbollah was born out of this conflict in 1985. Civil unrest also came from within the territories still occupied by Israel after the Six-Day War. In 1987 the First Intifada began. This was a series of violent uprisings until the Oslo Accords in 1993.

A second more deadly intifada took place between 2000 and 2005, after the 2000 Israeli–Palestinian peace talks failed. At least six incidences of armed conflict have occured since. A lasting settlement for Israel and Palestine remains elusive.

GREEK WONDERS 'OF THE WORLD'

Structure	Location	Year built	Year destroyed
Great Pyramid	Giza	c. 2570 BC	Still standing
Hanging Gardens	Babylon	6th c BC	?
Colossus	Rhodes	c. 280 BC	653 AD
Great Lighthouse	Alexandria	c. 250 BC	1323 AD
Temple of Artemis	Ephesus	7th c BC	401 AD
Statue of Zeus*	Olympia	c. 435 BC	475 AD
Mausoleum of Mausolus	Halicarnassus	350 BC	14th century

* The Statue of Zeus was moved from Olympia to Constantinople at the end of the 4th century.

The traditional Seven Wonders of the Ancient World were all standing in the early Hellenistic Period, after the conquests of Alexander the Great in the 4th century BC. Out of all of them, the Great Pyramid is both the oldest, and the only one still standing. The Statue of Zeus and Temple of Artemis were destroyed by fire, while the Mausoleum of Mausolus, Great Lighthouse and Colossus were all toppled by earthquakes. The existence of the Hanging Gardens of Babylon is debatable, as no archaeological evidence for them remains.

The poet Antipater of Sidon (2nd century BC) gives one of the original lists of the seven wonders, although it's unlikely that he saw them all:

'I have set eyes on the wall of lofty Babylon on which is a road for chariots, and the statue of Zeus by the Alpheus, and the hanging gardens, and the colossus of the Sun, and the huge labour of the high pyramids, and the vast tomb of Mausolus; but when I saw the house of Artemis that mounted to the clouds, those other marvels lost their brilliancy, and I said, "Lo, apart from Olympus, the Sun never looked on aught so grand."'

MAJOR ARCHAEOLOGICAL DISCOVERIES

Machu Picchu (1911)
On 24 July 1911, American archaeologist Hiram Bingham III redis-
covered the lost city of Machu Picchu, a 15th-century Incan settlement
in Peru. While the city hadn't been excavated, locals had been aware
it existed and some European explorers had likely reached the city
without excavating it.

The city of Machu Picchu is now one of the best-preserved Inca
monuments, partly due to its effective construction, but also as it was
never pillaged by Spanish conquistadors.

Tutankhamun's Tomb (1922)
Egyptologist Howard Carter had made several unsuccessful digs to
locate Tutankhamun's tomb in the Valley of the Kings, funded by
Lord Carnarvon.

During Carter's final attempt, local labourers found a step that
gradually revealed a door. Over the next few months, they excavated
the antechamber and annexe, finally opening the burial chamber.
Tutankhamun's tomb was largely intact, and included nearly 5,400
remarkably well-preserved items.

The Dead Sea Scrolls (1947)
These ancient manuscripts contain the earliest versions of the
Hebrew bible, maps to hidden treasure, and insight into John the
Baptist, Jesus and early Christians.

They were found in the Qumran caves in spring 1947 near an Essene
settlement by a young Bedouin shepherd searching for a stray sheep.
Other scrolls were located in nearby caves between 1947 and 1956.

The Terracotta Army (1974)
In March 1974, farmers digging a well in Xi'an, China unearthed a
life-sized clay human head, and called in archaeologists to investigate.
They discovered thousands of life-like terracotta figures from the Qin
dynasty, fashioned 2,000 years ago to protect the First Emperor of
China in the afterlife – the buried Terracotta Army. The discovery
was a complete surprise: there were no historical records suggesting
their presence at this tomb site.

Alexander the Great and Julius Caesar are two of the most famous warlords from ancient history. Both have been written about extensively, from antiquity to the present day. And both of these titanic figures have last words attached to them that have achieved immortal status. But did they actually say them?

'To the strongest' – Alexander the Great

When asked on his deathbed to whom he had left his empire, Alexander supposedly responded: 'to the strongest'. The quote alludes to the massive turmoil that engulfed his empire shortly after his death – the ancient *Game of Thrones* that was the Wars of the Successors.

These last words, spoken from Alexander's deathbed in Babylon in 323 BC, are almost certainly made up. According to our most reliable account of Alexander's last days, the king had already lost his ability to speak when he died on c. 11 June 323 BC.

'And you my child?' – Julius Caesar

'Kai Su Teknon' – the famous last words of Julius Caesar upon seeing Marcus Brutus, according to the Roman historian and biographer Suetonius. It was this that inspired Shakespeare's famous 'Et tu, Brute?'.

However, in all other sources that cover the assassination of Julius Caesar, the dictator says nothing at all in his dying breaths. His targeting of Marcus Brutus, too, is questionable. The Brutus that was closest to Julius Caesar wasn't Marcus Brutus, but Decimus Brutus.

Decimus was a key figure in the plot to assassinate Caesar; he had also been one of Caesar's closest allies over the preceding years. His betrayal was seismic indeed. If Julius Caesar did say 'and you my child', surely he would have targeted Decimus Brutus rather than Marcus.

TELEPHONE GREETING

Alexander Graham Bell, the inventor of the first practical telephone in 1876, decided that the correct salutation on answering should be 'Ahoy.'

FAMOUS MISQUOTES

'We are not amused' – Queen Victoria
Queen Victoria has a reputation for being sad after the death of her beloved Albert, but her diaries show she had a racy side. Victoria apparently insisted herself that she never uttered this phrase. It was made up by a courtier.

'I see no ships' – Admiral Horatio Nelson
Admiral Horatio Nelson famously ignored a signal from the flagship of his commanding officer during his victory over the Danish navy at the Battle of Copenhagen. But he did not say, 'I see no ships'. Instead, he said, 'I have a right to be blind sometimes. I really do not see the signal.'

'Let them eat cake' – Marie Antoinette
The last queen of France never said this. It was written by French philosopher Jean-Jacques Rousseau, before the French Revolution, about a fictional princess who looked at a starving crowd and said, 'Let them eat brioche!'

'Dr Livingstone, I presume?' – Henry Morton Stanley
There is no evidence that explorer and journalist Henry Morton Stanley said this upon first meeting the missing missionary Dr David Livingstone, on the shores of Lake Tanganyika in modern-day Tanzania. Stanley destroyed the relevant pages of his journal and Livingstone never mentioned it.

'We shall fight them on the beaches' – Winston Churchill
Winston Churchill's signature line is often quoted incorrectly. Instead he said, 'We shall fight on the beaches, we shall fight on the landing grounds, we shall fight in the fields and in the streets, we shall fight in the hills; we shall never surrender.'

'One small step for man, one giant leap for mankind' – Neil Armstrong
Patchy audio muddled the memory of the exact words that Armstrong spoke as he stepped onto the surface of the moon. Following the Apollo 11 mission, Armstrong himself insisted that he said, 'That's one small step for a man, one giant leap for mankind.'

Dynasty	Start Year	End Year
Xia	c. 2070 BC	c. 1600 BC
Shang	c. 1600 BC	1046 BC
Zhou	1046 BC	256 BC
Qin	221 BC	206 BC
Han	202 BC	220 AD
Six Dynasties Period	220 AD	589 AD
Sui	581 AD	618 AD
Tang	618 AD	906 AD
Five Dynasties Period	907 AD	960 AD
Song	960 AD	1279 AD
Yuan	1279 AD	1368 AD
Ming	1368 AD	1644 AD
Qing	1644 AD	1912 AD

Successive dynasties ruled China over the course of nearly 4,000 years, with the Qin dynasty establishing the role of the Emperor as a divine ruler with absolute power over a unified China in 221 BC. The longest-ruling dynasty was the Zhou, who ruled for 789 years, while the two dynasties who commanded the largest territories were the Yuan and the Qing.

With the abdication of Emperor Puyi in 1912, the Qing also became the last of China's ruling dynasties. In 1911, a revolutionary movement led by Sun Yat-sen and the Chinese Nationalist Party (KMT) succeeded in overthrowing the Qing dynasty and establishing the Republic of China. However, the new government faced numerous challenges, including ongoing foreign interference, warlords and economic instability. This led to a period of turmoil that lasted several decades, ultimately culminating in the rise of the Communist Party and the establishment of the People's Republic of China in 1949.

After the Qing dynasty ended in 1911, the Kuomintang (KMT)-led government of the Republic of China and forces of the Chinese Communist Party (CCP) decided to ally in an attempt to reunify the country. The alliance didn't last, and from 1927 the two sides fought in the Chinese Civil War. By the early 1930s, the Nationalists controlled most of China.

After Japan's surrender in 1945, the Republic of China (ROC) was given consent by its wartime allies, the United States and the UK, to begin ruling Taiwan. Separated from mainland China by the Taiwan Strait, the island of Taiwan was ceded to Japan after the First Sino-Japanese War (1894–95), and had been occupied ever since.

The Nationalists and Communists resumed their civil war. Backed by Soviet Russia, the CCP's army won, and in 1949 General Chiang Kai-shek's Nationalist forces, the remnants of his government and their 1.5 million supporters evacuated to Taiwan. There Chiang established a government-in-exile, named the Republic of China (ROC). Mao Zedong, leader of the Communists, consolidated control of the mainland, establishing the People's Republic of China (PRC). China and Taiwan have remained in a standoff ever since: China sees Taiwan as a renegade breakaway province that will ultimately return; Taiwan considers itself an independent country, whether officially declared or not.

Initially, Taiwan's government claimed to represent all of China, and intended to re-occupy it. It held China's seat on the UN Security Council and was recognised by many Western nations, including the United States, as the only Chinese government. As time passed, it became clear that Taiwan's government could not be considered genuinely representative of the hundreds of millions of people living in mainland China. Crucially, in 1971 the UN switched its diplomatic recognition to Beijing. In 1979, the US established diplomatic ties with Beijing under a 'One-China' policy, recognising Taiwan as part of China, though also arming Taiwan for self-defence. Today, Taiwan's economy is important globally for its production of computer chips, but only 13 countries recognise it as a sovereign country.

By the early 3rd century AD, the Han Dynasty had ruled over China for around 400 years. At its height this dynasty had overseen a golden age in China's history, boasting advances in science and economic prosperity, but its final decades were dominated by rebellion, betrayal, and a huge degree of internal fighting.

The Han Dynasty officially ended in 220 AD, when Emperor Xian was forced to abdicate by Cao Pi, the warlord who then controlled him. Cao Pi consequently declared himself Emperor of the new state of Wei, north of the Yangtze River. To the south, two other generals followed suit. Liu Bei established the Shu Han Dynasty and Sun Quan founded the Wu Dynasty.

By 230 AD, China was firmly divided between these three separate dynasties – hence the 'Three Kingdoms', a time of great strife later memorialised by the 14th-century novel *Romance of the Three Kingdoms*. China remained bitterly divided until 280, when it was reunified under the Jin Dynasty. The nationwide census undertaken by the Jin revealed a population that had shrunk by two-thirds, from 56 million to 16 million. It had been one of the bloodiest periods in Chinese history.

THE PLAIN OF JARS

Located in the Xieng Khouang province of northeastern Laos, the mysterious Plain of Jars is dotted with thousands of stone jars, some weighing as much as several tons. The site dates back to the Iron Age, and was likely in use from 500 BC–500 AD.

More than 100 jar sites have been discovered, with each site containing anywhere from a single jar to several hundred. The jars are made of various types of rock, including sandstone, granite and limestone. The smallest are about one metre in height, while the largest reach up to three metres. Many of the jars are cylindrical, with some featuring disc-shaped lids.

While the origins and purpose of the jars remain uncertain, they may have been used as part of a complex burial ritual. Human remains and burial goods have been found within and around the jars, leading archaeologists to hypothesise that they were used to store the remains of the deceased during a period of exposure to the elements. Once the soft tissue had decomposed, the bones may have been collected and buried in a separate location or placed back inside the jars for secondary burial. There is also a legend that a local king, Khun Cheung, won a great battle, and used the jars to store alcohol to celebrate.

This region of Laos was heavily bombed by the United States during the Vietnam War as it formed part of the Ho Chi Minh trail used by the North Vietnamese Army. As a result, the Plain of Jars is littered with unexploded munitions, leaving part of the site off-limits. The three most visited jar sites were cleared of munitions in 2005. In July 2019, the Plain of Jars was made a UNESCO World Heritage Site.

LARGEST PALACE EVER BUILT

In 200 BC, Emperor Gaozu of Han requested the building of Weiyang Palace complex north of modern Xi'an. Weiyang Palace has a claim to being the largest palace ever built on Earth: it covered 4.8 km² (1,200 acres), which is nearly seven times the size of the current Forbidden City in Beijing or eleven times the size of the Vatican City, though little remains of it today.

The Full English Breakfast is a bulwark of British cuisine, the roots of which date back to at least the 17th century. The greasy meal does few favours for the international standing of British kitchens, but at home on the archipelago the fry-up is as essential and jealously protected as fish and chips.

In the 18th century, the English breakfast referred to a substantial meal including hot bacon and eggs. It stood in contrast to the lighter 'continental' breakfast of mainland Europe. It was to such a meal that travel writer Patrick Brydone referred when in 1773 he delighted in having 'an English breakfast at his lordship's'.

Although Sir Kenelm Digby proclaimed how 'Two Poched Eggs with a few fine dry-fryed collops of pure Bacon, are not bad for breakfast' in a 17th-century recipe, eggs were generally regarded as a luxury on a par with chicken until the early 20th.

Eggs were a part of high-status Victorian breakfasts, however, and the popular cooked breakfast was to some extent an attempt by urbanites to imitate the lifestyle of a country estate. Meanwhile, cookery columns exhorted readers to eat fatty and filling foods, with books like T. C. Duncan's *How to Be Plump* (1878) featuring rather self-explanatory advice on 'healthy eating'. After World War Two, the dish embraced fried leftover potatoes. Soon avant-garde breakfasters were adding mushrooms, tomatoes, baked beans and black pudding.

The Full English is often claimed to originate among the medieval elite, while some of its constituent elements easily date back to the Bronze Age. Bread, for instance, was a staple in Egypt, Sumer and the Indus Valley, as common in Homer's Greece as Caesar's Rome.

On the other hand, tomatoes and potatoes are rather conspicuous due to being New World vegetables not introduced to European cooking until the 1500s. This rather brings into question just how English the English Breakfast is. The 'Full English Breakfast' as we know it appears to be early modern at best.

The Full English is the essential item on pejorative lists of British cuisine. But it is also one the few British meals to find favour abroad, resulting in a certain degree of pride over it.

Long breads, including baguettes, had been consumed in France since the mid-18th century. While the origins of the baguette are debatable, one legend is that Napoleon Bonaparte popularised the bread through making it a staple of army rations. Traditional bread loaves took up more space, so a baguette was easier to carry on long marches.

The popularity of the stick-like loaf was enhanced by cheaper flour and new steam oven baking techniques during the 19th century. In 1920, the Parisian authorities first defined the 'baguette' in regulations, setting its length, weight and price. During World War Two, the baguette became a symbol of resistance against the German occupation, with bakers secretly baking baguettes containing messages or supplies to aid partisans.

—— THE FAMOUS (AND SLIGHTLY FRENCH) PHO ——

French Indochina was established in 1887, initially comprising territory of Vietnam, and later adding Laos and Cambodia. There are clues to French influence within all these countries, but perhaps the biggest is the regular appearance of baguettes on food stalls, particularly in Vietnam and Laos.

Another Vietnamese street food staple is the pho, a beef noodle soup that has become the national dish. This appears to have originated in the capital of Hanoi in the early 20th century, after beef became more common in the Vietnamese diet. Its exact origins are unclear, and could be an amalgamation of French, Chinese and Vietnamese influences. The French theory is that it is derived from beef pot-au-feu. The final word sounds very much like 'pho' when spoken with a French accent.

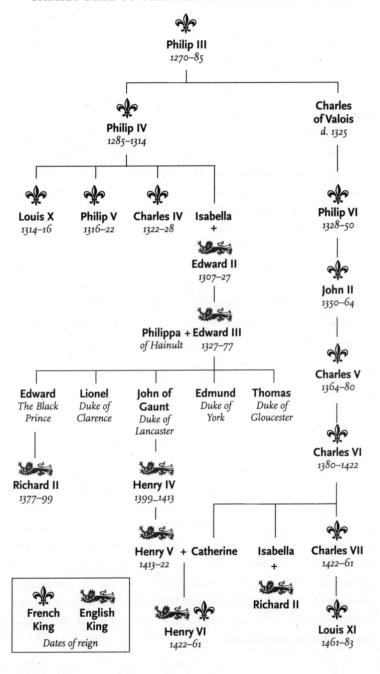

FAMILY TREE OF THE FRENCH MONARCHY IN 1328

Philip III
1270–85

Philip IV
1285–1314

Charles of Valois
d. 1325

Louis X
1314–16

Philip V
1316–22

Charles IV
1322–28

Isabella
+

Philip VI
1328–50

Edward II
1307–27

John II
1350–64

Philippa + **Edward III**
of Hainult   *1327–77*

Charles V
1364–80

Edward
The Black Prince

Lionel
Duke of Clarence

John of Gaunt
Duke of Lancaster

Edmund
Duke of York

Thomas
Duke of Gloucester

Charles VI
1380–1422

Richard II
1377–99

Henry IV
1399–1413

Henry V + **Catherine**
1413–22

Isabella
+

Charles VII
1422–61

Richard II

French King

English King

Dates of reign

Henry VI
1422–61

Louis XI
1461–83

→ 90 →

The Hundred Years' War erupted from a succession crisis in France and a personal dispute over land between the King of France and the King of England. King Philip IV of France died in 1314 and was succeeded by three of his sons in turn. Louis X ruled from 1314–16, then Philip V from 1316–22, and Charles IV from 1322–8. None of the brothers had a son to succeed them.

There were two candidates for the throne after the death of Charles. Louis, Philip and Charles's nephew, the son of their sister Isabella, was King Edward III of England. But there was strong resistance to giving the French Crown to an English king. The other candidate was a nephew of Philip IV. A French candidate was preferred, so Philip VI was selected as king. His father had been Charles, Count of Valois, so Philip VI became the first King of France of the House of Valois.

At this time, England still retained control of Gascony, a reduced version of the Duchy of Aquitaine on the southwest coast of France, famed for its wine. On 24 May 1337, as a result of ongoing arguments, Philip declared Gascony forfeited and seized it from Edward. Edward responded by resurrecting his claim to the throne of France, and a series of conflicts known as the Hundred Years' War began. The first significant engagement was the naval Battle of Sluys on 24 June 1340, an unexpected victory at sea for England. It was followed by crushing French defeats on land at Crecy in 1346 and Poitiers in 1356, with numerous French and English victories in between.

The Black Death and the minority of Richard II saw the war stutter. It was resurrected in 1415 when Henry V led an invasion that culminated in the Battle of Agincourt on 25 October. In 1420, the Treaty of Troyes made Henry heir to the French Crown, but he died just weeks before the French king and left behind a 9-month-old heir. Henry VI is the only person in history crowned King of England and King of France in both countries, but his youth and emerging preference for peace made the war unsustainable. The end of the Hundred Years' War, a term applied later to a series of conflicts that is usually divided into three phases (1337–60, 1369–89 and 1415–53), is usually given as the Battle of Castillon, a French victory on 17 July 1453.

The 'Wars of the Roses' began as a dynastic conflict between cadet branches of the Plantagenet family – the Yorkists, descended from Lionel Duke of Clarence, and Lancastrians, descended from John of Gaunt. They were the second and third sons of Edward III respectively.

Trouble had begun brewing from 1399 when Richard II was deposed by his cousin Henry Bolingbroke, who crowned himself as the first of the Lancastrian line, Henry IV. However, this line found itself in trouble after England's de facto defeat in the Hundred Years' War. Henry VI had come to the throne as a baby, and his court was heavily influenced by the Beaufort family, who were also descended from John of Gaunt.

By the 1450s, Richard Duke of York was beginning to see the weaknesses of the Lancastrian regime. As a descendant of Edward III's second son, he also had a strong claim to the throne. By 1455, the Yorkists were in rebellion, starting with the First Battle of St Alban's.

The 'Wars of the Roses' was not called that at the time. It was a series of rivalries and disputes that took place between 1455 and 1487 among the English nobility, largely between Lancaster and York, with many switching sides. Although roses feature in imagery from Tudor times onwards, the moniker first appeared in Sir Walter Scott's novel *Anne of Geierstein* in 1829. The name the Cousins' War was first applied to the conflict in the 20th century.

By 1460, it had become a question of who had the better right to the Crown between the Houses of Lancaster and York, both of whom were descended from King Edward III. In 1461, the first Yorkist king, Edward IV, deposed Henry VI but was in turn deposed in 1470. Henry's restoration was named the Readeption, a made-up word, and only lasted six months before Edward returned. In 1483, Edward died and his brother succeeded him as Richard III, only to be defeated and killed at the Battle of Bosworth; the victorious Henry Tudor became King Henry VII, beginning the Tudor era. The Battle of Stoke Field, on 16 June 1487, was the result of a Yorkist invasion and the last pitched battle of the Wars of the Roses.

MAJOR BATTLES OF THE WARS OF THE ROSES

Battle of	Date	Ruler	Winner
(First) St Albans	22 May 1455	Henry VI	York
Blore Heath	23 Sep 1459	Henry VI	York
Ludford Bridge	13 Oct 1459	Henry VI	Lancaster
Northampton	10 Jul 1460	Henry VI	York
Wakefield	30 Dec 1460	Henry VI	Lancaster
Mortimer's Cross	2 Feb 1461	Henry VI	York
(Second) St Albans	17 Feb 1461	Henry VI	Lancaster
Towton	29 Mar 1461	Edward IV	York
Hedgeley Moor	25 April 1464	Edward IV	York
Hexham	15 May 1464	Edward IV	York
Edgcote	24 Jul 1469	Edward IV	Lancaster
Losecoat Field	12 Mar 1470	Edward IV	York
Barnet	14 April 1471	Henry VI	York
Tewkesbury	4 May 1471	Edward IV	York
Bosworth	22 Aug 1485	Richard III	Tudor
Stoke Field	16 Jun 1487	Henry VII	Tudor

The see-sawing of political power between the houses of York and Lancaster began at Saint Albans in 1455, after which Richard of York took control of Henry VI's government. Four years of tense peace later, the Yorkists were driven into exile after Ludford Bridge, but returned to claim the throne after Northampton. York was killed at Wakefield, but his son won the Battle of Towton three months later and was crowned Edward IV. His cousin, Warwick the Kingmaker, then drove Edward from England and restored Henry VI. At Barnet, Warwick was killed, and Edward won a decisive victory over the Lancastrians at Tewkesbury. Yorkist rule ended after Henry Tudor's forces defeated Edward's brother, Richard III, at Bosworth.

The origins of the longbow are unclear. Ötzi the Iceman, discovered on the Austrian border and dating from 5,300 years ago, had something very similar to a longbow in his grave. In the British Isles, it is often considered to have originated in Wales. By the 14th century, it had become closely associated with English armies, and became the new superweapon on the European battlefield.

Many nations preferred the crossbow. It was much easier to learn to use, had a range of around 300 yards, and could shoot two to three bolts a minute. In comparison, using the longbow took years to perfect. However, since every Englishman could use one, archers were relatively cheap to employ. A bowshot was a genuine medieval measure of distance, set at around 204 yards. Some modern replica longbows have fired up to 450 yards. It could pierce mail armour at around 100 yards, and archers were expected to shoot eight to ten arrows a minute. 5,000 archers could therefore fire up to 50,000 arrows a minute.

Edward I (r. 1272–1307) ordered the construction of archery butts, ranges for practising, across England. His grandson Edward III (r. 1327–77), at the height of the Hundred Years' War with France, ordered every Englishman to practice on a Sunday after church. The English army developed a tactic that seemed simple, but proved devastatingly effective, particularly against larger forces.

The first major use of it came at the Battle of Dupplin Moor in August 1332, the opening engagement of the Second War for Scottish Independence. An English army outnumbered ten to one fought with a centre of dismounted men-at-arms flanked by archers. As the Scots poured forward, their numbers worked against them and the trapped men were picked off by archers. The tactic was repeated in France at Crecy (1346), Poitiers (1356) and Agincourt (1415). Once they finished shooting, archers employed daggers or mallets to deliver the coup de grâce – killing blows, often through the helmet visors of the wounded.

For a century, this simple formula dominated battlefields. The French answer was to invest heavily in gunpowder weapons, which saw them defeat the English and drive them out of France after the Battle of Castillon in July 1453.

DATES OF WOMEN'S SUFFRAGE

New Zealand 1893
Australia 1902
Germany 1918
United States of America 1920
Sweden 1921
United Kingdom* 1928
France 1945
Italy 1946
Japan 1947

*Britain had limited suffrage in 1918, and full suffrage in 1928.

While the woman's right to vote was granted on the dates above, it could be restricted by criteria like age or property ownership, or exclude ethnic minorities. Sweden allowed women to vote in some local elections as far back as 1718, and other countries granted similar local rights in the 18th century, but many of these allowances were rescinded.

Political turmoil after World War One meant some European countries lost democratic freedoms altogether. Germany granted full suffrage as part of the founding of the Weimar Republic, but rights were severely restricted under the Nazis from 1933. Suffrage returned in 1949 with the formation of the Federal Republic of Germany. In Russia, women over 20 were given the right to vote and hold public office in July 1917. However, the October 1917 Revolution and ensuing civil war led to the end of democracy in the newly formed USSR.

MEGA-TSUNAMI

In July 1958 the tallest tsunami ever recorded crashed through the quiet fjord of Lituya Bay in Alaska. A massive tremor 13 miles away caused 30 million cubic metres of rock to fall into the Lituya Glacier, resulting in a huge wave of displaced water. At 1,720 feet, the mega-tsunami was higher than the Empire State Building.

Although often associated with the medieval period, torture methods were 'finessed' further in Tudor times. Burning at the stake and beheading continued, but many other grisly forms of punishment were also introduced.

Boiled alive

In 1531 Henry VIII forced through the 'Acte of Poysoning' in response to the case of Richard Roose – a Lambeth cook accused of serving poisoned gruel to two people in a botched attempt to assassinate John Fisher, the Bishop of Rochester. It declared murder by poison an act of high treason, with the punishment of being boiled alive. The act was made retroactively, and Roose met his bubbling end.

Pressed to death

You couldn't face a jury unless you entered a plea of guilty or not guilty. Being pressed to death involved the placing of heavy stones onto the accused until they decided to make a plea or expired under the weight. Due to a legal loophole, some people chose this punishment despite its lethality, hoping to evade the confiscation of lands that usually followed a court conviction.

Broken on the wheel

This punishment was popular in Europe, and made its way over to Scotland. In 1603 one Robert Weir was found guilty of murdering the Lord of Warriston. He was tied to a wooden wheel in spread-eagle fashion, then his limbs were broken with the coulter of a plough. Once the body had been shattered, the condemned person would either be strangled, given a mortal blow or left to die in agony.

Beheaded by the Halifax gibbet

This Yorkshire invention was essentially a large axe attached to a wooden block, and was 200 years ahead of the guillotine's adoption in Revolutionary France. The town of Halifax adopted it to punish even lowly crimes like petty theft, and it remained in use until the mid-17th century. It inspired another device – the maiden – first used in Scotland during Mary Queen of Scots' reign.

THE VENETIAN ARSENAL

By the 15th century Venice was the most powerful of Europe's port cities, whose giant commercial fleet made a Venetian Lake of the Adriatic, and whose colonies steadily spread across the Eastern Mediterranean. Venice's ambitions rested on its navy, based at the Venetian Arsenal, a walled 45-hectare industrial complex, possibly the largest in Europe before the Industrial Revolution. It's not a coincidence that Venice became the first European state to have a permanent navy.

OH DEER! THE ORIGINS OF HUMBLE PIE

One explanation for the origins of the phrase 'eating humble pie' comes from the medieval hunt. As well as providing valuable practice in riding and using weapons, it offered the elite a way to reinforce the strict social hierarchy. When a stag was killed, there was a very specific ritual for unmaking the deer, also known as breaking or undoing the animal. The process is described in the 15th-century Boke of Seynt Albans.

Firstly, the stag's genitalia and organs were removed and placed on top of a pole called a forchée to be paraded on the way home. The right hind hoof was then removed and given as a prize to the highest-status person on the hunt, man or woman. The stag was next skinned, and the hide used to protect the meat and to collect the blood. It was then cut into pieces that were ceremonially distributed. The rear haunches were the prime cut for the top table. The left shoulder was given to the forester who cared for the land as his payment. The kidneys, intestines, windpipe and blood were mixed with bread and fed to the hounds, who were held on leads by their masters as they ate so that they would associate the reward with the hunt.

The word venison is derived from the Old French word vene-soun, which comes from the Latin venari, meaning to hunt. It is the product of the hunt. While the top table dined on the finest cuts, lower-status members of the household were fed the offal and the entrails, which were also known as the umbles, so that eating humble pie was a demonstration of low status.

In 31 BC, following his defeat of Mark Antony and Cleopatra at the Battle of Actium, Octavian became the sole ruler of the Roman Republic.

Over the next decades, he consolidated his control as princeps (chief) of the restored Roman 'Republic'. He also received the title of Augustus ('the increaser'). This 'restoring the Republic' agenda all ultimately proved a facade to him becoming a near absolute ruler. He slowly solidified his control as this superpower's first Emperor. What followed him was an imperial dynasty – the first of many that would define the Roman Empire. There were, however, many violent changes of Emperor and changes of dynasty over the next four centuries.

Emperor	Dynasty	Reign
Augustus	Julio Claudian	27 BC–14 AD
Tiberius	Julio Claudian	14–37 AD
Caligula	Julio Claudian	37–41 AD
Claudius	Julio Claudian	41–54 AD
Nero	Julio Claudian	54–68 AD
Vespasian	Flavian	69–79 AD
Titus	Flavian	79–81 AD
Domitian	Flavian	81–96 AD
Nerva	Nerva Antonine	96–98 AD
Trajan	Nerva Antonine	98–117 AD
Hadrian	Nerva Antonine	117–138 AD
Antoninus Pius	Nerva Antonine	138–161 AD
Lucius Verus	Nerva Antonine	161–169 AD
Marcus Aurelius	Nerva Antonine	161–180 AD
Commodus	Nerva Antonine	180–192 AD

Emperor	Dynasty	Reign
Septimius Severus	Severan	193–211 AD
Geta	Severan	211 AD
Caracalla	Severan	211–217 AD
Macrinus	Severan	217–218 AD
Elagabalus	Severan	218–222 AD
Severus Alexander	Severan	222–235 AD
Valerian	Constantinian	253–260 AD
Gallienus	Constantinian	253–268 AD
Constantius I	Constantinian	305–306 AD
Constantine I	Constantinian	306–337 AD
Constantine II	Constantinian	337–340 AD
Constans	Constantinian	337–350 AD
Constantius II	Constantinian	337–361 AD
Valentinian I	Valentinian	364–375 AD
Valens	Valentinian	364–378 AD
Gratian	Valentinian	367–383 AD
Valentinian II	Valentinian	375–392 AD
Theodosius I	Theodosian	379–395 AD
Arcadius	Theodosian	383–408 AD
Honorius	Theodosian	393–425 AD
Theodosius II	Theodosian	402–450 AD

There are a few caveats to the preceding table. Galba, Otho and Vitellius also ruled in 69 AD in what was known as 'The Year of the Four Emperors' but none formed a dynasty as Vespasian did. Similar chaos ensued after the assassination of Commodus in 192 AD. Marcinus briefly overthrew the Severan dynasty and claimed their titles, but he was not from the Severan family.

——————— THE REAL GLADIATOR ———————

The first time the Roman imperial crown passed from father to son, with the son being born in the Emperor's lifetime, was when Commodus succeeded his father Marcus Aurelius in 180 AD. The pair had reigned jointly since 177. This was over 200 years after Augustus had first established the role.

Commodus was a megalomaniac and it ended badly. Ridley Scott's swords and sandals epic *Gladiator* (2000) provides a Hollywood version of his reign – although he was not killed by an ex-general-cum-gladiator named Maximus Decimus Meridius. That said, Commodus did fight as a gladiator in the Colosseum. He was strangled by his wrestling partner and personal trainer, Narcissus, in December 192.

In early 193, an experienced magistrate called Pertinax succeeded Commodus, but he was assassinated by his personal bodyguard after just three months. He was succeeded by a rich Roman aristocrat called Didius Julianus, who was also quickly assassinated and replaced by a governor and general called Septimius Severus.

Severus seized power in Rome by the point of a sword. Over the next few years, he vied with two other powerful contenders for the emperorship. He first had to march his forces east, to present-day Anatolia, where he fought and defeated the powerful governor of Syria – Pescennius Niger.

He then had to march west to the area around present-day Lyon, to fight his final great rival: Clodius Albinus, the Governor of Britain, at the Battle of Lugdunum.

LUGDUNUM: ROME'S BIGGEST BATTLE

In February 197, Severus and Albinus fought one of the largest battles of Roman history near Lyon (Roman Lugdunum). The Roman historian Cassius Dio claimed that 150,000 soldiers were fighting on either side. So 300,000 men in total. This number is almost certainly an exaggeration, but the battle was probably still one of the biggest in antiquity.

Severus won the battle, but only just, and Albinus perished in the aftermath. Seeking to make an example of his rival, Severus found Albinus's body and had the man's head cut off and placed on top of a pike in Rome. The rest of Albinus's mutilated remains were thrown into a river.

EXTERNAL ENEMIES OF ROME

Name	People	When They Fought
Brennus	Gaul	c. 390 BC
Pyrrhus	Epirote / Greek	280–275 BC
Hannibal	Carthaginian	218–c. 183 BC
Arminius	German (Cherusci)	9–21 AD
Boudica	Celtic Briton (Iceni)	60–61 AD
Tacfarinas	Berber	19–24 AD
Shim'on Bar Kokhba	Jewish	132–135 AD
Surena	Parthian	53 BC
Zenobia	Palmyrene	270–272 AD
Attila	Hun	444–453 AD

TEUTOBURG FOREST

One of Rome's most significant defeats during the Empire period came in 9 AD at the hands of Arminius's alliance of Germanic tribes. A Roman army was marching along a track in the Teutoburg Forest, in a line close to 10 miles long. Arminius ambushed and destroyed three legions. Some 20,000 Roman soldiers were killed or captured.

Cats have somehow achieved a monopoly over Internet memes. But 100 years prior to the Internet, Victorian artist Louis Wain gained widespread popularity with his illustrations of anthropomorphic cats.

At the turn of the 20th century, it was uncommon for a family home to have a cat. Cats were free-roaming animals, given that cat litter didn't exist and spaying and neutering was uncommon.

Louis Wain's drawings helped to balance the appreciation of cats with that of dogs. His first cat illustration, *A Kittens' Christmas Party*, was published in the *Illustrated London News* in 1886. Over the next three decades, Wain was a prolific artist, sometimes producing over 1,000 cat paintings and drawings a year. His cats would be engaged in many forms of human adventure, from wearing the latest fashions to having parties and making speeches.

He illustrated around 100 children's books, and his work appeared across newspapers and magazines. The *Louis Wain Annual* ran from 1901 to 1915, and he was Chairman of the National Cat Club between 1898 and 1911. His life was the subject of a 2021 film, *The Electrical Life of Louis Wain*, starring Benedict Cumberbatch and Claire Foy.

He made the cat his own. He invented a cat style, a cat society, a whole cat world. British cats that do not look and live like Louis Wain cats are ashamed of themselves.

H.G. Wells

DICK WHITTINGTON THE CAPITALIST

Those familiar with the pantomime circuit will likely have heard of the tale of Dick Whittington and his cat. This legendary rags-to-riches tale dates back to the early 17th century in the form of a play and a ballad. In its simplest form 'Dick' Whittington, a poor boy from the shires, comes to London in search of his fortune, but only finds work as a dishwasher. Finding himself rather above this work, he runs away, but hears the sound of Bow Bells of East London telling him he is destined for greatness if he stays. He then sends his cat on a merchant ship to a foreign land, where it ends up in a royal court with an infestation of vermin. The cat keeps the court mice-free, and Dick is sent a fortune in thanks, and he becomes Mayor of London three times.

A likely tale, you might say. The real Richard Whittington was a serial entrepreneur, and a key player in England's striving medieval merchant class. Born around 1350 as the son of a knight, the young Whittington soon got into the wool and cloth business, which was probably the biggest industry in the realm. By the 1380s he had become wealthy enough to begin loaning money to the London authorities, and soon took public office, serving as Mayor of London for three terms (and part of another), just like his pantomime persona. He went on to become a mercer (a fabric merchant) for the lavish royal court of Richard II, who had quite a penchant for fine silks and garments.

When Richard II was deposed in 1399, the new Lancastrian King Henry IV invited Whittington into the royal council. He became a major exporter of wool, as well as collecting wool tax for the Crown. When Henry's son Henry V came to the throne and invaded France, Whittington loaned him £1,600, a very substantial sum at the time.

Richard Whittington was also well known for his charity, through providing money for numerous public works in the capital. When he died a childless widower in 1423, he insisted that his entire estate of £7,000 was given to charity. The Charity of Sir Richard Whittington was formed in 1423 and entrusted to the Mercer's Company, and is still active, providing communities for the elderly in London and Surrey.

HISTORICAL CONNECTIONS

British literature

In 1895, when Robert Graves was still a baby, he received a kiss on the head from Algernon Charles Swinburne, who was already 70 years old at the time. When Swinburne was a younger man he had met Walter Savage Landor, when he was an old man. Landor had also been a friend of Charles Dickens and Robert Browning. When Landor was a child he received a pat on the head from Dr. Samuel Johnson, who had received the 'Royal Touch' by Queen Anne during his childhood, who gave it as a cure for scrofula.

Prussian military

German President Paul von Hindenburg served in the Prussian Guards, during which time he met Kaiser Wilhelm I. Wilhelm had fought at Waterloo under the leadership of Captain von Blücher, who had served under Frederick the Great during the Seven Years' War but was forced to resign in 1773. Frederick declared that 'Blücher can take himself to the devil!' in reply to the 1773 petition in which Blücher demanded Frederick's retirement from the Prussian Army.

Well-connected artist

Gertrude Stein lived in Paris from 1903 to 1938, sharing an apartment with Alice B. Toklas. The apartment's salon became famous for hosting writers Ernest Hemingway, F. Scott Fitzgerald, and Ezra Pound who would gather to discuss their work. Henri Matisse and Pablo Picasso also visited the salon, and Matisse painted Stein on Saturday evenings. Picasso then took his turn to paint her, followed by Man Ray, who came to photograph her.

While living in the apartment Stein wrote *The Autobiography of Alice B. Toklas,* which made her a sensation in the United States. Upon arriving back in the United States Stein had dinner with Charlie Chaplin.

20th century dictators

In 1913 Joseph Stalin, Adolf Hitler, Leon Trotsky and Josip Tito all lived in Vienna for a couple of months. Hitler, aged 24, had by then failed twice to study painting at the Vienna Academy of Fine Arts.

SUNGLASSES AT NIGHT

In early September 1859 a massive solar flare hit the Earth. Telegraphists could transmit messages without plugging in their machines, the northern lights were seen in Jamaica. Elsewhere the sky appeared to be on fire and you could read in the middle of the night.

TOUCHING THE KING'S EVIL

Scrofula is a swelling of the bones and lymphatic glands in the neck, sometimes caused by tuberculosis. Edward the Confessor believed that, as king, he had a divinely gifted healing touch to rid his subjects of scrofula, known as the 'King's Evil'. He also ensured patients were looked after at his expense until they were cured. In the 13th century, this was replaced by the monarch giving a gold coin to each patient. Known as an Angel, it would be hung round the sufferer's neck as a healing charm.

The practice continued until the Commonwealth period under Oliver Cromwell, when touching stopped completely. Scrofula sufferers instead travelled in droves to Europe to receive 'the touch' from the exiled Charles II. With the Restoration of the monarchy, the king quickly re-established the practice, touching almost 100,000 people during his reign.

Queen Anne continued touching but its popularity was diminishing. A 2-year-old boy touched by Queen Anne grew up to be the distinguished man of letters, Samuel Johnson, but the monarch had clearly lost her healing touch and Johnson's sight and hearing were permanently impaired. Touching the King's Evil ended when Queen Anne died.

REPETITIVE PLOTTING

There were more than 600 plots to kill Cuban dictator Fidel Castro. Castro was targeted by a range of foes, including political opponents, criminals and the USA. Tactics included an exploding cigar and a poisoned diving suit.

2 IMPORTANT CAR CRASHES IN 1931

On 13 December 1931, Winston Churchill was struck by a car while crossing Fifth Ave in New York City. He had looked the wrong way before crossing the street and was dragged for several yards, sustaining bruises, sprains and cuts. At that time, Churchill was prescribed unlimited alcohol for his recuperation, as America was under the grip of prohibition.

In the same year, a 19-year-old British aristocrat named John Scott-Ellis was driving a red Fiat in Munich and almost hit the future Führer, Adolf Hitler. Scott-Ellis jumped out of his car and apologised, and Hitler only suffered minor bruises. They shook hands, and Scott-Ellis later remarked, 'For a few seconds, perhaps, I held the history of Europe in my rather clumsy hands. . . [Hitler] was only shaken up, but had I killed him, it would have changed the history of the world.'

THE FIRST AFFORDABLE CAR

When the first Ford Model T was wheeled out of Ford Piquette Avenue Plant in Detroit, Michigan on 27 September 1908, it wasn't the first automobile on the market. Nor was it the first Ford.

But with the Model T, Henry Ford aimed to 'build a motor car for the great multitude. It will be large enough for the family, but small enough for the individual to run and care for. It will be constructed of the best materials. . . But it will be so low in price that no man making a good salary will be unable to own one.'

By 1918, half of the cars in the United States were Model Ts. The explosion in production was possible thanks to a revolution in manufacturing at Ford's Highland Park factory. Here Henry Ford made an early and influential stab at what became known as the mass production system. By producing lots of standardised products, made with standardised parts, by specialised machinery and workers at different stages of the production line, production costs were significantly reduced. On 26 May 1927, Ford and his son drove the 15-millionth (and last) Model T out of the factory. It remained the most sold car in history until 1972, when it was surpassed by the Volkswagen Beetle.

THE QUIRKY HISTORY OF CARS

Any customer can have a car painted any colour
that he wants, as long as it is black.

Henry Ford

The world's first recorded speeding ticket

On 28 January 1896, Walter Arnold drove his 'horseless carriage' through Paddock Wood, Kent, at a reckless 8mph – four times the 2mph speed limit. He also had no man with a red flag preceding him, as required by law. Arnold was chased down by a police officer on a bicycle, and later fined £4 7s, of which 10 shillings was for speeding.

Steam-powered land speed record

In 1906, a steam-powered car known as the 'Stanley Rocket' driven by American Fred Marriott set a land speed record of 127.659 mph, becoming the fastest car in the world. This steam powered record was held for 103 years.

First car accident mortality

The first recorded fatality as a result of riding in a car occurred in Parsonstown in County Offaly, Ireland on 31 August 1869. Mary Ward, a celebrated polymath, fell from a steam carriage and died after being crushed by its heavy iron wheels.

Hand-cranked wipers

Early self-propelled vehicles lacked windscreens, so motorists wore goggles to protect themselves from the elements. In the early days of cars, windshield wipers were not powered by motors, but were manually operated using a hand crank. Drivers or passengers had to manually move the wipers back and forth to clear the windshield.

It'll all be over by Christmas

This line is remarkably common in film and literature about the war, relating to the naive optimism of a quick win for the Allies. On the opposing side, Kaiser Wilhelm II declared that it would be over before the leaves fell from the trees.

But not everyone shared this sentiment, particularly experienced soldiers. General Smith-Dorrien told a crowd of cadets that 'the whole of Europe and more besides would be reduced to ruin; the loss of life would be so large that whole populations would be decimated'.

Lions led by donkeys

This idea related to the brave everyman soldier being led by fools of the officer class. While some generals were clearly incompetent, rarely in history have commanders had to adapt to a more radically different technological environment.

British commanders had been trained to fight small colonial wars; now they were thrust into a massive industrial struggle unlike anything the British Army had ever seen. After the war Field Marshal Haig was revered as a national hero, particularly in his lobbying for better support for veterans.

No one won

Swathes of Europe lay wasted, millions were dead or wounded after years of stalemate. Empires had collapsed, and even the 'victors' were bankrupt. It is odd to talk about 'victory'.

But the Allies did win militarily. By late September 1918 the Kaiser and his military mastermind Erich Ludendorff admitted that there was no hope and Germany must beg for peace. The 11 November Armistice was essentially a German surrender, the Kaiser abdicating and fleeing to the Netherlands.

If I should die, think only this of me:
    That there's some corner of a foreign field
That is for ever England. There shall be
    In that rich earth a richer dust concealed;
A dust whom England bore, shaped, made aware,
    Gave, once, her flowers to love, her ways to roam;
A body of England's, breathing English air,
    Washed by the rivers, blest by suns of home.

 And think, this heart, all evil shed away,
    A pulse in the eternal mind, no less
        Gives somewhere back the thoughts by England given;
Her sights and sounds; dreams happy as her day;
    And laughter, learnt of friends; and gentleness,
        In hearts at peace, under an English heaven.
Rupert Brooke, 'The Soldier', 1914

What passing-bells for these who die as cattle?
 — Only the monstrous anger of the guns.
 Only the stuttering rifles' rapid rattle
Can patter out their hasty orisons.
No mockeries now for them; no prayers nor bells;
Nor any voice of mourning save the choirs,—
The shrill, demented choirs of wailing shells;
And bugles calling for them from sad shires.

What candles may be held to speed them all?
Not in the hands of boys, but in their eyes
Shall shine the holy glimmers of goodbyes.
The pallor of girls' brows shall be their pall;
Their flowers the tenderness of patient minds,
And each slow dusk a drawing-down of blinds.
Wilfred Owen, 'Anthem for Doomed Youth', 1917

In the early phases of World War One, post-traumatic stress disorder (PTSD), as we now define it, was not well understood. The term 'shellshock' originates from soldiers being blasted by shells, and thus going into a kind of physical shock.

After the Battle of the Somme in 1916 a significant number of British soldiers were returning from the front with a difficult-to-diagnose mental disorder, and more soldiers were admitted into psychiatric institutions.

Initially the condition was defined as 'neurasthenia', which was first coined in 1829 as a physical disease of the nerves. There was little understanding that combat stress could lead to a mental disorder. At Craiglockhart Hospital, in Edinburgh, Dr W.H. Rivers saw the link, and began to address it with Freudian talking therapy.

After the war, 'shellshock' was still not widely accepted. *A War Office Committee of Enquiry into 'Shell-Shock'* was completed in 1922, and much of the testimony from both military and the medical officials illustrates the ongoing confusion around the term.

> 'The term shellshock has been wrongly used, and has popularly become accepted to include any man suffering from nerves. It really means the effect of the explosion of a shell so near as to knock a man silly.'

> Lieut-Colonel E Hewlet

Some senior officers continued to downplay the condition, considering it akin to a lack of discipline or general morale. Men who suffered from shellshock in such a way that they couldn't work also didn't get the same level of disability pensions as men who returned from the front with debilitating physical injuries.

'Shellshock' or PTSD is not unique to World War One, and it is almost a certainty that combat stress has always been a feature of warfare. However, the grim conditions in the trenches and the anxiety-inducing position of stalemate under shellfire, along with the sheer number of men in the army in combat, led to combat stress being a significant problem for all combatants.

SOLDIER'S DECLARATION

I am making this statement as an act of wilful defiance of military authority, because I believe that the war is being deliberately prolonged by those who have the power to end it.

I am a soldier, convinced that I am acting on behalf of soldiers. I believe that this war, upon which I entered as a war of defence and liberation, has now become a war of aggression and conquest. I believe that the purposes for which I and my fellow soldiers entered upon this war should have been so clearly stated as to have made it impossible to change them, and that, had this been done, the objects which actuated us would now be attainable by negotiation.

I have seen and endured the sufferings of the troops, and I can no longer be a party to prolong these sufferings for ends which I believe to be evil and unjust.

I am not protesting against the conduct of the war, but against the political errors and insincerities for which the fighting men are being sacrificed.

In behalf of those who are suffering now I make this protest against the deception which is being practised on them; also I believe that I may help to destroy the callous complacence with which the majority of those at home regard the continuance of agonies which they do not share, and which they have not sufficient imagination to realise.

Siegfried Sassoon, July 1917

The war poet Siegfried Sassoon wrote the above declaration in June 1917, and it was read out in Parliament on 30 July. Given Sassoon was a decorated soldier, the army opted against court-martialing him; instead they summoned him for examination by the Medical Board. This found him unfit for service and referred to Craiglockhart Hospital near Edinburgh. There he met Wilfed Owen, another war poet. He returned to the frontline in November 1917, but was wounded for a third time in July 1918. Unlike Owen, he survived the war, and died in 1967, aged 80.

This letter to the *Morning Post* was published on 14 August 1916, during the Battle of the Somme. It appears in Robert Graves's (who was a friend of Siegfried Sassoon) classic war memoir, *Goodbye to All That* to illustrate the disconnection between returning soldiers and the homefront. It is not clear if the letter was genuine or the work of a patriotic journalist, but it was soon heaped with praise across the press, and a pamphlet version sold 75,000 copies. Below, it appears in slightly edited form.

Sir, – As a mother of an only child– a son who was early and eager to do his duty – may I be permitted to reply to Tommy Atkins, whose letter appeared in your issue of the 9th inst.? Perhaps he will kindly convey to his friends in the trenches, not what the Government thinks, not what the Pacifists think, but what the mothers of the British race think of our fighting men. It is a voice which demands to be heard, seeing that we play the most important part in the history of the world, for it is we who 'mother the men' who have to uphold the honour and traditions not only of our Empire but of the whole civilized world.

To the man who pathetically calls himself a 'common soldier', may I say we women, who demand to be heard, will tolerate no such cry as 'Peace! Peace!' where there is no peace. . . We only need that force of character behind all motives to see this monstrous world tragedy brought to a victorious ending. The blood of the dead and the dying, the blood of the 'common soldier' from his 'slight wounds' will not cry to us in vain. They have all done their share, and we, as women, will do ours without murmuring and without complaint. Send the Pacifists to us and we shall very soon show them, and show the world, that in our homes at least there shall be no 'sitting at home warm and cosy in the winter, cool and "comfy" in the summer'. There is only one temperature for the women of the British race, and that is white heat. . . We women pass on the human ammunition of 'only sons' to fill up the gaps, so that when the 'common soldier' looks back before going 'over the top' he may see the women of the British race at his heels, reliable, dependent, uncomplaining.

The reinforcements of women are, therefore, behind the 'common soldier'. We gentle-nurtured, timid sex did not want the war. It is no pleasure to us to have our homes made desolate and the apple of our eye taken away. We would sooner our lovable, promising, rollicking boy stayed at school. We would have much preferred to have gone on in a light-hearted way with our amusements and our hobbies. But the bugle call came, and we have hung up the tennis racquet, we've fetched our laddie from school, we've put his cap away, and we have glanced lovingly over his last report, which said 'Excellent '– we've wrapped them all in a Union Jack and locked them up, to be taken out only after the war to be looked at. A 'common soldier', perhaps, did not count on the women, but they have their part to play, and we have risen to our responsibility. We are proud of our men, and they in turn have to be proud of us. If the men fail, Tommy Atkins, the women won't.

> Tommy Atkins to the front,
> He has gone to bear the brunt.
> Shall 'stay-at-homes' do naught but snivel and but sigh?
> No, while your eyes are filling
> We are up and doing, willing
> To face the music with you – or to die!

Women are created for the purpose of giving life, and men to take it. Now we are giving it in a double sense. It's not likely we are going to fail Tommy. We shall not flinch one iota, but when the war is over he must not grudge us, when we hear the bugle call of 'Lights out', a brief, very brief, space of time to withdraw into our secret chambers and share with Rachel the Silent the lonely anguish of a bereft heart, and to look once more on the college cap, before we emerge stronger women to carry on the glorious work our men's memories have handed down to us for now and all eternity.

Yours, etc.

A Little Mother

War fever swept Britain in August 1914, and many took to the streets to celebrate going to war as if it was a kind of victory. Of course, few of these optimists could foresee what carnage awaited.

However, many did oppose the war – when conscription was introduced in 1916 around 16,000 men refused to serve on moral grounds. Many prominent intellectuals throughout Europe were also against it.

Virginia Woolf, author

She wrote that the war was 'the end of civilization. . . Rendering the rest of our lives worthless.' One of her most famous novels – *Mrs Dalloway* (1925) – features a First World War veteran, Septimus Warren Smith, who suffers badly from shellshock.

Bertrand Russell, philosopher

In August 1914 he 'discovered to my amazement that average men and women were delighted at the prospect of war'. He was prosecuted in June 1916 for an anti-conscription pamphlet, and imprisoned in 1918 for lecturing against the United States joining the Allies.

Albert Einstein, physicist

Teamed with physician Georg Friedrich Nicolai as a signatory of a 'Manifesto to the Europeans', written to oppose the pro-war address 'To the World of Culture'. However, the manifesto gained little support.

Sigmund Freud, psychoanalyst

Initially supported the war, but later attacked 'the belligerent state' for 'permit[ting] itself every such misdeed, every such act of violence, as would disgrace the individual.'

John Maynard Keynes, economist

While he worked in the service of the British war economy for the duration of the conflict, Keynes privately thought the war a mistake. In December 1917 he told artist Duncan Grant: 'I work for a government I despise for ends I think criminal.'

In the 1920s and 30s, the First World War was often referred to as 'The War for Civilisation' and British society was very anxious of another war. Many politicians and academics put forward the treatise that another war could well end civilisation, with some referring to a societal collapse on a similar level to the fall of the Roman Empire. The advancements in long-range bombers and the potential of these dropping poison gas on civilians was of particular concern.

A policy now known as appeasement was adopted. Belligerent powers like Germany, Japan and Italy were allowed to rearm and even make certain conquests in the hope that their ambitions could be satisfied and war avoided.

In 1934–5, British anti-war sentiment manifested itself in the 'Peace Ballot', with the official title being 'A National Declaration on the League of Nations and Armaments, and organised by the League of Nations Union'. Over 500,000 volunteers went door to door to ask people who were registered to vote in parliamentary elections to answer five questions with a Yes or No response.

In total 11.6 million people, or 38% of the adult population, voted in the ballot. In answer to questions relating to Britain's role in the League of Nations and disarmament, votes were cast in 90% favour of supporting both of these aims. However, when asked the following question:

> Do you consider that, if a nation insists on attacking another, the other nations should combine to compel it to stop if necessary, by military measures.

Those who voted Yes numbered 6.7 million.

The ballot both supported disarmament, but also supported war for a cause led by the League of Nations. Appeasement, therefore, became an ambiguous political minefield.

TUNGUSKA EVENT

In 1908, an explosion in Siberia had a yield about 1,000 times more powerful than the atomic bomb dropped on Hiroshima. Eighty million trees were flattened. The most likely explanation was a meteor strike.

A BRIEF HISTORY OF TIME

Timepiece	Date	Region
Sundial	1500 BC	Egypt
Water clock	1500 BC	Greece
Hourglass	8th century	Middle East
Candle clock	9th century	England
Incense clock	10th century	China
Mechanical clock	11th century	Europe
Astronomical clock	15th century	Europe
Spring clock	16th century	Europe
Pocket watch	16th century	Europe
Pendulum clock	1656	Netherlands
Stopwatch	1695	England
Marine chronometer	1761	England
Electric clock	1840	Scotland
Railroad watch	1890s	United States
Atomic clock	1940	United States
Smartwatch	2010	United States

Lost time is never found again.

Benjamin Franklin

TIME IMMEMORIAL

Law in medieval England relied heavily on the idea of long use and custom. Retaining grazing rights on a piece of land relied on proving that they had been enjoyed since time immemorial. The problem was how to prove something had happened in a time out of all memory. That issue was resolved by the Statute of Westminster in 1275. Time immemorial was given a date: 6 July 1189.

Edward I was the king who issued the Statute of Westminster and the date he chose was the first day of the reign of his great-uncle, Richard I, the Lionheart. Edward had been a crusader and perhaps chose the date to recall the last great crusading king. So, a legal test of whether a right had been enjoyed since time immemorial meant proving it had existed since 6 July 1189. Courts stated that where a long-standing custom exists, it will be presumed to have existed since time immemorial unless it can be proven otherwise.

OLDEST MECHANICAL CLOCK

Salisbury Cathedral lays claim to housing the world's oldest mechanical clock. It's a rather large contraption and has no dials or hands, telling the time by striking a bell every hour. The clock was created in 1386 or earlier on the orders of Bishop Erghum.

BRITAIN'S OLDEST DOOR

The oldest door in Britain is on a corridor leading to the Chapter House in Westminster Abbey. It was dated for the first time in 2005 using dendrochronology. The wood was felled after 1032 and the door was made in the 1050s during the reign of Edward the Confessor. It is the only surviving door from the Anglo-Saxon period. The oak tree from which the door was made could have been standing as far back as Roman times.

In the 19th century fragments of cowhide were found on the door, and a legend grew that the skin was human. Allegedly someone had been caught committing robbery in the church and his skin was nailed to the door as a deterrent to other criminals.

The Percys are a noble house who dominated the north of England from the reign of Edward III, despite a very very violent family history. They usually didn't die in their beds:

The first Earl was Henry Percy, made Warden of the Marches, the man in charge of border defence against Scotland. He rebelled against Henry IV and was killed in battle in 1408.

His son was Henry 'Hotspur' Percy, one of England's greatest knights. He joined his father's rebellion and was killed before his old man in battle in 1403.

His son was Henry Percy, Second Earl, who decided to be loyal to the king. So loyal that he was killed fighting for the king in the opening battle of the Wars of the Roses in 1455.

His son, Henry Percy, Third Earl, also took the king's side in the Wars of the Roses and was killed in the terrible battle at Towton in 1461.

His son, Henry Percy, Fourth Earl, was sent to the Tower as a child, but won his land and titles back, holding on to them through the upheavals at the end of the Wars of the Roses and the coming of the Tudors. But he was beaten to death by a mob of rioters in 1489 while trying to collect taxes.

His son, Henry Percy, Fifth Earl, stayed close to Henry VIII and died in his bed.

His son, Henry Percy, Sixth Earl, was engaged to Anne Boleyn but quickly ditched in favour of Henry VIII – he was lucky to escape with his life. Henry died in his bed leaving no children. His brother Thomas had joined the rebellion against the king known as the Pilgrimage of Grace. He was executed.

His brother Ingelram had also joined the rebellion, and died a prisoner in the Tower.

His son, Thomas Percy, Seventh Earl, rebelled against Elizabeth I and was executed in 1572.

His brother, Henry Percy, Eighth Earl, was sent to the Tower three times for plotting against Elizabeth. On the last occasion he was found dead, shot through the heart. A verdict of suicide was recorded.

His son, Henry Percy, Ninth Earl, spent 16 years as a prisoner in the Tower on suspicion of supporting the Gunpowder Plot, but was eventually released and died in his bed.

His son, Algernon Percy, Tenth Earl, supported Parliament in the Civil War but did not approve of the execution of Charles I. A slippery survivor, he died in his bed in 1668.

His son, Josceline Percy, Eleventh Earl, died young with no male heirs.

The Northumberland title was resurrected as a dukedom in the 18th century, through the female line, and things got a little more peaceful, although the Percys have never been far from the battlefield.

BALL LIGHTNING

The church of St Pancras in Widecombe-in-the-Moor, Dartmoor, was struck by ball lightning on 21 October 1638, in an event known as 'The Great Thunderstorm'. The church was packed with around 300 worshippers, of whom four were killed and 60 injured. A wall-panelled poem within the church reads (this is the first panel of four):

In token of our thanks to God, these tables are erected,
Who in a dreadful thunder from, the persons here protected
Within this church of Widicombe, 'mongst many fearful signs
The manner of it is declared in these enduring lines.
In sixteen hundred thirty eight, october twenty first
On the Lords day at afternoon, when people were addressed
To their devotion in this church while singing here they were.
A Psalm distrusting nothing of the danger then so near;
A crack of thunder suddenly with lightning hail and fire,
Fell on the church and tower here, and ran into the choir;
A sulphurous smell came with it and the tower strangely rent,
The stones abroad into the air, with violence were lent.

A GLOSSARY OF ECCLESIASTICAL TERMS

Abbey: A community of monks or nuns presided over by an abbot or abbess.

Advowson: The right to nominate someone to a vacant position.

Anathema: The exclusion of heretics from all Christian services and society.

Apostate: A person who leaves holy orders.

Benefice: A paid post within the Church.

Benefit of Clergy: The right of clergy to be tried by Church courts.

Canonical Hours: Services held at specific times through the day: matins, lauds, prime, terce, sext, none, vespers, compline.

Cellerer: The member of a monastic community responsible for provisions.

Chantry Chapel: A chapel where prayers are said for a person or family.

Chapter: clergy within a cathedral, or daily assembly of a monastic community.

Crypt: A room beneath a church, often found in the eastern end.

Grange: A monastic farm.

Infirmary: A place for the sick and infirm to be cared for, led by the infirmarian.

Interdict: A punishment that required the withdrawal of religious services.

Lavatorium: A trough with running water for washing hands before meals.

Oblate: A person given into a monastic life as a small child.

Peculiar: Outside the jurisdiction of the local bishop, often a Royal Peculiar such as Westminster Abbey.

Prebend: The income assigned to a member of the clergy.

Quire: Part of a church where services are held.

Refectory: A monastery's dining hall.

Sacrist: A monk responsible for the care of buildings, books and vestments.

Sanctuary: A right to protection within the walls of a church.

Simony: Giving or accepting a payment for a job within the church.

Synod: An assembly of clergy.

Tithe: One-tenth of produce paid to the church.

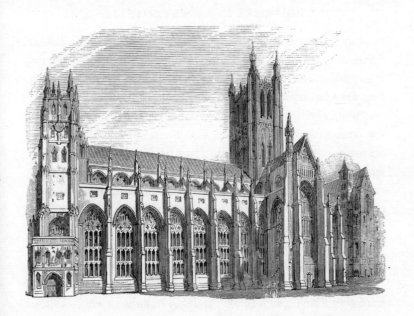

MERCY SEATS FOR MONKS

Choir stalls in some churches still have misericords – carved wooden
scenes or symbols that represent a wide variety of things. Some might
be the badges of prominent local families, while others might show
wrestling matches, farming activities or drinking scenes reflecting
everyday life. The carvings are visible when the seat of the choir stall
is folded away and they often have a flat shelf at the top of the carving.
The reason misericords were popular is that they helped monks to
bend the rules.

Monks were required to stand for long periods during services.
The seats in the choir stall could be folded down when sitting was
permitted, but at all other times they were required to be folded away.
The misericords were a decorative touch, but the shelf on top of the
carvings also provided a perch for weary monks to allow them to
take the weight off their feet during long services when they weren't
supposed to sit down. That's why misericords are also sometimes
called mercy seats or pity seats.

POMPEII'S INDIAN STATUETTE

In 1938, a team of archaeologists led by Amedeo Maiuri were excavating a high-end Roman house in Pompeii. In its garden, they
uncovered an ivory-object – small and shattered. What they had discovered was a beautifully crafted statuette, rich in decoration on all sides.

The statuette itself is around 24 cm tall, depicting a naked woman.
It was originally believed that the figurine represented Lakshmi – the
consort of the Hindu god Vishnu. Now, however, the identity of the
figurine is much less clear. The statuette also includes two smaller
maidens – one on either side of the 'Lakshmi'. A mysterious symbol
on the statuette's underside is perhaps the signature of the artist.

Its function is also unclear, but what's really interesting is where
it came from. The discovery of a very similar statuette in Bhokardan,
India, suggests that this was where the object was crafted. Two thousand years ago, Bhokardan was part of the Satavahana Kingdom that
ruled over a large swathe of the Indian subcontinent and had strong
trade connections with the Roman Empire in the 1st century AD.

These trade connections allowed a Pompeiian to ultimately acquire
this Indian object almost 2,000 years ago.

THE GLASS ROMAN BRAIN

Vitrification is the process of turning substances into glass – but you
wouldn't think this could happen to any parts of a human body. In the
1960s archaeologists made an intriguing discovery in the Collegium
Augustillium in Pompeii. One of the victims of the 79 AD eruption of
Mount Vesuvius had their brain 'vitrified'.

Experts from the Roma Tre University in Rome and Federico
II University of Naples finally solved the brain of glass mystery in
April 2023, after studying carbonised wood from trees, buildings and
furniture also burned in the eruption. The heat-induced effects the
victims suffered indicated an early extremely high thermal, short-lived
blast of a 550-Celsius volcanic ash cloud – hotter than the 500-Celsius
previously estimated – which engulfed them, followed by a rapid
cooling phase.

From the 13th century onwards, the Habsburg dynasty ruled over large parts of Europe. But for a family to consolidate its power and influence – or to make new alliances – its members had to make politically advantageous matches.

The genetic issues of marriages between relatives were not then understood. Normally, a child is the product of two very different gene pools, but if your parents are cousins the chances are they share the same recessive genes. Continually mixing them can cause them to become dominant, sometimes with rather unpleasant results.

In the case of the Habsburgs, this manifested itself most overtly in an enlarged lower jaw (known as mandibular prognathism) – creating a pronounced underbite, a large humped nose and a protruding lower lip. This trait – known as 'The Habsburg Chin' – became increasingly apparent in successive generations due to extensive intermarriage within the family. Marie Antoinette was part of the Austrian Habsburgs, but her protruding lower lip simply gave the appearance of a constant pout. Other Habsburgs fared worse.

Carlos II was the last of the Spanish Habsburgs. He was born with several physical disabilities, including a lower jaw so pronounced that he struggled to eat and talk. Historians and geneticists both believe that these stemmed from centuries of inbreeding. Carlos's physical deformities were so noticeable, he earned the nickname El Hechizado – literally meaning the hexed one. While he did marry twice, Carlos never produced an heir: some scientists think he was incapable of doing so, and his autopsy seemed to raise more questions than it answered. The physician who conducted it is supposed to have said: 'His [body] did not contain a single drop of blood; his heart was the size of a peppercorn; his lungs corroded; his intestines rotten and gangrenous; he had a single testicle, black as coal, and his head was full of water.'

The Brown Lady of Raynham Hall

This famous ghost is said to haunt Raynham Hall in Norfolk, England, and is believed to be the spirit of Lady Dorothy Walpole, who died in 1726.

The Tower of London

Said to be one of the most haunted places in England, some of the Tower's most famous include the ghost of Anne Boleyn, who was beheaded there in 1536, and the ghost of Sir Walter Raleigh, who was imprisoned there in the 17th century.

Versailles Palace

Among the Versailles ghosts is Marie Antoinette, who was executed during the French Revolution in 1793. In August 1901, two English women were convinced they saw the French Queen in the gardens.

Ghosts of Gettysburg

The bloodiest battle of the American Civil War took place at Gettysburg in July 1863. The Herr Tavern, used as a Confederate hospital during the fighting, is said to have four haunted guest rooms. Eight ghost tour companies operate in the town.

The Flying Dutchman

A legendary ghost ship that is said to sail the seas forever. Its origins date back to the 17th century, and it has been reported in various locations around the world, including by George V.

Hampton Court Palace

This royal palace is said to be haunted by several ghosts, including that of Catherine Howard, the fifth wife of Henry VIII, who was executed. She allegedly runs through the Haunted Gallery, begging for mercy.

The Ancient Ram Inn

The 12th-century pub in Gloucestershire lays claim to more than twenty ghosts, including a witch who was burned at the stake, a cavalier and several monks.

LION MAN

In 1939 fragments of a carved ivory mammoth tusk were discovered in Stadel Cave on Hohlenstein Mountain in southern Germany. Analysis of the fragments was delayed because of the subsequent outbreak of the Second World War. For decades, they remained undisturbed in a museum archive. During the 1970s and 80s, archaeologists attempted to piece the fragments together. It was only then that they realised what this object actually was: a part-human, part-animal sculpture – carved from a mammoth tusk. Complete with eyes, ears, arms, a nose and mouth, the 31-cm-tall sculpture depicts a bipedal lion. We today know it as the Löwenmensch – 'lion man'. The German 'mensch' here just means human.

What makes this artefact so fascinating is that the lion is bipedal. Lions standing upright do not exist in nature, and the sculpture possibly represents a mythological character. Ice Age hunter-gatherers may have created the sculpture based upon a powerful animal that they were competing against. A reconstruction experiment by Wulf Hein using Neolithic tools, found that the sculpture would have taken around 400 hours to carve.

At around 40,000 years old, Lion Man is the oldest known evidence of human religious beliefs, and could be the oldest mythical figure that we know of.

THE ICE MUMMIES

More than 2,000 years ago, a nomadic Ice Age culture called the Pazyryks lived in the area of Central Asia that we now call the Altai Mountains. They built many of their tombs high up in the mountains, and they became natural freezers.

When these tombs started being discovered, archaeologists found the frozen bodies within, with tattooed skin and clothing still visible. The most famous of these mummies is the Siberian Ice Maiden. Discovered by a team of Russian-led archaeologists in 1993, the maiden had been buried with gold jewellery, and had a mark of a deer-style tattoo on one of her shoulders and on her wrist and thumb.

INTERESTING AVIATION FACTS

Fewer than ten people witnessed the first powered flight by the **Wright Brothers** on 17 December 1903.

Harriet Quimby was the first American woman to earn a pilot's licence, in 1911. A year later she became the first woman to fly across the English Channel.

The first airline meals were served by **Handley Page Transport**, on the London–Paris route in October 1919. They were pre-packed lunch boxes at 3 shillings each (15p).

The first African American woman to earn a pilot's licence was **Willa Brown** in 1939.

Qantas Airways was the first airline in the world to introduce business class – in 1979

In 1987, **American Airlines** saved $40,000 by removing one olive from each salad served in first-class.

In 1996, the **Concorde** set the record flying time from New York to London, making the journey in only 2 hours, 52 minutes and 59 seconds and travelling at speeds of up to 1,354 mph.

There have been more astronauts than pilots who have flown the **Concorde**, which is now out of service.

The largest building in the world is an aircraft-production factory. **Boeing's Everett Factory** was named by *The Book of Guinness World Records* as the largest building on the planet. It's so big that clouds formed inside it until the installation of a state-of-the-art air circulation system.

— KEY MOMENTS IN THE HISTORY OF AIR TRAVEL —

19 September 1783: Montgolfier Brothers' first hot air balloon flight.

1891–6: Otto Lilienthal's glider flights (some 2,000 flights were made).

17 December 1903: First successful powered flight by the Wright Brothers, lasting 12 seconds and covering 36.8 metres.

October 1911: Italy becomes the first country to significantly incorporate aircraft into military operations.

1 January 1914: World's first scheduled passenger airline service takes off, operating between St Petersburg and Tampa, Florida.

2 September 1916: Aeroplanes in flight communicate with each other directly by radio for the first time.

15 June 1919: First non-stop transatlantic flight, by John Alcock and Arthur Whitten Brown.

7 October 1919: KLM is established in the Netherlands. It is the world's oldest operating airline.

20–21 May 1927: First solo, non-stop transatlantic flight, by Charles Lindbergh.

1930: Frank Whittle registers the patent for the first the jet-engine.

20 May 1932: Amelia Earhart becomes the first woman to pilot a solo transatlantic flight.

1933: First modern airliner flies (Boeing 247).

1937: The *Hindenburg* crashes, bringing the age of airships to an end.

14 October 1947: Chuck Yeager breaks the sound barrier.

1949: First jet-powered passenger aircraft.

1954–1957: Boeing ushers in the age of modern jet travel.

20 July 1969: Apollo 11 moon-landing: US astronauts Neil Armstrong and Edwin 'Buzz' Aldrin are the first to walk on the moon.

22 January 1970: First commercial Boeing 747 flight ushers in the dawn of the jumbo jet age.

21 January 1976: First supersonic Concorde flight with commercial passengers.

THINGS NAMED AFTER JULIUS CAESAR

Julius Caesar left an indelible mark on history, declaring himself dictator of Rome in 49 BC, marking the Roman Republic's end. His heir, Octavian, became the first Emperor. Testament to his legacy are the many things named after him.

July

The Roman month Quintilis was renamed Julius in honour of Caesar following his death. We know it today as July.

The Julian Calendar

Caesar's academics reformed the Roman calendar in 46 BC. Before then, the calendar was misaligned to the seasons. 46 BC is also the longest year in history, having 445 days in total.

Caesar / Czar / Kaiser

Caesar's name is the title for Roman, Russian and German monarchs.

Caesarism

Caesarism is a recognised form of government behind a powerful, usually military leader – Napoleon was arguably a Caesarist and Benjamin Disraeli was accused of it.

HMS *Caesar*

The British warship was one of several named after Caesar. The Italian battleship *Giulio Cesare* saw service in World War Two.

The Caesarsboom (Caesar's Tree)

Located in the Belgian town of Lo, Caesarsboom is a yew tree believed to be more than 2,000 years old. A local legend has thus emerged that Julius Caesar once rested under the tree.

Limited Companies

There are nearly 700 limited companies (LTD) registered in the UK with the name 'Caesar'. Many are associated with Italian food.

Not Caesar

As much as you might wish it, the Caesar salad was not named after Julius Caesar, but the Italian who created it – Caesar Cardini.

WHEN THE GLOBE BURNED DOWN

Elizabethan playgoers loved special effects as much as we do today, and the Globe Theatre prided itself on its cannon, used to herald the arrival of important characters. On 29 June 1613, during a performance of Shakespeare's *All Is True* – later renamed *Henry VIII* – sparks from the cannon landed in the thatched roof.

Sir Henry Wotton penned this eyewitness account, four days later:

'. . . I will entertain you at the present with what happened this week at the Banks side. The King's players had a new play called All is True, representing some principal pieces of the reign of Henry the Eighth, which set forth with many extraordinary circumstances of pomp and majesty even to the matting of the stage; the knights of the order with their Georges and Garter, the guards with their embroidered coats, and the like: sufficient in truth within awhile to make greatness very familiar, if not ridiculous. Now King Henry making a Masque at the Cardinal Wolsey's house, and certain cannons being shot off at his entry, some of the paper or other stuff, wherewith one of them was stopped, did light on the thatch, where being thought at first but idle smoak, and their eyes more attentive to the show, it kindled inwardly, and ran round like a train, consuming within less than an hour the whole house to the very ground. This was the fatal period of that virtuous fabrick, wherein yet nothing did perish but wood and straw, and a few forsaken cloaks; only one man had his breeches set on fire, that would perhaps have broyled him, if he had not by the benefit of a provident wit, put it out with a bottle of ale.'

HISTORICAL HOBBIES

Isaac Newton: The renowned physicist and mathematician had a fascination with alchemy and spent years conducting experiments in this field.

Napoleon Bonaparte: Found time during his military career to write a romance novel, *Clisson et Eugénie*, in 1795. It went unpublished in his lifetime.

Nikola Tesla: The inventor and electrical engineer had a passion for pigeons, and was known to care for injured birds and feed them in the park.

Adolf Hitler: Applied to the Vienna Academy of Fine Arts twice, but was rejected both times. Prior to World War One he struggled to make a living as an artist.

Winston Churchill: The former British Prime Minister had a hobby of bricklaying and constructed a number of structures on his estate. Like his adversary in World War Two, he was also a keen painter.

Salvador Dali: The surrealist artist was passionate about cooking, and published a cookbook, *Les Diners de Gala*, in 1973.

George Washington: The 1st President of the United States enjoyed ballroom dancing in 1799, once dancing for three straight hours.

Abraham Lincoln: The 16th President of the United States was a skilled wrestler and reportedly won 300 bouts and had only one known defeat.

Mahatma Gandhi: The Indian political leader had a love of spinning and weaving, and often used this as a form of meditation and relaxation.

Elvis Presley: The musician loved collecting police badges and was known to have amassed a collection of over 200 by the time of his death.

Sigmund Freud: The father of psychoanalysis was a passionate collector of antiquities, and amassed thousands of ancient artefacts.

Imelda Marcos: The former First Lady of the Philippines was famous for her extensive collection of shoes, reportedly owning over 3,000 pairs, and building a museum to display her collection.

MEDIEVAL PROVERBS

The Well-Laden Ship was a poem composed by Egbert of Liège in the 11th century to help students learn Latin. It contained proverbs, fables and folktales that would have been familiar to those reading. The book contains the first known version of 'Little Red Riding Hood' and the nursery rhyme 'Jack Sprat'. Some of the proverbs are familiar today. 'When a horse is offered for free, you should not open its mouth' is the literal translation equivalent to 'Don't look a gift horse in the mouth'. 'The apple never falls far from the tree' and 'While the cat's away, the mice shall play' also appear.

Other proverbs have not stood the test of time so well, though their meaning remains clear. 'A poor man extends his poverty when he has regular recourse to wine.' 'The crow, by not crowing, could have the corpse to himself.' 'A living dog is better than a dead lion' is a similar notion to a bird in the hand being worth two in the bush. 'Calves should not play with an ox as they are outmatched in horns.'

Other medieval proverbs crop up in various sources. John Warkworth, a 15th-century London merchant, used a couple in his chronicles. 'Such goods as are gathered with sin, are lost with sorrow', and 'A castle that will speak and a woman that will hear, they shall both be won.' Other sources include such proverbs as 'He who serves two masters, serves neither', 'God meets every man, but few recognise Him', and 'Nature surpasses art without effort or anxiety'.

HAPPY FAMILY

Several animals appear listed as family members in the 1921 census. They include three goldfinches, a cat called Ginger, a tortoise and a rooster.

Henry and Edward 8
George 6
William 4
Richard 3
Charles 3
Mary, Elizabeth and James 2
John, Stephen, Victoria and Anne 1

Lady Jane Grey also reigned for nine days in 1553. However, the country rallied to Queen Mary I and Jane was deposed and executed with her husband in 1554.

Queen Mary II reigned jointly with her husband, William III.

— YEARS OF MAJOR DYNASTIES ON THE THRONE —

The length of reign for the Norman kings is contested, as there was a civil war period known as 'The Anarchy' from 1135–53. Stephen of Blois was technically King of England throughout this period.

Dynasty	Period	Years
Plantagenet	1154–1485	331
Hanoverian	1714–1901	187
Windsor	1901–present	122+
Tudors	1485–1603	118
Stuart	1603–1714	111
Norman	1066–1154	88

The name of the British Royal Family was Saxe-Coburg-Gotha from 1901 until 1917. Fearing it sounded too German, King George switched the family name to Windsor. He also asked his relatives to relinquish any German-sounding names or titles and suspended British peerage titles for any pro-German relatives. Windsor has remained the Royal Family and the dynasty remains on the throne.

James 6
Robert, Malcolm, Alexander and Robert 3
David, Donald, Duncan and John 2
Kenneth, Lulach, Macbeth, Margaret, Mary and William 1

This list includes the names used by Scottish monarchs from the House of Dunkeld (beginning in 1034 with Duncan I) up to James VI, when the Crowns of England and Scotland were combined.

Margaret, Maid of Norway, was not inaugurated as Queen, and thus her status is contested. There was an interregnum upon her death (1290–92) before John Balliol ruled for four years. A second interregnum took place from 1296–1306 while Edward I of England attempted to conquer Scotland. Robert the Bruce restored the Scottish monarchy in 1306 and defeated the English at the Battle of Bannockburn. England accepted Scottish independence in 1328.

Further turmoil came in 1332 when Edward Balliol led an English-backed invasion of Scotland against the regency of David II (son of Robert the Bruce) – he was a disputed claimant, but renounced his claim to the throne in 1356 and peace was restored in 1357 with the Treaty of Berwick.

The Stuart dynasty began with the accession of Robert II in 1371 and lasted until 1651, when Scotland became part of Oliver Cromwell's Commonwealth. The Stuarts were restored in 1660 and reigned until 1707. While there was a break, the Stuarts lasted 427 years on the Scottish throne, making that house the longest-ruling house in either England or Scotland.

ANGLO-SAXON DOOM

The almost total eclipse of the old Anglo-Saxon elite after the Norman conquest is revealed in the pages of the Domesday Book. Of the thousand or so individuals who held their lands directly from the king in 1086, only thirteen were English. All the rest were foreign newcomers.

THE UNFORTUNATE STUART FAMILY

Killed

James I murdered in a sewer.

James II blown up by his cannon.

James III killed in battle.

James IV killed in battle.

James V died after his army was humiliated invading England.

Mary executed by her cousin.

Charles I executed.

Near Misses

James VI and I narrowly avoided getting blown up.

Charles II narrowly escaped with his life after hiding in the Royal Oak.

James II deposed by his daughter and her husband.

NEITHER HOLY, ROMAN NOR AN EMPIRE

This agglomeration which was called and which still calls itself the Holy Roman Empire was neither holy, nor Roman, nor an empire.

Voltaire, 1756

The Holy Roman Empire emerged when Otto I was crowned by Pope John XII in 962. It sought to resurrect the old Roman Empire and Charlemagne's Carolingian Empire. Covering much of modern Germany and central Europe into Italy, it was the most powerful European monarchy until the 12th century. It reached its greatest extent under Frederick I (r. 1155–90), also known as Barbarossa (red beard), of the House of Hohenstaufen. It became a loose collection of states that was often unwieldy and rebellious, with an Emperor frequently at odds with the Pope. The Emperor was elected from among his peers, who considered their own states semi-autonomous, making it a prestigious position, but one often lacking in the real authority other monarchs held. It faced terminal decline after the Thirty Years' War (1618–48), which caused population declines of 50% in certain areas. It was dissolved in 1806, having been subjugated by Napoleon.

TALLEST BUILDINGS IN HISTORY

Building	Completed	Height (m)	Country
Great Pyramid of Giza	c. 2550 BC	146.6	Egypt
Lincoln Cathedral	1311	159.7	England
Ulm Minster	1890	161.5	Germany
Philadelphia City Hall	1901	167	USA
Singer Building	1908	192	USA
Metropolitan Life Tower	1909	213	USA
Woolworth Building	1913	241	USA
40 Wall Street	1930	282	USA
Chrysler Building	1930	318.9	USA
Empire State Building	1931	381	USA
World Trade Center	1972	417	USA
Sears Tower	1974	442	USA
Petronas Towers	1998	452.9	Malaysia
Taipei 101	2004	510	Taiwan
Burj Khalifa	2010	828	Dubai

The Great Pyramid is an anomaly in the above list, as it is not a habitable building, but it was the tallest structure for over 3,800 years. Lincoln Cathedral surpassed it as the world's tallest building when its spire was completed in 1311. The central spire collapsed in 1548, but there was no taller building constructed until Ulm Minster was finished in 1890.

DICK TURPIN'S CHICKEN DOWNFALL

Having adopted the identity of John Palmer and posing as a horse trader in Yorkshire, highwayman Dick Turpin instigated his own demise by murdering hunting associate John Robinson's game-cock on 2 October 1738. When Robinson angrily responded, Turpin threatened to also kill him, which brought the incident to the attention of three local justices.

The World's Oldest

The oldest confirmed 'message in a bottle' was found in 2018 on a beach in Western Australia. The bottle, which had been tossed into the sea in 1886, contained a rolled-up piece of paper with information about the German ship *Paula* and its coordinates at the time. It was confirmed to be authentic by the Western Australian Museum, beating the previous record holder by five years.

Goodbye from the *Titanic*

Jeremiah Burke was a passenger on the *Titanic* who, at some point before its disastrous sinking, wrote a message and placed it in a bottle. He threw the bottle overboard in the hope that it would reach his family in Ireland, close to where the *Titanic* departed. It read: 'From Titanic, Good Bye all, Burke of Glanmire, Cork.' Burke did not survive the wreck. His message was found, extraordinarily, a few miles from his family's home in 1913, a year after the disaster. Though the *Irish News* had observed in 1912 that 'very many' message-bearing bottles turn out to be 'cruel hoaxes', Burke's family believed in its authenticity.

A Message for Mary

In 2013, a 23-year-old kite surfer, Matea Medak Rezic, found a half-broken bottle while clearing debris from a beach in Croatia. Inside the bottle was a message from Jonathan, from the Canadian province of Nova Scotia, written 28 years ago, expressing his admiration for a woman named Mary and hoping to keep in correspondence.

The message read: 'Mary, you really are a great person. I hope we can keep in correspondence. I said I would write. Your friend always, Jonathan, Nova Scotia, 1985.'

The bottle had travelled approximately 6,000 kilometres across the Atlantic Ocean, entered the Mediterranean Sea, and then drifted into the Adriatic Sea. The identities of Jonathan and Mary, as well as how they knew each other, remain unknown.

PLAGUE VILLAGE

In 1665 London was racked by bubonic plague. That summer, the plague travelled north and reached the village of Eyam in the Derbyshire Dales, through a contaminated parcel to the village tailor, Alexander Hadfield.

The plague spread through the village during the autumn of 1665, but slowed in winter. The next year's wave proved stronger than the first. By May, the village rector William Mompesson organised a strict quarantine to stop the plague spreading beyond the village boundary. This meant people remaining in the village and burying their dead near their homes rather than on consecrated ground. Provisions were left by outsiders at the boundary. While this quarantine worked, the villagers paid a heavy price.

The peak of infections came in August 1666, when 78 people died in one month. At least 260 residents succumbed to the plague, with 273 victims being on the church record, out of a population of around 800.

There are several 'Plague Cottages' in Eyam that have plaques detailing the outbreak, along with graves in the churchyard. The nearby 'Riley Graves' is a small graveyard on a hillside where seven members of the Hancock family are buried. It takes its name from the nearby farm. Elizabeth Hancock survived, while her six children and husband succumbed in eight days.

The nursery rhyme 'Ring-a-ring-o-roses' has been associated with the tragedy, with the 'ring' representing a mark on the cheek that those who caught the plague exhibited. However, folklorists contest the link because there are many variations of the rhyme, and there is no record of it becoming commonplace until at least 100 years later.

ROMAN WIGS

Wigs were not an uncommon sight at the Roman forum. Near the temple of Hercules, merchants would sell hair imported from the reddish-blond heads of Germans and Britons. Full wigs were available for those who were completely bald (or who sought a sly disguise), while smaller hairpieces could be used to create extravagant hairstyles.

137

Since 1324, every whale, dolphin, porpoise and sturgeon found on England's shores has become the property of the monarch. The right for these 'royal fish' was enshrined during the reign of Edward II.

It endures today, administered by the official Receiver of Wreck, although by the 19th century scientists had decided that whales, dolphins and porpoises were mammals, not fish.

MACHIAVELLIAN BEHAVIOUR

In his book *The Prince* (1532), the Italian Renaissance diplomat Niccolò Machiavelli considered the nature of political power and the strategies that can be deployed to gain and maintain it.

So-called Machiavellian behaviour is characterised by a focus on self-interest, a lack of moral scruples, and a willingness to manipulate and deceive others. In politics, it can be seen as a necessary trait for successful leadership in what is a highly competitive and often ruthless environment.

Here are some of the characteristics of Machiavellian behaviour:

1. **Deception:** Deceive and manipulate others for your own benefit.
2. **Exploitation:** Exploit the weaknesses and vulnerabilities of others for your own gain.
3. **Lack of empathy:** Do not concern yourself with the feelings or well-being of others.
4. **Ruthlessness:** Use whatever means necessary, including violence and coercion, to achieve your goals.
5. **Strategic thinking:** Be skilled at planning and executing complex schemes.
6. **Calculated risk-taking:** Do not be afraid to take calculated risks and be willing to accept the consequences if your plans fail.
7. **Manipulation:** Become skilled at manipulating others to do your bidding, often using flattery or other forms of persuasion.
8. **Pragmatism:** Be highly pragmatic and focused on achieving your goals, regardless of the ethical implications.

27 May 1798: Prime Minister William Pitt fought a duel on Putney Common with George Tierney, MP, Treasurer of the Navy, President of the Board of Control. Both men missed.

1794 to 1813: Pierre Dupont de l'Étang and François Fournier-Sarlovèze fought over 30 duels, all stemming from Fournier-Sarlovèze taking exception to a message from Dupont de l'Étang to a friend and fellow officer. Dupont de l'Étang finally, decisively beat his opponent two decades later and forced Fournier-Sarlovèze to swear an oath that he would never ask for another duel.

11 July 1804: Vice President Aaron Burr duelled former Treasury Secretary Alexander Hamilton. Hamilton was killed.

30 May 1806: Andrew Jackson duelled Charles Dickinson. Jackson was wounded but Dickinson was killed. Andrew Jackson went on to become the only US President who had killed a man in a duel.

21 September 1809: Foreign Secretary George Canning fought Minister for War Viscount Castlereagh. Canning was hit in the leg, while a button on Castlereagh's coat deflected a shot.

23 March 1829: Prime Minister the Duke of Wellington fought a duel in Battersea against the Earl of Winchelsea. Wellington missed, Winchelsea fired his pistol into the air.

DAVID HASSELHOFF AND THE BERLIN WALL

David Hasselhoff's hit song 'Looking for Freedom' became an anthem for a newly unified Germany during the fall of the Berlin Wall. Hasselhoff, an American television actor known for his roles in *Knight Rider* and *Baywatch*, had released the cover song in 1988. It was a hit in West Germany, remaining number one for eight weeks. The song's timely release and the wall's destruction soon afterwards made Hasselhoff a Cold War icon.

On New Year's Eve 1989 a crowd of over 500,000 people gathered at the Brandenburg Gate to watch the actor perform the song. Hasselhoff hovered in a bucket crane over a crowd of thousands who had gathered to celebrate the fall of the wall. Germans from both sides of the border sat astride the hated barricade, and thousands more watched the performance live on national television. 'Looking for Freedom' was eventually certified Platinum in Germany, and became the best-performing single of 1989 in the country.

THE WORLD'S BIGGEST RESTAURANT CHAIN

McDonald's is the world's largest fast-food restaurant chain, with more than 35,000 outlets globally. Its logo, the familiar golden arches, has become a symbol of globalisation. The first restaurant was founded by Richard and Maurice McDonald in May 1940 in San Bernardino, California.

Entrepreneur Raymond A. Kroc bought out the founding brothers' equity in 1961 and began aggressively expanding its operations through franchising, introducing a standardised menu and deploying innovative marketing techniques. He is credited with revolutionising the fast-food industry. By the time of Kroc's death in 1980, there were 7,500 restaurants in the United States.

The oldest operating McDonald's is located in Downey, California, and was opened in 1953. As it was franchised from the McDonald brothers, not Ray Kroc, it did not modernise alongside the McDonald's Corporation until its acquisition in 1990, when it was the only remaining independent McDonald's.

MCDONALD'S SYMBOLIC ROLE IN COMMUNISM'S END

On 31 January 1990, after nearly 14 years of negotiations, the Soviet Union's first McDonald's opened in Moscow's Pushkin Square. Its arrival was a sign that change was on the horizon as part of 'glasnost', the opening up to the world's ideas and products – yet the establishment of this iconic American capitalist fast-food chain in the communist country's capital city also signalled the end of the Soviet Union.

McDonald's Moscow opening was greeted enthusiastically – 27,000 people responded to McDonald's newspaper advert to fill jobs on salaries of 1.5 rubles an hour. On its opening day, hundreds of people queued to spend sometimes the equivalent of several days' wages on Big Macs, milkshakes and French fries at what was then the largest McDonald's in the world at 900 seats. To average Soviet workers, McDonald's was a high-class meal – they'd need to work for 2.5 hours to earn 3.85 rubles for a Big Mac ('Bolshoi Mak') – something that took the average US worker under 20 minutes.

For many Russians, visiting McDonald's was more of an opportunity to enjoy a small pleasure than a political statement. Soviet restaurants were renowned for their unfriendly service, bad hygiene and menu shortages, so this (along with plans to open 19 more outlets in Moscow over the next few years) was exciting. McDonald's famous golden arches were seen as symbolic of capitalist society, which many Russians longed for after a life of queues, inferior products and shortages.

The appearance of McDonald's and its enthusiastic reception signalled times were changing, signifying greater Russian engagement with the world, both economically and democratically. Less than two years later, the Soviet Union ceased to exist as a nation, Gorbachev had resigned, and many Soviet republics proclaimed their independence.

However, in May 2022, after more than 30 years of operations in Russia, McDonald's announced its complete withdrawal from the Russian market. The war in Ukraine led McDonald's to conclude that continued business in Russia was no longer tenable, nor consistent with their values.

Magna Carta is a well-known document that set out key legal principles, but it was also essentially a list of complaints from a small number of high-ranking nobles that, almost accidentally, offered a small benefit to other people. Of far more importance to contemporaries was the Charter of the Forest, issued by King Henry III's regency council on 6 November 1217. This charter sought to claw back some of the vast increases in land designated as royal forest. This didn't only mean wooded areas, but might include fields, heaths and other open spaces. Royal forest, in this context, simply meant an enclosed area of land reserved for the king, mainly for hunting. Under William the Conqueror and his sons, this area had become much larger across England, and was further extended by King John, with harsh penalties for anyone else caught using the land.

The Charter of the Forest reset the extent of the Royal Forest to what it had been under Henry II (r. 1154–89). Clause 9 of the Charter restored the right to collect wood, to graze pigs, and to leave pigs overnight within Royal Forest lands. Clause 10 removed the death penalty for poachers and replaced it with a fine, or a year in prison if the fine was not paid. This reopened access to land for grazing and foraging that had been shrinking for 150 years. However, like Magna Carta, the Charter of the Forest expressly applied only to free men, which was around half the population of England at the time. Serfs were excluded. The Charter of the Forest was reissued in 1225, and remained on the statute books until 1971, making it the longest piece of legislation to remain in force in English history.

CROMWELL'S HEAD

In 1649, King Charles I lost his head. For the first time in British history, the king was tried for treason, found guilty and executed. In 1661, Charles's son, Charles II, took vengeance on one of his father's leading enemies – Oliver Cromwell. Eighteen months after he had been buried, he dug up Cromwell's corpse, then had it decapitated and hanged. His head remained on a pole outside Parliament for 20 years.

SOME 20TH-CENTURY MYTHS

Titanic's owners never said it was 'unsinkable'
Neither the White Star Line nor shipbuilders Harland and Wolff had advertised the *Titanic* as unsinkable. Three trade publications had described *Titanic* as 'practically unsinkable', and a promotional item from White Star Line stressed the *Olympic* and *Titanic*'s safety, claiming that 'as far as it is possible to do so, these two wonderful vessels are designed to be unsinkable'; similar claims had been made about other ocean liners. Harland and Wolff claim the 'unsinkable' myth was the result of misinterpretations of articles in the *Irish News* and the *Shipbuilder* magazine, which grew after *Titanic* sank.

The 'Spanish flu' didn't come from Spain
The 1918/19 'Spanish flu' was one of the world's deadliest pandemics, killing over 50 million people. While its origin is uncertain, it probably started in America and spread quickly among troops during World War One. Spain's neutral status and free press meant their newspapers were first to report the outbreak, leading to 'Spanish flu', even though the virus likely did not originate in Spain.

It wasn't illegal to drink alcohol during Prohibition
The 18th Amendment and subsequent Volstead Act prohibited the production, sale and transport of 'intoxicating liquors' within America, but their possession and consumption were never outlawed. Any alcohol already stashed away could be enjoyed in people's own homes. During the Prohibition era, from 1920 to 1933, speakeasies flourished as secret establishments where people clandestinely gathered to enjoy alcohol. They were primarily located in major cities.

President Kennedy never announced he was a German pastry
President Kennedy's famous phrase 'Ich bin ein Berliner' means 'I am a citizen of Berlin' in standard German. The inclusion of the indefinite article 'ein' did not change the meaning of the sentence to 'I am a Berliner', referring to a type of German pastry. The pastry has many names in Germany, and is not even commonly called 'Berliner' in the Berlin area.

Medieval manuscripts are filled with drawings of fantastic beasts. Bestiaries, books that detail types of animals, also include monsters and races believed to exist beyond the known edges of the world. These were sometimes the spark for discussion about whether some humanoid beings possessed souls, and therefore ought to be preached to, or whether they belonged to the animal kingdom. Here are a few examples from the medieval mind.

Manticores: Medieval bestiaries were packed with monsters made up of parts of real animals. A manticore was usually shown in manuscript illustrations as having the head of a man, the body of a lion, and the tail of a scorpion.

Blemmyae: A race of human-like beings, the Blemmyae were thought to live in Africa, somewhere beyond Ethiopia. They were headless humanoids, with eyes, a nose and a mouth in the centre of their chests.

Giants: With their roots in the biblical story of David and Goliath, it seemed reasonable to the medieval mind that giants must exist. Geoffrey of Monmouth wrote in the 12th century of a giant named Gogmagog who was the last surviving member of his race in the British Isles and was killed by Corineus, who threw him from a cliff into the sea.

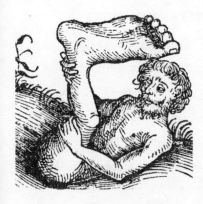

Monopods: Another humanoid race, the Monopods, or Skiapodes, were believed to have one thick leg and one large foot, which they are often pictured using as a shade from the sun. No one seemed to give any thought to the sunburn they might get on the soles of their feet.

Basilisk: Believed to originate from Ethiopia, they were frequently pictured as a cockerel with a snake's tail, or as a snake with a large crest.

Dog Heads: Also known as Cynocephali, this was a race of humanoids who had the head of a dog or wolf. They were perhaps a representation of the pagan Scandinavians who, as Vikings, terrorised Christian Europe and some-times wore animal pelts.

2022 was not the first time Britain had three different Prime Ministers.

1782: Britain was reeling from its worst defeat in its history. A French fleet saw off a British relief fleet in Chesapeake Bay, USA, which led to the surrender of Britain's beleaguered army in Yorktown, Virginia to George Washington and his French allies. The War of Independence was effectively over. Lord North, the British Prime Minister, resigned in March 1782, he was succeeded by Lord Rockingham, who died after a couple of months. The Earl of Shelburne took over making it three in the calendar year. Interestingly, both he and his successor Portland lasted under a year each, meaning that Britain ended up with five Prime Ministers in two years.

1827: Long-serving Lord Liverpool had a debilitating stroke; Canning took over but died in just over three months. Lord Goderich took over as the third that year. He only just saw out the year and there were two more Prime Ministers in the next two years.

1834: A bit ambiguous. Grey resigned, Melbourne took over, despite the expectation that it would be a 'damned bore'. The king kicked out Melbourne and the Whigs that autumn and asked the Tories to form a government. The Duke of Wellington didn't want to be Prime Minister but Robert Peel was on holiday in Sardinia so while he was on the way back Wellington did the job for him, sort of. Historians can't agree whether he was Prime Minister or not!

1852: A year of crisis during the Irish Potato Famine saw Whig Prime Minister Lord Russell hand over the reins to Lord Derby, who called an election that he failed to win. Needing to turn back to the Whigs but with Russell an unpopular choice and another candidate pleading ill health, it fell to Lord Aberdeen.

1868: Prime Minister Lord Derby was incapacitated by bad health so Queen Victoria summoned Benjamin Disraeli to form a government. He was thrilled, boasting that he had 'climbed to the top of the greasy pole'. He soon slid down because Gladstone's Liberals won the General Election towards the end of the year.

CRY HAVOC!

The verbal commands used to control medieval armies on the battle-field are largely unknown as they were poorly recorded. One of the few that is noted is the order 'Montez!', which was an instruction for all those with a horse to get into the saddle.

One other battlefield order that is known is the cry of 'Havoc!'. Shakespeare uses the instruction in the line 'Cry havoc! and let slip the dogs of war!' in *Julius Caesar*. Havoc was an order that often featured prominently in ordinances prepared for medieval armies because it was considered so dangerous that it was expressly forbidden without permission from the army's commander.

Havoc released the army from any formation and gave freedom to loot. It was an order only ever to be given when it was utterly certain that a battle was won and discipline was no longer required. A wrongly timed cry of havoc could cost a battle and ordinances often prescribed a severe punishment for crying havoc without permission – sometimes extending to beheading.

AUGUSTUS THE PROPAGANDIST

The first Emperor of Rome was a successful general, great statesman and a clever propagandist. During the Last War of the Roman Republic against Mark Antony, he falsified Antony's will and produced coinage holding slogans against his adversary.

'Augustus' wasn't his real name either. The Emperor was formerly known as Octavian or Octavius Caesar, as he was the nephew of Julius Caesar. 'Augustus' means 'the increaser' and thus Octavian thought it most appropriate. He also commissioned very fine statues of himself, and sent youthful busts throughout the empire. Even by his 80th birthday, the year that he died, the young Augustus was still popping up throughout Europe.

MARK TWAIN PREDICTED HIS OWN DEATH (KIND OF)

In 1909, Mark Twain said:

> 'I came in with Halley's Comet in 1835. It is coming again next year, and I expect to go out with it. It will be the greatest disappointment of my life if I don't go out with Halley's Comet. The Almighty has said, no doubt, "Now there are these two unaccountable freaks; they came in together, they must go out together".'

He died of a heart attack on 21 April 1910 – one day after the comet had come again and appeared at its brightest. Halley's comet only passes by Earth approximately every 76 years, and has been the subject of a string of predictions since 1705.

SOME 'CLANDESTINE' ORGANISATIONS

Lollards: A 14th-century pre-Protestant religious movement in England that advocated for reform within the Catholic Church.

Cathars: A Christian sect that emerged in the 11th century in southern France, persecuted as heretics by the Catholic Church for their belief in two Gods – one good, and one evil.

Freemasons: A fraternal organisation from the 17th century, promoting moral and social values and providing mutual support and fellowship among its members.

Illuminati: A secret society founded in Bavaria in the late 18th century, promoting Enlightenment ideals and advocating for political and social change.

Underground Railroad: A network of secret routes and safe houses used by enslaved African Americans to escape to freedom in the 19th century.

Luddites: A group of 19th-century English textile workers who protested against the introduction of new machinery and technology, which they saw as a threat to their livelihoods.

In case you thought *Titanic* was
the most famous shipwreck
ever, there were many others
that captured the public's attention in previous centuries.

Mary Rose (1545)

Henry VIII's warship served the
king and country for 33 years.
But she sank in the Solent,
between Portsmouth and the Isle of Wight during an attack on a
French fleet. Some 500 crew members died. Large parts of *Mary Rose*
were raised in 1982, but why she went down still remains a mystery.

Batavia (1629)

The Dutch East India Company ship *Batavia* was wrecked on 4 June
1629 when the vessel struck a reef off the western coast of Australia.
After she ran aground, 300 of its 341 passengers made it ashore but
a mutiny broke out, resulting in around 125 people being massacred.
The mutineers were the first Europeans legally executed in Australia.

Vasa (1628)

The most heavily armed vessel of its time, this Swedish warship was
lost on its maiden voyage just 1,400 yards out to sea. Being top-heavy
and unstable, she capsized just minutes after setting sail.

Whydah Gally (1717)

Originally built as a passenger, cargo, and slave ship, *Whydah Gally*
was captured by the infamous pirate 'Black Sam' Bellamy. She was
caught in a violent storm and wrecked off the coast of Massachusetts.
In 1984, she was found off the coast of Cape Cod.

HMS Victory (1744)

One of the worst naval disasters in British history, *Victory* sank in
the English Channel after being caught in a storm, in which its 1,150
sailors were lost. It's possible that *Victory* was carrying gold and silver
worth hundreds of millions of pounds.

Stalin's eldest son died in a German concentration camp

Stalin's son, Yakov Dzhugashvili, was raised by an aunt and didn't meet his father until he was 14. During the war, Yakov fought as a Russian soldier and was captured by the Nazis. After he was revealed to be Stalin's son, the Nazis attempted to use Yakov as leverage, but Stalin refused to negotiate, stating: 'You have in your hands not only my son Yakov but millions of my sons. Either you free them all or my son will share their fate.' Yakov died at Sachsenhausen concentration camp while attempting to climb the camp's electric fence.

Hitler's half-nephew served in the US Navy

The son of Adolf Hitler's half-brother, Alois, William Patrick Hitler was born in England in 1911 but moved to Germany in the 1930s. He was something of a problem for the German Führer, and in July 1939 he published an article in *Look* magazine titled 'Why I hate my uncle. . .' He moved to America in 1939. It has been reported that in 1944 he appealed directly to President Roosevelt to join the fight against his uncle and the FBI deemed it sincere. Though he never saw combat, Hitler served until 1947. He changed his name to William Stuart-Houston and died in 1987.

Hermann Goering's brother reportedly saved hundreds of Jews

Albert Goering had not been indoctrinated by the Nazis like his brother Hermann (Hitler's deputy and chosen successor), and instead set about working to aid persecuted Jews. He would often seek help from Hermann in releasing prisoners or removing arrest warrants for him, and Hermann is said to have assisted Albert many times.

Theodore Roosevelt Jr. stormed the Normandy beaches

Theodore Roosevelt Jr., son of President Roosevelt, was a respected veteran of World War One, where he'd been shot and gassed. Despite being in his mid-50s, he participated in D-Day as the only US general to storm the Normandy beaches in the first wave. He was the oldest soldier there. One month later, he suffered a fatal heart attack and was buried at the Normandy American Cemetery near Omaha Beach.

STRANGE WAYS TO DIE

From 1592 to 1595 – and then from 1611 onwards – the weekly mortality statistics of London were regularly recorded in the Bills of Mortality. Among the more curious causes of death noted were:

Appoplex and Suddenly : Blasted and Planet : Bloody Flux : Chrisomes : Collick and Winde : Cut of the Stone : Distracted : Dropsie and Timpany : Fistula : French Pox : Frighted : Griping in the Guts : Headmouldshot : Itch : Kild by several accidents : Kings Evill : Lethargy : Lunatick and Frenzy : Mouldfallen : Purples : Rising of the Lights : Scalded in a Brewer's Mash at St Giles, Cripplegate : Strangury : Sore Legge : Teeth and Worms : Tissick : Wen

THE VANISHING OF EDISON'S RIVAL

Louis Le Prince, a French inventor and filmmaker, disappeared under mysterious circumstances on 16 September 1890. On the day of his disappearance, Le Prince boarded a train from Dijon to Paris, but he never arrived at his destination.

There have been suggestions that he staged his own disappearance to escape debt and financial troubles. A drowned man resembling Le Prince was recovered from the Seine, although the body was never formally identified as Le Prince. That he could have been a rival to Thomas Edison has led some to cry foul play, including Le Prince's widow, but there is no concrete evidence to support these claims.

BAD NOMINATIONS

Among the nominees for the Nobel Peace Prize are Adolf Hitler and Benito Mussolini (both 1939) and Joseph Stalin (1945 and 1948). Hitler's nomination was submitted by a Swedish MP, while Mussolini's came from an Italian professor. Stalin's nominations were made by a British MP and a group of Norwegian politicians. No prize was awarded in 1939 or 1948. The 1945 prize was awarded to Cordell Hull, for his work establishing the United Nations.

On 26 November 1922, Howard Carter peered through a gap into Tutankhamun's tomb and laid eyes upon 'wonderful things'. What his team had discovered was the first ever sealed, ancient Egyptian tomb in the Valley of the Kings. Overall the tomb included more than 5,000 objects, interred with the boy king for his journey into the afterlife.

The death mask

The most famous artefact uncovered from the tomb. Made of gold, electrum, glass, obsidian, lapis lazuli and other precious stones, the mask was originally placed on top of Tutankhamun's mummy, protecting the boy king's fragile remains.

Chariots

Tutankhamun was buried with six of these. Some were lightweight, built for speed and agility across desert terrain. Others were more heavily decorated – used for sumptuous ceremonies.

The crook and flail

The crook and the flail were the royal regalia for an ancient Egyptian pharaoh. Symbolising animal husbandry and agriculture, they evoked the pharaoh's control over the natural world. We often see pharaohs holding these items in ancient Egyptian art, but Tutankhamun's crook and flail are the only surviving examples.

The volcanic pectoral

Among the many items of jewellery found in Tut's tomb was a very special pectoral, complete with a beetle decoration made from natural, green glass. The ancient Egyptians quarried this glass from a meteorite crater deep in the Sahara Desert. More than 3,000 years ago, the ancient Egyptians knew of this crater hundreds of miles away from the Nile.

TUTANKHAMUN'S CURSE

The unveiling of Tutankhamun's tomb was one of the greatest archaeological discoveries of all time, and caused a media frenzy. However, *The Times of London* had exclusivity of the story, meaning only they could report the discovery. Starved of objective reporting, many newspapers turned to speculative stories, with the most persistent being 'Tutankhamun's Curse'.

The boy king died in 1323 BC, leaving a gap of over 3,000 years before his tomb was unsealed. The story went that the tomb then unleashed a 'curse', killing people connected to the discovery. Lord Carnarvon, who funded the excavations, died just six months after the unsealing. Many other people who died after the event were associated with the curse:

Name	Cause of Death	Age	Year of Death
Lord Carnavon	Blood poisoning	57	1923
Ali Fahmy Bey	Fatally shot	23	1923
Audrey Herbert	Blood poisoning	43	1923
Hugh Evelyn-White	Suicide	40	1923
Georges Bénédite	Possible stroke	69	1926
Arthur Mace	Pneumonia	53	1928
Richard Bethel	Natural causes	46	1929
Mervyn Herbert	'Malarial pneumonia'	46	1929
Richard Bethell Snr	Suicide	78	1930
Albert Lythgoe	Arteriosclerosis	66	1934
Howard Carter	Hodgkin's disease	64	1939

But this supernatural tale doesn't stand up to much scrutiny. Of 26 people who were present at the opening of Tutankhamun's tomb, six died within a decade. Average life expectancy for males in the 1920s was just under 57 years of age.

Spiritualism was a mid-19th century phenomenon, largely originating in America. For some it became a quasi-religion, with spirit contact via medium-led seances and later Ouija boards.

Sherlock Holmes creator Sir Arthur Conan Doyle was one of Spiritualism's greatest advocates. His interest in the paranormal began in 1887 with his first seance attendance, and in 1893 he became a member of the Society for Psychical Research.

Doyle publicly presented himself as a Spiritualist in 1916 – a year when Britain's involvement in the First World War was heightened by the Battle of the Somme. He published his first book on his spiritualist beliefs, *The New Revelation*, in 1918, and it became something of a bible for the Spiritualist cause in Britain.

He suffered family bereavement in 1918 and 1919 when both his son and brother died of Spanish flu. Seeking solace in his belief in the afterlife, he embarked on a lecture tour of Australia and New Zealand in 1920, followed by a 50,000-mile Christian Spiritualist tour of North America in 1923. In 1920 he met Harry Houdini, and they formed a friendship, but they would later fall out over Conan Doyle's beliefs and alleged trickery.

Like Houdini, not all the public and media were enamoured with Conan Doyle's Spiritualist lectures. In September 1921 the *Sunday Express* ran a tactless headline asking 'Is Conan Doyle Mad?'

Conan Doyle also got involved in King Tutankhamun's Curse by speculating that Lord Carnavon had been killed by an 'elemental'. Asked why no one else involved in the dig had suffered such a fate, Conan Doyle famously said:

'It is nonsense to say that because 'elementals' do not harm everybody, therefore they do not exist. One might as well say that because bulldogs do not bite everybody, therefore bulldogs don't exist.'

ARTHUR CONAN DOYLE'S GOALKEEPING

Quite the polymath, Sir Arthur Conan Doyle was a medical doctor, bestselling author and Spiritualist advocate. He also played as a football goalkeeper for Portsmouth Association Football Club under the pseudonym A. C. Smith. The club was amateur, and disbanded in 1896. Portsmouth FC, the now professional club, was founded in 1898.

HELEN DUNCAN: BRITAIN'S LAST WITCH

Helen Duncan was one of the last people to be imprisoned under the Witchcraft Act of 1735. 'Hellish Nell' was a Scottish medium who earned a living conducting seances across Britain in the mid-1920s.

Her act was notable for the spiritual 'materialisations' she appeared to conjure. As Duncan slipped into a trance-like state and took on the persona of one of her spirit partners, spectral figures appeared and she produced 'ectoplasm' from her mouth. Duncan's act naturally attracted plenty of scepticism, and her stagecraft was exposed several times when flash photos showed her materialisations to be dolls. Later her 'ectoplasm' was revealed to be a combination of cheesecloth, paper mixed with the white of egg and loo paper, which she regurgitated at the appropriate time.

In November 1941, during World War Two, she performed a seance in Portsmouth where she summoned the spirit of a sailor who had just gone down with the battleship HMS *Barham*. The *Barham* had indeed been sunk by a German submarine off the Egyptian coast on 25 November 1941, but its fate had been kept from the public. Duncan's revelation of a state secret during wartime initially passed without censure but made her a person of interest.

Two years later, police lieutenants found evidence she was acting fraudulently and arrested her. By then it was clear Duncan's HMS *Barham* revelation was probably obtained via a leak. Eager to make an example of her, the authorities used section 4 of the Witchcraft Act of 1735, triable before jury, on the grounds of fraudulent spiritual activity. Duncan was found guilty and sentenced to nine months in prison. She died in 1956, five years after the Witchcraft Act was repealed.

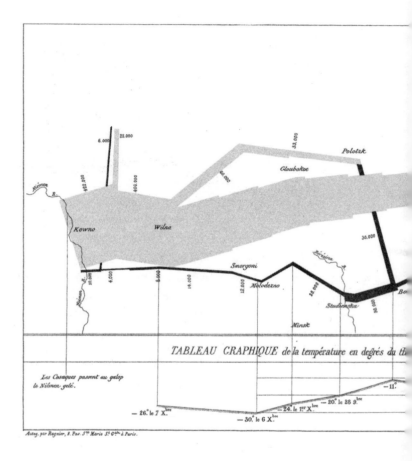

Charles Minard's famous infographic of Napoleon's invasion of Russia in 1812-13 shows the strength of Napoleon's army, numbering 422,000 men, as it crossed the Niemen river in Lithuania on 24 June 1812. The Russians refused to engage with Napoleon and retreated into their homeland, deploying scorched earth tactics that starved the French Army. The first major engagement was at Smolensk in August, followed by the Battle of Borodino on 7 September. This was probably the bloodiest battle in history up to that point,

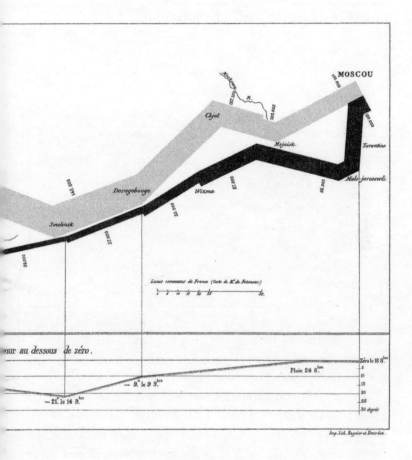

with 45,000 Russians and 35,000 French dead. In the aftermath, Napoleon entered Moscow assuming its capture would end the war. However, the Mayor of Moscow ordered the city to be burned, and the Russians refused to negotiate. Concerned about his position in France, Napoleon left Moscow after five weeks. The black returning line shows the depletion of Napoleon's force as it retreated, facing the Russian winter and harrying attacks by Russian forces. Only around 10,000 French troops crossed the Niemen again in December 1812.

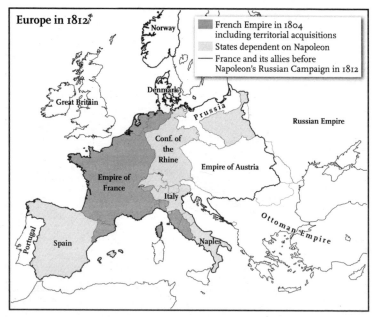

By 1812 France had direct control over much of Western Europe, with client states in the east up to the Russian border. The British Empire remained opposed to Napoleon. After the Battle of Trafalgar in October 1805, Britain was dominant at sea.

French power over Europe led Napoleon to create the Continental System, which was a large-scale trade embargo against the British Empire from November 1806. Britain was already blockading the French coast from May 1806. While the embargo caused some damage to the economy, the British Empire's control of the Atlantic meant it could trade with the Americas. The Continental System was also hard to police, and there was extensive smuggling.

The Portuguese, a long standing British ally, refused to join the Continental System. Napoleon invaded in 1807 leading to the Peninsula War, which sapped French resources. Other European economies were damaged by the embargo and began ignoring it. Napoleon invaded Russia in 1812 after realising it was trading with Britain. This proved to be a fatal mistake, from which Napoleon never recovered.

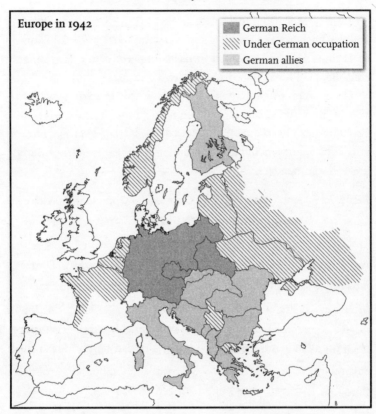

Europe in 1942

German Reich
Under German occupation
German allies

Hitler's Nazi Germany reached its maximum territorial expansion in mid-1942. In a series of successful military campaigns, Germany had absorbed or subdued Czechoslovakia, Poland, France, the Low Countries, Norway, Yugoslavia and Greece. Western Russia was under military occupation from late 1941.

The tables turned in February 1943 with Germany's decisive defeat at the Battle of Stalingrad – the deadliest battle of the Second World War. Germany and Italy also suffered defeat in North Africa in May 1943, and by the summer of 1944 the Soviets had turned the tide and entered Poland, while the Western Allies had successfully invaded Normandy. Paris was liberated in August 1944. It would take until 2 May 1945 for Germany to finally surrender.

MAJOR BATTLES OF THE NAPOLEONIC WARS

The Napoleonic Wars took place from 1803 to 1815, after Napoleon had established the French Republic as the most powerful country in Europe. He soon crowned himself Emperor of the French, and consolidated French dominance, at least on land, in 1805.

There were seven Napoleonic Wars in total, starting with the War of the Third Coalition and ending with the War of the Seventh Coalition (also known as the Hundred Days). Napoleon fought over sixty battles, he won all but a handful of them. He is one of history's greatest commanders.

Battle	Date	Location	Opponent	Victor
Ulm	16–19 Oct 1805	Germany	Austria	France
Trafalgar	21 Oct 1805	Spain	Britain	Britain
Austerlitz	2 Dec 1805	Czechia	Coalition	France
Jena-Auers	14 Oct 1806	Prussia	Prussia	France
Eylau	7–8 Feb 1807	East Prussia	Russia	Stalemate
Friedland	14 Jun 1807	East Prussia	Russia	France
Wagram	5–6 Jul 1809	Austria	Austria	France
Salamanca	22 July 1812	Spain	Coalition	Coalition
Borodino	7 Sep 1812	Russia	Russia	Stalemate
Leipzig	16–19 Oct 1813	Germany	Coalition	Coalition
Waterloo	15 June 1815	Belgium	Coalition	Coalition

The tides turned on Napoleon after the disastrous 1812 invasion of Russia. A year later, with French forces seriously weakened, the biggest battle in Europe before World War One was fought at Leipzig. Napoleon was defeated, and the Sixth Coalition moved on to Paris, forcing him to abdicate. He escaped exile and returned to Paris on 20 March 1815, gathering an army to march on Brussels, but he was decisively defeated by the Duke of Wellington and Gebhard Leberecht von Blücher's Seventh Coalition at Waterloo. On Napoleon's recapture the British exiled him to the remote island of St Helena, where he died in May 1821, aged 51.

In September 1943, Mussolini's regime adopted some of the Nazi state's antisemitic policies and began arresting and deporting Italian Jews to concentration camps in central and Eastern Europe. 8–9,000 Italian Jews were killed during the Holocaust.

The Fatebenefratelli Hospital in Rome had previously protected some of the city's Jewish residents. On 16 October 1943, Nazi soldiers began a raid on the Jewish ghetto in Rome, deporting around 1,200 Jews. This prompted the hospital to open its doors to help hide a number of Jews seeking shelter from the Nazi raid.

Knowing the hospital would be searched, a trio of doctors – Vittorio Sacerdoti, Giovanni Borromeo and Adriano Ossicini – duped the authorities into believing they were quarantining these Jewish patients who had been stricken with a highly contagious disease known as 'Syndrome K', whose symptoms included convulsions and paralysis and could lead to disfiguration and death. Syndrome K was entirely fictitious, but all patients were advised to cough violently if a Nazi soldier came close. The name Syndrome K was used so that staff could differentiate which people were actually patients and which were Jews in hiding.

When the Nazis came to search the hospital, they were warned about the highly contagious disease. Scared of contracting it, the Nazi soldiers didn't dare enter the building. The doctors were then later able to move the Jewish hideaways to various safe houses around the city. Borromeo and his co-conspirators also installed an illegal radio transmitter in the hospital's basement to communicate with partisans. However, this was thrown in the Tiber after they suspected the Nazis had identified its position.

In May 1944, the Nazis finally raided the hospital, but the ruse over Syndrome K had been so carefully executed that only five Polish Jews were caught hiding on a balcony (all went on to survive the war). Over a half-century later, the fabricated illness was finally revealed and the doctors at Fatebenefratelli Hospital were recognised for their life-saving actions. Estimates suggest the Syndrome K cover story saved a couple of dozen lives.

CULTURAL BRITISH UNESCO SITES

Site	Location
Castles and Town Walls in Gwynedd	North Wales
St Kilda+	Outer Hebrides
Durham Castle and Cathedral	County Durham
Ironbridge Gorge	Shropshire
Stonehenge and Avebury	Wiltshire
Studley Royal Park*	North Yorkshire
Frontiers of the Roman Empire	Northumberland
Blenheim Palace	Oxfordshire
City of Bath	Somerset
Palace of Westminster**	London
Canterbury Cathedral***	Kent
Tower of London	London
Old and New Towns of Edinburgh	Midlothian
Maritime Greenwich	London

+The uninhabited island of Saint Kilda is a 'mixed' entry with both cultural and natural categorisation.

* Includes Fountains Abbey

** Includes St Margaret's Church

*** Includes St Augustine's Abbey, and St Martin's Church

Oldest surviving English town in the New World

The UK's UNESCO list includes Historic Town of St George and Related Fortifications, Bermuda (a British Overseas Territory), admitted in 2000. St George's Town was originally called New London and was settled in 1612, founded by the Virginia Company near the site of the shipwrecked *Sea Venture*, incidentally the likely inspiration for William Shakespeare's play *The Tempest*

Abandoned islands

St Kilda is an archipelago on the Outer Hebrides. People have lived there for 4,000 years, but by 1930 there were only 36 residents living on the island of Hirta, and it was evacuated. There are around 1,200 abandoned homes on Hirta, and the residents of St Kilda now amount to some livestock and close to 1 million birds.

CULTURAL BRITISH UNESCO SITES

Industrial landscape

Many of the UK world heritage sites are industrial. Places like the Forth Bridge, opened in 1882, and the Derwent Valley Mills, where the water-powered mill invented by Richard Arkwright was first put into large-scale production, recall Britain's unique industrial history.

THE FIRST WRITING

Today, Ice Age cave sites such as Lascaux, Chauvet and Altamira are famous – first and foremost – for their beautiful animal depictions, drawn, painted and engraved on cave walls more than 15,000 years ago. But next to many of these animal depictions – usually showing the prey of hunter-gatherers – are strange markings.

It's believed some of the most frequently observed marks represent the number of months (lunar cycles) after the beginning of spring that these various prey animals mated and gave birth. For hunter-gatherers, the beginning of spring was one of the only, clear fixed points in the landscape – when the ice began to melt.

In some cases a 'Y' sign can be seen next to these markings. It's believed that the 'Y' sign indicates giving birth. The position of Y in a sequence of marks indicates how many months after the beginning of spring the prey animal gave birth. For hunter-gatherer societies, where hunting large groups of these prey animals was central to their way of life, having a system like this that told them when in the year large herds of these animals came together was vital.

This Ice Age early proto-writing system was cracked by archaeologists in the early 2020s. The recent breakthrough means that these markings are the earliest form of writing that we know about.

DAYLIGHT SAVING

Daylight-saving time was introduced during World War One to conserve energy and increase daylight hours. Germany adopted it in 1916, the UK a few weeks later, then France and the USA. After the war, most countries abandoned it until World War Two.

However, the UK continued to use it and made the change permanent in 1925, calling it 'British Summer Time'. During World War Two, the UK implemented 'Double British Summer Time' (two hours ahead of GMT in summer and one hour ahead in winter), and in 1968 began an experiment with staying one hour ahead of GMT for three years. In 1971, the UK reverted to just the summer-time switch, which remains in use to date.

HISTORIC HATS

St Thomas More's Bonnet

Napoleon's Bicorne

Guy Fawkes's Sugarloaf

Abraham Lincoln's Stovepipe

*Davy Crockett's
Coonskin Cap*

Winston Churchill's Homburg

Jackie Kennedy's Pillbox

Frank Sinatra's Fedora

Elvis Presley (1935–77), the 'King of Rock and Roll', revolutionised music in the mid-1950s by popularising the niche genre of rock and roll, which had roots in blues and country music. He rose to fame quickly and became one of the most influential musicians of the 20th century.

Elvis Presley released a total of 24 studio albums between 1956 and 1977, with his debut album, *Elvis Presley* (1956), the first of many to reach number one on the Billboard 200 chart. He achieved this feat with ten of his studio albums, a record that stood for over three decades.

Elvis Presley (1956): *Elvis* (1956)

Elvis' Christmas Album (1957)

Elvis is Back! (1960) : *His Hand in Mine* (1960)

Something for Everybody (1961) : *Pot Luck* (1962)

Elvis for Everyone! (1965) : *How Great Thou Art* (1967)

From Elvis in Memphis (1969)

From Memphis to Vegas / From Vegas to Memphis (1969)

That's the Way It Is (1970) : *Elvis Country*
(I'm 10,000 Years Old) (1971)

Love Letters from Elvis (1971)

Elvis Sings The Wonderful World of Christmas (1971)

Elvis Now (1972) : *He Touched Me* (1972)

Elvis (aka The Fool Album) (1973)

Raised on Rock / For Ol' Times Sake (1973)

Good Times (1974) : *Promised Land* (1975)

Today (1975) : *From Elvis Presley Boulevard,*
Memphis, Tennessee (1976)

Moody Blue (1977)

In the late 1970s, Elvis Presley suffered declining health and personal problems. He died on 16 August 1977, at the age of 42.

Born in the mid-1250s in the Republic of Venice, Marco Polo was a merchant and explorer who became famous for writing about his travels in Asia. Marco's father Niccolò and uncle Maffeo had travelled into the Mongol Empire and found success before returning home in 1269. When they left again in 1271, they took Marco, then around 15 years old, with them. The Polo family travelled east through modern Turkey, Iran and Afghanistan, before returning to the Mongol court of Kublai Khan.

Marco lived in the empire for the next two decades and was shown great favour by Kublai Khan. He was employed as a diplomat, visiting present-day Burma, India, Indonesia, Sri Lanka and Vietnam among other places. In 1291, the Polo family accompanied a princess travelling to Persia to be married. As Kublai Khan was around 80 years old, and times of succession could be dangerous and disruptive in the Mongol Empire, they may have decided the time was right to leave.

In 1293, they arrived back in Venice after 22 years away to find family and friends had believed them dead. Marco became involved in the ongoing war between Venice and Genoa and was captured. While in prison, he shared a cell with a writer named Rustichello da Pisa. Marco dictated stories of his journeys and descriptions of what he had seen to Rustichello, who created the first edition of *Il Milione* ('The Million'), also known as *The Travels of Marco Polo*. Marco was soon released and died a wealthy and famous man in 1324.

Doubt has been cast on whether Marco actually visited the places he describes. Although Marco's account includes the first European references to paper money, gunpowder, porcelain and burning coal, he does not mention the Great Wall of China or tea at all, leading some to suggest he was merely reporting stories he had heard without visiting any of the places. For example, Marco Polo's account of the Assassin clan of Isma'ili Muslims is the origin of the false idea that they engaged in drug-taking, using opium to trick members into believing they were in a secret paradise, which they could only access if they followed their orders to assassinate their victims.

The Ark of the Covenant (10th century BC)
According to biblical accounts, the Ark of the Covenant was a sacred chest that housed the Ten Commandments given to Moses by God. It was believed to be located in the Temple of Solomon in Jerusalem, but it disappeared after the Babylonian invasion in 587 BC. Despite extensive searches, its whereabouts remain unknown.

Cleopatra's Tomb (30 BC)
One of the most famous queens in history, Cleopatra VII ruled over Ptolemaic Egypt at the height of its power. After her death, Egypt became a province of the Roman Empire, and Cleopatra's tomb was said to have been hidden somewhere in Egypt's deserts. Though searches have taken place, its exact location remains unknown.

The Library of the Moscow Tsars (16th century)
This collection of gold-covered books is supposed to have belonged to the Russian tsars. The earliest reference to the mysterious archive is by Michael Trivolis, who remarked on Tsar Basil III's 'countless multitudes of Greek books' in 1518. In 1978 engineers reportedly located underground passageways containing weapons stored by Ivan IV, but as yet no legendary library has been found.

The Lost Da Vinci Mural (16th century)
This famed work of art, supposed to have been created by the Italian Renaissance master Leonardo da Vinci, was commissioned to depict the 1440 Battle of Anghiari. A flag with the words 'Cerca trova' (He who seeks, finds) on a mural in Florence's town hall led some to believe Leonardo's painting lay beneath, but art historians have since cast doubt on whether Leonardo ever got round to painting it at all.

The Amber Room (18th century)
This stunning chamber, decorated with amber panels, gold leaf and precious gemstones, was installed in the Catherine Palace in Pushkin, Russia, in the 18th century. It was looted by German soldiers during World War Two and relocated to Königsberg, which was destroyed by Allied bombing in 1944. If it survived, its ultimate fate is a mystery.

The Treasure of Lima (1820)

The Treasure of Lima, also known as the 'Cocos Island Treasure', is said to be a vast fortune in gold, silver and jewels that was removed from Lima, Peru, in 1820 and buried on Cocos Island off the coast of Costa Rica. It is estimated to be worth some £160 million in today's money.

The Lost Fabergé Eggs (19th–20th centuries)

The House of Fabergé, a renowned jewellery firm in Russia, created a series of intricate and opulent Easter eggs for the Russian imperial family. However, after the Russian Revolution in 1917, many of these precious eggs were lost or stolen. Today, several of these eggs are still missing, and their value is estimated to be in the millions of dollars.

The Irish Crown Jewels (1907)

The Irish Crown Jewels were presented by King William IV for use by the Lord Lietenant of Ireland in 1831, and comprised a jewelled star and badge. They were reported missing from Dublin Castle in July 1907. With an estimated value of several million euros, the missing jewels are considered one of the biggest heists in Irish history.

The Florentine Diamond (1940s)

Though its origins are disputed, the documented history of the Florentine Diamond began in the 16th century in the possession of the influential Medici family. It passed through various royal families until some time after 1918, when it accompanied the Austrian Imperial family into exile. The diamond then vanished from the record, with later rumours claiming it lost, stolen or sold.

The Missing Jules Rimet Trophy (1983)

Awarded to winners of the FIFA World Cup from 1930 onwards, the Jules Rimet Cup was renamed after a former FIFA president in 1946. It was famously held by Brazil for winning three World Cup championships in 1958, 1962 and 1970, which made them the permanent owners of the trophy. However, in 1983 the trophy was stolen from a display case in Rio de Janeiro, Brazil, and has never been recovered.

CONQUESTS OF THE MONGOL EMPIRE

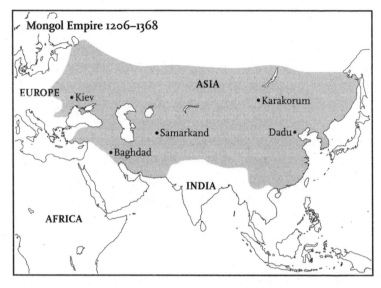

The Mongols built the largest contiguous empire in history. Emerging on the Mongolian steppes it stretched from China, to the Levant, and India. Genghis Khan, or Chingis Khan, was born Temüjin in around 1162. Between 1195 and 1205, Temüjin unified the steppe clans. His reputation for sharing the spoils of war with all of his men cemented his popularity. In 1206, Temüjin was crowned Emperor of the Great Mongol State and took the title Genghis Khan, which means something like 'the universal leader'.

From 1207 to 1211 the Mongols completed a conquest of Western Xia, in what is now China, giving the empire a tribute-paying vassal state and increasing their control over the Silk Road trade routes. Moving east, the Jin Dynasty was conquered at the Battle of Yehuling, where hundreds of thousands were reported killed. The Mongol capital was moved to Zhongdu, modern Beijing.

When Genghis sent embassies west to the Muslim Khwarazmian lands, the Shah attacked them. Furious, Genghis led around 100,000 men over the Tien Shan Mountains. Adapting their military tactics as they went, the Mongols seemed unstoppable. Genghis died in 1227 and his sons, led by Ögedei Khan, continued to expand the empire.

In 1230, Mongol forces pushed into Persia. Cities were offered the choice to surrender or be obliterated. Most chose to pay tribute. To the north, Georgia and Armenia were conquered, followed by attacks into Poland, Croatia, Serbia, Bulgaria, Austria and the Byzantine Empire. They reached as far north as Kyiv, where the Rus' surrendered and paid tribute. Baghdad's fall in 1258 shocked the Middle East, and Seljuk Turks, Armenians and Christian Crusader states submitted.

Under Genghis Khan's grandson Möngke, expansion continued. In 1259, Möngke was succeeded by his brother Kublai Khan, who completed the unification of China. On Kublai's death, the empire fractured into four Khanates. One was pushed back from the Middle East, another ruled China as the Yuan Dynasty until it was overthrown by the Ming dynasty in 1368, and the Golden Horde in the north maintained control of the Rus lands until the 15th century.

MR LOVERMAN

As was traditional for powerful Mongol men, Genghis Khan took many wives and concubines. Many were princesses of captured territories. Genghis's first wife was Börte, to whom he was betrothed when he was ten. They had three sons together, Chagatai, Ögedei and Tolui, as well as several daughters, and only Börte's children were considered legitimate successors to Genghis.

The total number of children fathered by Genghis Khan is unknown, but estimates range from several hundred to over a thousand. DNA evidence has suggested that one in every 200 people in the world today is a descendant of Genghis Khan. That's around 16 million people.

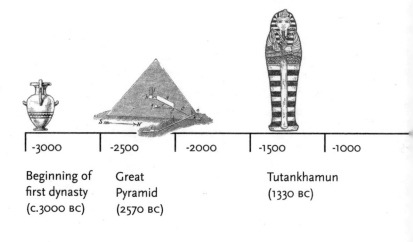

-3000	-2500	-2000	-1500	-1000

Beginning of
first dynasty
(c.3000 BC)

Great
Pyramid
(2570 BC)

Tutankhamun
(1330 BC)

EGYPT, BC

Egypt has one of the longest histories of any nation. Some 4,500 years ago, Egypt's Old Kingdom was established, and over the course of the next two millennia, farmers on the fertile banks of the lower River Nile combined to construct the pharaonic state, as well as four giant pyramids.

The Old, Middle and New Kingdoms differentiate the regimes that came to power over the next few thousand years. The relics that have defined the popular image of ancient Egypt mostly derive from the New Kingdom, the age of pharaohs Tutankhamun and Ramesses the Great, and the queen Nefertiti.

Conquest by the Achaemenid Empire, the Persians, in the 6th century BC ended native Egyptian rule. They were ousted in 332 BC by the Macedonian ruler Alexander the Great, who gave his name to the city of Alexandria. This led to the Ptolemaic kingdom (305–30 BC), whose most famous leader was also its last: Cleopatra VII. Cleopatra brought prosperity to a country that had been bankrupt and riven by civil war, but the end of her reign also saw Egypt succumb to annexation by Rome in 30 BC.

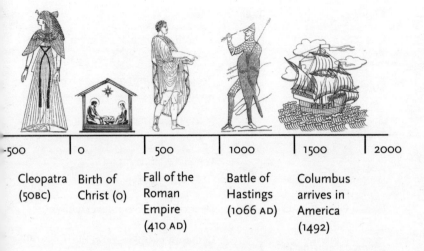

-500	0	500	1000	1500	2000

Cleopatra (50BC)

Birth of Christ (0)

Fall of the Roman Empire (410 AD)

Battle of Hastings (1066 AD)

Columbus arrives in America (1492)

EGYPT, AD

Roman rule in Egypt endured into late antiquity as a province of the Eastern Roman (later Byzantine) Empire. By far the wealthiest of Rome's provinces, Egypt yielded a massive amount of grain to feed the population of Alexandria, the empire's largest port, and for export to the Roman capital. That was until 641 AD, when Islamic conquest led to rule by successive caliphates, starting with the Rashidun Caliphate (632–61) and ending with the Mamluk Sultanate (1250–1517).

From Egypt, the Mamluks turned back invading Mongols in 1260 and recaptured the Crusader Kingdom of Jerusalem. Yet in 1517 Egypt was absorbed into the Ottoman Empire. Except for occupation under Napoleon Bonaparte (1798–1801), Egypt remained in Ottoman hands until the late 19th century, at which point the British began to dominate what they saw as an important node in their global empire.

In 1953, the monarchy established in 1922 was overthrown, along with the British. Gamal Abdel Nasser became the first President of the modern Republic of Egypt. Despite enduring social strife and political instability, Egypt remains a regional power, with a national identity drawing on its rich cultural heritage.

LEGAL CHANGES OF THE 1960S

Change	Year	Effect
Obscene Publications Act	1959	Liberalised regulation in publishing against 'obscenity' and censorship
Suicide Act	1961	People attempting suicide would no longer be prosecuted
Family Planning Act	1967	Made the contraceptive pill available to unmarried women
Abortion Act	1967	Legalised abortion on certain grounds
Sexual Offences Act	1967	Decriminalised homosexuality
Divorce Reform Act	1969	Unhappy couples could file for a no-fault divorce.

The 1960s was marked by social change throughout Western European countries and America.

In Britain there were significant changes in the law that had a liberalising effect towards the so-called 'Permissive Society.' The changes are often credited to two Home Secretaries under both Conservative and Labour governments. Rab Butler took office between 1957 and 1962, while Roy Jenkins took over for Labour in late 1965, holding the office until 1967.

The 'Permissive Society' is sometimes marked between two famous obscenity trials. The first notable prosecution under the Obscene Publications Act was the *Lady Chatterley's Lover* trial. D.H. Lawrence's novel was originally privately published in 1928, but also with key passages censored. Penguin Books then published an unexpurgated edition in 1960, but they were prosecuted under the law. However, the trial reached a not guilty verdict in November 1960.

In 1971, the publishers of a *Schoolkids* issue of the countercultural magazine *Oz* were also prosecuted. After the longest obscenity trial in British history, the publishers were found guilty under the act. Many see this as the end of a particularly permissive decade.

Vietnam had been under French colonial rule since the 1850s. In spring 1954, the French were defeated by communist Vietnamese forces at the Battle of Dien Bien Phu and the French agreed to withdraw according to the Geneva Accords, signed on 20 July 1954. The country was to be partitioned along the 17th parallel, with the communist Viet Minh controlling the north and a non-communist government (backed by the United States) in the south. The partition was meant to be temporary, but the South Vietnamese government refused to hold elections to reunify the country.

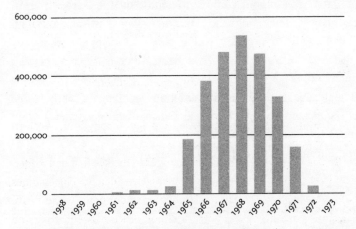

In 1959, the communist forces began an insurgency in the south. The United States began to up its military aid to the south with the placement of military advisers. There were fears, known as the 'Domino Theory', that if one country fell to communism, others would follow. The US opted for a policy of containment.

In 1964, US ships reported that they were under attack from North Vietnamese torpedo boats in the Gulf of Tonkin and the war began to escalate. Despite an immense amount of aid to the South Vietnamese and the vast resources of the United States, there was no decisive victory. Domestic opposition, cost and international pressure pushed the US to negotiate. The war ended after the US withdrawal in 1973 following the Paris Peace Accords, and Saigon falling to the communists on 30 April 1975. Vietnam has been a country united ever since.

1967 was a year of significant political, social and cultural change. Along with key liberalising law changes, the year was marked by a more visible 'counterculture' and civil protest, particularly for racial equality and against the Vietnam War. It is often considered the watershed year of the 'Swinging Sixties'.

Tens of thousands of young free spirits converged in the Haight-Ashbury neighbourhood of San Francisco to celebrate art, music and counterculture in what became known as 'The Summer of Love'. The movement later spread to other areas of America and Europe. Associated with hippie culture, the movement featured musical performances, including the Monterey Pop Festival. Although its significance to ordinary young people is disputed (especially in Britain), the Summer of Love helped define 1960s American counterculture.

The Beatles released their iconic album *Sgt. Pepper's Lonely Hearts Club Band* in June 1967 – considered a masterpiece and a landmark in the history of popular music. Nicknamed 'The Soundtrack of the Summer of Love', the album was number one in the charts throughout the summer.

Over 150 race riots broke out across America, sparked by long-standing racial tensions and frustrations over social and economic inequalities, and the lack of civil rights progress for African Americans. The riots were some of the most violent and destructive in US history, particularly in July in Detroit and Newark.

On 21 October there was a massive demonstration against the Vietnam War, involving more than 100,000 protestors in Washington DC. Around 50,000 of these crossed the Potomac River from the Lincoln Memorial to the Pentagon, where they were confronted by on-guard paratroopers. A similarly large anti-war protest occurred in London in October 1968.

1967 saw many other trends and events: colour television's introduction, mini-skirts, flowing skirts, velvet bell-bottoms, exuberant Afros, Sandie Shaw's Eurovision win, Elvis's wedding, and the capture of Che Guevara.

In 1989, the World Wide Web was launched. In 2007, after eighteen years, it came of age. This was the year that the first Apple iPhone arrived, but alongside this innovation in smartphone technology, Facebook and Twitter went global, IBM released an Artificial Intelligence system called Watson and Google bought YouTube.

Familiar applications and services like Amazon Kindle, Google's operating system Android and Airbnb were all released in 2007. Many of these releases and expansions were possible due to advances in cloud computing, with notable launches being Apache Hadoop in April 2006, and Amazon Elastic Compute Cloud in August 2006.

INVENTIONS THAT SOLVED HOUSEHOLD CHORES

Several inventions from the 20th century transformed household chores, making them more efficient and less time-consuming. This also freed up time for other activities, enabling many women to enter the workplace. Despite their early 20th century origins, many appliances did not enter the majority of homes in industrial societies until the 1950s.

Electric washing machine, 1907: Early models were produced by Orlando B. Woodrow of the Automatic Electric Washer Company. An original advertising slogan was, 'Everybody Works but Mother.'

Electric vacuum cleaner, 1908: Credited to American inventor James Spangler, who sold his idea to William Hoover. The Hoover Company's first UK factory opened in the 1930s.

Domestic refrigerator, 1913: The DOMELRE was one of the first domestic fridges, gradually replacing ice delivery and cool boxes. It initially cost a rather steep $24,000 in today's money.

Microwave Oven, 1945: This invention came about accidentally, after engineer Percy Spencer found radio waves emitted by a radar set he was working on melted a chocolate bar.

Of the eight planets in the Solar System, Mercury, Venus, Mars, Jupiter and Saturn were observed by Babylonian astronomers as early as the 2nd millennium BC. The Greek Aristarchus of Samos (310–230 BC) also correctly observed the position of Earth in relation to the planets – known as the heliocentric model.

A geocentric model was developed by Aristotle (384–22 BC), which purported that Earth was the centre of the universe, and that all celestial bodies rotate around it. This was standardised by Claudius Ptolemy (c.100–170) in the 2nd century, in his treatise *The Almagest*. The geocentric model was accepted by most for the next 1,200 years, and was central to the Catholic Church's interpretation of the universe, with mankind at its centre.

The Polish astronomer Nicolaus Copernicus (1473–1543), who was also a Catholic canon, revived heliocentrism in the 16th century. The Italian Galileo Galilei (1564–1642) championed the theory, and observed the four largest moons orbiting Jupiter, which did not conform to the geocentric model. While Pope Paul V was initially supportive of Galileo, in 1616 the Inquisition ordered that Copernican doctrine should not be taught. Galileo then upset the Church further in 1632 with the publication of the popular *Dialogue Concerning the Two Chief World Systems*.

Pope Urban VIII, who had also shown favour to Galileo, had the book banned. Galileo subsequently went on trial for heresy in 1633 and spent the rest of his life under house arrest. Of course, Galileo was right, and the heliocentric model eventually won out as the accepted theory.

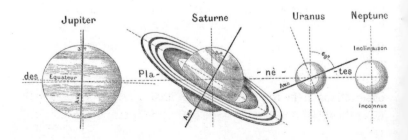

Until 1781, the coldest and farthest outer planets were largely unknown to science. Saturn and Jupiter are many times further away from Earth than either Mars or Venus (our closest neighbours), but it helps that they are the two largest planets in the Solar System. Saturn's diameter is nine times that of Earth's, while Jupiter's diameter is eleven times. This vast size meant they were visible before Renaissance-era telescopes.

Saturn sits at around 1.5 billion km from Earth, but Uranus is twice as far, and Neptune three times as far. They are also both less than half the size of Saturn. Hence they took much longer to observe than Saturn, Jupiter and their moons. That said, Uranus and Neptune were observed earlier than the Enlightenment era, but they were mistaken as stars rather than planets.

After Galileo, the moons of Saturn were observed by Christiaan Huygens (1629–95) and Giovanni Domenico Cassini (1625–1712). It took nearly 97 years between the discovery of Saturn's fourth moon (Dione) and the observation of Uranus as a planet by German-born British astronomer William Herschel (1738–1822).

Body	Year of Discovery	Discovered by
Uranus	1781	William Herschel
Neptune	1846	Johann Galle
Pluto	1930	Clyde William Tombaugh

Neptune's position was predicted by John Couch Adams (1819–92) and Urbain Le Verrier (1811–77), who worked independently. It was observed with a telescope on 23 September 1846 by Johanne Galle (1812–1910).

Pluto was hailed as the ninth planet upon its discovery by American astronomer Clyde William Tombaugh (1906–97) in 1930. However, observations in the 1990s found it was smaller than expected, and it was declassified as a planet in 2006 by the International Astronomical Union.

Isaac Newton (1642–1726)

Mathematician, physicist and astronomer whose groundbreaking work laid the foundation for classical mechanics. Inspired by an apple falling from a tree, his laws of motion and universal gravitation, as well as his development of calculus, revolutionised science and influenced subsequent generations of thinkers.

Michael Faraday (1791–1867)

Made groundbreaking discoveries in electromagnetism and electrochemistry. His experiments on electromagnetic induction in 1831 led to the development of the electric motor, generator and transformer. Faraday also established the basis for understanding the relationship between electricity and magnetism, leading to the formulation of Faraday's Law.

Charles Darwin (1809–82)

Famous for his theory of evolution by natural selection, Darwin visited four continents on HMS *Beagle*, including the Galapagos Islands. His groundbreaking work, *On the Origin of Species*, transformed our understanding of life on Earth and had a lasting impact on various fields, including biology, geology and anthropology.

Marie Curie (1867–1934)

Polish-born physicist and chemist who, along with her husband Pierre, won the 1903 Nobel Prize in Physics for discovering polonium and radium. Curie later won the 1911 Nobel Prize for Chemistry, the only winner in both fields. The Curies' research was crucial in the development of X-rays in surgery, and radiation as a cancer treatment.

Albert Einstein (1879–1955)

German-born theoretical physicist who developed the theory of relativity. His most famous equation, $E=mc^2$, highlights the equivalence of mass and energy, laying the groundwork for nuclear energy development. Einstein received the 1921 Nobel Prize in Physics for his work on the photoelectric effect, which contributed to the development of quantum theory.

John Locke (1632–1704)

The 'Father of Liberalism' emphasised the importance of the individual, who he believed should enjoy protected rights within a political system. Individuals should be protected from tyrannical governments by restrictions on government power, and a separation of powers into different branches, which strongly influenced the American Founding Fathers.

Voltaire (1694–1778)

Born François-Marie Arouet, Voltaire was an influential figure in the French Enlightenment and a critic of censorship, the Catholic Church and slavery. He was a prolific writer and satirist, with more than 20,000 letters and 2,000 books and pamphlets to his name.

Jean-Jacques Rousseau (1712–78)

Known for his work *The Social Contract*, Rousseau was convinced that humans were naturally good and sympathetic to each other and that war and competition were the result of social structures like religion, property and hierarchies. He believed that people should have the power to make laws, contributing to ideas that prompted the French Revolution.

Mary Wollstonecraft (1759–97)

Mary Wollstonecraft believed that society was wasting potential because it forced women to stay as 'convenient domestic slaves' with no political, economic or social freedom. The founder of modern feminism, she demanded education and greater equality.

Friedrich Nietzsche (1844–1900)

Best known for works such as *Thus Spoke Zarathustra* and *Beyond Good and Evil*, Nietzsche introduced influential concepts like the 'will to power', the 'Ubermensch' (super-human) and 'eternal recurrence'. Upon his death, his sister became the editor of his work, redacting it towards German nationalist ideology. Later scholars disputed this position, and his views on individualism, scepticism and questioning of morals had a profound impact on later 20th-century thought.

Born around 1412 in Domrémy, France, Jeanne (anglicised to Joan) was first referred to as Jeanne d'Arc in 1455, 24 years after her death. Charles VII of France called her Jeanne d'Ay de Domrémy in a letter of 1429. Much of Joan's story comes from her interrogation after her capture and a subsequent retrial to exonerate her. In 1428, aged around 16, Joan claimed to have received a vision from the Archangel Michael, St Catherine and St Margaret instructing her to help the disinherited Charles the Dauphin to become king instead of Henry VI of England.

To validate her claims, Joan underwent various tests. She successfully identified Charles among his courtiers, and appeared before a panel of theologians in Poitiers, who declined to comment on the origin of her visions. Next, she was sent to Tours for physical examination by a group of women led by Charles's mother-in-law to confirm her virginity. Eventually Charles accepted Joan's claims, equipping her with armour, a banner and a sword. In April 1429 he sent her to Orléans to relieve the English siege.

Nine days after Joan's arrival, the English fled. The unexpected victory was seen as proof of Joan's claims. Her forces achieved a decisive victory at the Battle of Patay on 18 June, enabling access to Reims, where French monarchs were traditionally crowned. After Charles VII's coronation on 17 July, and failures at Paris and La Charité, he distanced himself from Joan. Continuing to fight, Joan was captured by Burgundian forces in 1430 and sold to the English.

The English were desperate to paint Joan as a heretic rather than a  prophet, and she was tortured and interrogated before a church court. While a single conviction for heresy did not warrant a death sentence, Joan was accused on a number of counts. Joan was burned as a heretic in Rouen on 30 May 1431, and her ashes discarded into the river to prevent relic veneration. In 1456, a French inquisition overturned the verdict and Joan became a symbol of French freedom. Canonised as a saint in 1920, in 1922 Joan was adopted as patron saint of France.

*Their leading men have moulded them into rival factions.
Indeed, there is nothing that helps us more against such
very powerful peoples than their lack of unanimity.*

Tacitus on the Britons, 2nd century AD

*Anything that looks like a fight is a thing of utter
delight to an Englishman.*

**Henri Misson, a Frenchman writing up
his journeys round England in 1698**

*We made him welcome as all Englishmen do
their friends, damnably drunk.*

A naval seaman during the 18th century

*. . . the people have a special character, common to the
whole nation, which makes them think they are superior
to everyone else. It is a belief shared by all nations, each
thinking itself the best. And they are all right.*

Casanova, late 18th century

*There are two types of English gentlemen, some are
knowledgeable and therefore awkward but some are not
knowledgeable but become the height of fashion.*

Montesquieu, 18th century

*I feel justified in saying that by and large the
British are a race of very bad losers.*

**Roald Amundsen on the attitude towards him
when he returned from the North Pole, 1927**

*The English always get other people to do their fighting
for them. The Canadians, the Australians, the
New Zealanders, the South Africans.*

Erwin Rommel, German General, 1944

Titanic's sinking may be the most famous maritime disaster in history, but it's far from the deadliest. While over 1,500 people were killed after the *Titanic* sank in April 1912, an estimated 9,500 people perished in the sinking of Nazi military transport ship the *Wilhelm Gustloff*.

Originally a cruise ship, purpose-built for Nazi leisure organisation Kraft durch Freude ('Strength through Joy') in 1937, the *Gustloff* was acquisitioned by the military during World War Two and converted to a hospital ship before becoming a barracks ship in Gdynia on Poland's Baltic coast.

By mid-January 1945 the Soviets had advanced significantly into occupied Poland, liberating Warsaw. Subsequently, the Germans launched 'Operation Hannibal', one of the largest seaborne evacuations in history, to take wounded soldiers and refugees pushed westwards by the Red Army. The Nazis used almost any ship they could find, including the *Gustloff*.

On the night of 30 January 1945 while cruising westwards 20 miles off the north Polish coast, the *Gustloff* was torpedoed by a Soviet submarine. Hit three times, it sank in just 40 minutes. By the time vessels arrived offering help, most of those on board had died; the rescue boats carried just 1,252 survivors.

The exact number of fatalities is unknown as those who'd let refugees on board had stopped counting around 8,000. However, based on the estimated 11,000 people on board and survivor numbers, it's believed about 9,500 people perished, making it the largest maritime disaster in history. The majority never left the ship, trapped within the promenade deck's sealed glass panels, while those who did faced the freezing temperatures of the Baltic Sea.

The Soviet attack isn't considered a war crime as the ship was carrying military personnel and anti-aircraft guns, and travelling through a war zone (with its lights periodically off), which made it a legitimate military target.

The *Gustloff*'s sinking wasn't widely recognised for decades as incidents involving German victimhood were considered distasteful after Germany initiated World War Two.

Arthur Priest was a stoker on the *Titanic*. He laboured away deep in the hull of the ship, shovelling coal into the furnaces that heated up the steam that drove the ship's mighty engines.

Stokers were among the unlikeliest crewmen to survive a sinking ship, or even a badly damaged one. Sea water would flood their compartments first, drowning them. The rest of the crew would scramble to shut watertight doors to save the ship, trapping their comrades in the compartments below. Somehow though, despite the deaths of many of his fellow stokers, Priest was picked up by a lifeboat after the *Titanic* sank on 15 April 1912. It was miraculous. But compared to the rest of his career, it was nothing.

Priest did not just survive the *Titanic*. He was involved in two other major collisions, and three other sinkings.

In chronological order Priest survived:

» A collision on RMS *Asturias'* maiden voyage, 1908

» A collision on *Titanic*'s sister ship, RMS *Olympic*, 1911

» The sinking of RMS *Titanic*, 1912

» The First World War sinking of HMS *Alcantara*, 1916

» The First World War sinking of *Titanic*'s other sister ship, HMHS *Britannic*, 1916

» SS *Donegal* First World War sinking, 1917

The four sinkings were caused by an iceberg, enemy shells, a mine and a torpedo respectively. He struggled to find work after the war, claiming that no one wished to sail with him after these disasters.

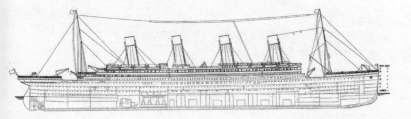

Hali Meithhad (A Letter on Virginity) was written in the West Midlands of England c.1220s. This snippet is an illustration of the number of chores a frantic medieval housewife may have had to tend to.

> Ant hwet yef ich easki yet — thah hit thunche egede — hu thet wif stonde the ihereth hwen ha kimeth in hire bearn schreamen, sith the cat et te fliche ant ed te hude the hund, hire cake bearnen o the stan ant hire kelf suken, the crohe eornen i the fur, ant te cheorl chideth? Thah hit beo egede i sahe, hit ah, meiden, to eggi the swithre therfrommart, for nawt ne thuncheth hit hire egede thet hit fondeth!

Translation:

> And what if I ask yet – though it seems shameful – how the wife behaves when she hears her child screaming, sees the cat in the timbers, the dog biting the carpet, her cake burning on the stove and her calf sucking, the crock running into the fire, and her husband still complaining? Although it may seem shameful to say so, it is necessary, maiden, to draw great strength from it, for she is not afraid that it feels that it tests her!

TERROR IN THE ARCTIC

Two handwritten messages, written almost a year apart on the same piece of paper. The first, dated May 1847, ends in high spirits: 'Sir John Franklin commanding the Expedition. All Well.' The second message is a stiff scribble in the margins, added the following April.

It tells of the death of 24 men, including Franklin, the abandonment of his expedition's ships HMS *Erebus* and *Terror*, and a desperate plan to trek overland to safety. Found in 1859 inside a cairn on King William Island, the Victory Point Record is one of the most evocative documents in the history of Arctic exploration. It is crucial evidence in unpicking the mystery of what happened to the Royal Navy's failed 1845 attempt to chart the Northwest Passage through the Arctic, from which 129 men never returned.

JFK'S ASSASSINATION:
THE MAGIC BULLET THEORY

The 'magic bullet theory' is a term used to describe the official explanation of how President John F. Kennedy was assassinated on 22 November 1963.

According to this theory, a single bullet (known as CE 399) fired by Lee Harvey Oswald passed through Kennedy's neck and then through the chest, wrist and thigh of Texas Governor John Connally, causing multiple injuries (seven entry/exit wounds in both men), before finally coming to rest in pristine condition on Connally's stretcher at the Parkland Memorial Hospital.

The theory was first presented by the Warren Commission, which was tasked with investigating the assassination, and it has been widely criticised and debated ever since. Critics argue that the trajectory of the bullet and the injuries sustained by both Kennedy and Connally suggest that multiple shots were fired, and that the idea of a single bullet causing all the damage is implausible.

Despite the controversy surrounding the magic bullet theory, it remains the official explanation of how Kennedy was killed, and it continues to be the subject of ongoing debate and speculation.

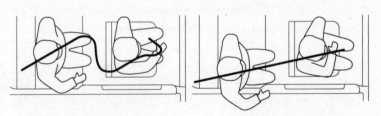

Trajectory of CE399 according to some critics   *Trajectory according to some modern theorists*

WHERE CREDIT IS DUE

More locations and living things are named after the 19th-century German explorer and scientist Alexander von Humboldt than anyone else, including mountain ranges, animal species and a lunar sea.

In May 1588, King Philip II of Spain sent his *Grande y Felicísima Armada*, 'Great and Most Fortunate Navy', to conquer England in an event remembered as the Spanish Armada. Made up of roughly 150 ships and 18,000 men, it was the largest fleet ever seen in Europe. Philip II of Spain considered it invincible. An English sailor reported that the ocean itself seemed to groan under the weight of the ships.

Famously, it proved disastrous. The Armada was scattered by English fireships, defeated in the Battle of Gravelines and was battered by gales as it returned to Spain around the north of Scotland and Ireland. Almost a third of its ships were destroyed.

But King Philip did not give up. There were three other Armadas:

In 1596 a Second Spanish Armada was sent to assist Irish rebels fighting the English, an attempt at revenge by Philip after the English sacked the Spanish city of Cádiz in 1596. But less than a week after leaving port that October, it was smashed by a terrible storm off Spain's Cape Finisterre. Nearly 5,000 men died, dozens of ships were sunk, and more badly needed repairs. The catastrophe pushed Philip's government into bankruptcy.

In 1597 a Third Spanish Armada was assembled with enormous difficulty. Around 140 ships were sent towards the unprotected coasts of England while the English fleet was raiding in the Azores. An autumn Channel storm lashed the fleet for three days. Ships were wrecked in Cornwall, the Scilly Isles and Wales. A few scattered ships sent their men ashore on the English and Welsh coasts, but they were quickly killed or forced to retreat. The English fleet returned safely, unaware of Philip's designs. When the surviving ships brought the terrible news to Philip, he was devastated. His health collapsed and he died the following year.

In 1601 the Fourth Armada, a much more modest one, was sent to help Irish rebels in Kinsale. Bad weather, you guessed it, led to the fleet becoming scattered and a third of the troops never got to Ireland. The other 4,000 Spaniards landed but were besieged by Ireland's English garrison. After suffering severe losses, and seeing the defeat of their Irish allies, the Spanish negotiated terms and sailed home.

Empress Matilda (1102–1167)
Tragedy struck the Norman nobility in 1120 in the White Ship Disaster, when Matilda's brother (and Henry I's heir) drowned. Henry I then named her his heir. However, upon her father's death, Matilda was in Normandy, and her cousin Stephen of Blois had himself crowned king. Matilda then contested her claim in a period known as 'The Anarchy', which lasted from 1135 to 1153. Stephen agreed that her son, also called Henry, would be his heir.

Arthur, Prince of Wales (1486–1502)
If Arthur had not died, history would have turned out completely differently. The death of the Tudors' greatest hope made way for his younger brother Henry to become England's most notorious monarch. Arthur was married to Catherine of Aragon for five months before his death – so the Crown was not the only thing that Henry VIII inherited.

Juan, Prince of Asturias and Girona (1478–97)
King Ferdinand II of Aragon and Queen Isabella I of Castille lavished attention on their eldest son and heir. Married to Margaret of Austria, Juan confessed that he could not contain his lust and the excessive time the couple spent in bed led to worries about his health. He died aged just 19.

Henry Frederick, Prince of Wales (1594–1612)
The heir to King James VI and I, Henry was a bright and promising boy, with a penchant for politics and playing golf. He became so popular that his father felt threatened. His death from typhoid fever aged 18 meant that his younger brother became King Charles I.

James Stuart, Duke of Cambridge (1663–67)
The nephew of Charles II – who had no legitimate heirs – James Stuart was being raised to be the future monarch after the reign of his father, Charles's brother James II. But the boy became ill with either smallpox or bubonic plague before he turned four. His demise, reported by Samuel Pepys, was a blow to the country, which saw it as a sign of the end of the Stuarts.

NICKNAMES FOR BRITISH PRIME MINISTERS

Robert Walpole – 'Sir Blue-String'
Duke of Newcastle – 'Hubble-Bubble'
William Pitt the Elder – 'The Great Commoner'
William Pitt the Younger – 'Pitt the Younger'
Duke of Grafton – 'The Turf Macaroni'
Arthur Wellesley, Duke of Wellington – 'The Iron Duke'
Robert Peel – 'The Peeler'
Benjamin Disraeli – 'Dizzy'
William Ewart Gladstone – 'The Grand Old Man'
Bonar Law – 'The Unknown Prime Minister'
Herbert Henry Asquith – 'Squiffy'
David Lloyd George – 'The Welsh Wizard'
Neville Chamberlain – 'The Coroner'
Winston Churchill – 'The British Bulldog'
Harold Macmillan – 'Supermac'
Margaret Thatcher – 'The Iron Lady'
John Major – 'Grey Man'
Tony Blair – 'Bambi'
Gordon Brown – 'The Broon'
Theresa May – 'Maybot'
Boris Johnson – 'BoJo'
Liz Truss – 'The Human Hand Grenade'

DUKES OF NORMANDY NICKNAMES

William the Conqueror son of
Robert the Magnificent son of
Richard the Good son of
Richard the Fearless son of
William Longsword son of
Rollo

Rollo won Normandy from the King of the West Franks,
Charles the Simple.

ODD FACTS ABOUT MONARCHS

Richard the Lionheart only spent six months of his ten-year reign in England.

King Henry VIII of England had a suit of armour made for his dog.

Queen Elizabeth I of England had a particular taste for candied violets. Eventually, the sugar cane caused many of her teeth to go black.

King Charles VI of France believed he was made of glass and would shatter if anyone touched him.

Queen Margrethe II of Denmark was such a fan of the Lord of the Rings that she drew illustrations and sent them to J.R.R. Tolkien.

King Louis XIV of France had a personal perfume maker who created a unique scent just for him.

Queen Victoria of England was a collector of human hairwork jewellery, a trend linked to public mourning.

King George IV of England had a specially designed bed that was 10 feet wide and required 20 servants to make.

Queen Anne of England was so overweight that she required a special chair with an opening in the back to accommodate her large frame.

Marie Antoinette built an entire village at Versailles as a retreat – a myth circulated that she dressed up as a peasant when attending.

THE MARCH ON WASHINGTON

The 1963 March on Washington was a pivotal event in the Civil Rights Movement in the United States, credited with spurring the passage of the 1964 Civil Rights Act, which outlawed segregation and discrimination.

Around 250,000 people of all races participated in the march for Jobs and Freedom on 28 August 1963 (the centennial of the Emancipation Proclamation), to highlight racial injustice and put pressure on Congress to pass John F. Kennedy's Civil Rights Bill. The participants packed the 1.9-mile strip from the Lincoln Memorial to the Washington Monument, while many thousands of others also offered support behind the scenes. During the event, Martin Luther King Jr, a leading figure in the US civil rights movement, delivered his famous 'I Have a Dream' speech, on the steps of the Lincoln Memorial, calling for racial harmony and equality.

The march had faced fierce opposition from the JFK administration and the FBI, and there had been widespread concerns it would incite racial violence, chaos and disturbance. Nevertheless, it was organised and executed peacefully.

After the march, King and other civil rights leaders met with President Kennedy and Vice President Lyndon Johnson at the White House. Although passed after Kennedy's death, the provisions of the Civil Rights Act of 1964 and Voting Rights Act of 1965 reflect the demands of the march in improving the issues of discrimination, segregation and disenfranchisement that King had highlighted.

A FOUNDING FATHER

'The problem of the twentieth century is the problem of the color-line,' begins *The Souls of Black Folk* (1903), the seminal work of W.E.B. Du Bois, whose prolific writings challenging racism made him one of the most significant black scholars in American history. The first African American to earn a doctorate, Du Bois confronted prevailing philosophies from accommodation to discrimination, insisting instead on full civil rights and, in 1909, co-founding the NAACP.

1909: Creation of the National Association for the Advancement of Colored People (NAACP).

1948: President Truman desegregates the armed forces.

1954: Supreme Court outlaws segregation in public schools in *Brown v. Board of Education*.

1955–7: Montgomery Bus Boycott in Alabama, sparked by Rosa Parks and organised by Martin Luther King. (In November 1956, the Supreme Court rules segregated seating unconstitutional.)

1957: The 'Little Rock Nine' are escorted to and from classes at Central High School in Little Rock, Arkansas, highlighting the issue of desegregation.

1957: President Eisenhower signs the Civil Rights Act of 1957, allowing prosecution of anyone trying to prevent someone from voting.

1962: James Meredith enrols at University of Mississippi after President Kennedy sends in troops.

1963: Images of police using fire hoses and dogs on black demonstrators in Birmingham, Alabama, gain widespread sympathy for the civil rights movement.

28 August 1963: Around 250,000 people gather for the March on Washington. Martin Luther King delivers his 'I Have a Dream' speech.

1964: President Johnson signs sweeping Civil Rights Act, forbidding discrimination in many areas of life including employment, and in public facilities including restaurants, theatres and hotels. The law also limits the use of voter literacy tests.

1965: Martin Luther King leads a march from Selma to Montgomery, Alabama, in support of black voter registration.

1965: Malcolm X assassinated.

1965: President Johnson signs Voting Rights Act, banning all voter literacy tests.

4 April 1968: Martin Luther King assassinated, sparking riots in more than 100 cities.

OFFICE FORTRESS

Walter Schellenberg, head of foreign intelligence in Nazi Germany from 1944, and incidentally a romantic liaison of Coco Chanel, was infamous for his 'office fortress' desk. He claimed that it had two automatic guns built into it, which could 'spray the whole room with bullets' at the touch of a button.

ATOMIC NATURE RESERVE

Cold War history in Britain is difficult to spot – there's the occasional and somewhat hidden nuclear bunker to explore, but these rarely compare to the swathes of abandoned ex-Soviet sites that are scattered throughout Eastern Europe.

Perhaps the most intriguing of all Britain's Cold War sites is Orford Ness, on the remote Suffolk Coast and Heaths. The expansive shingled waste land was used as a military test site from 1913, when it was purchased by the War Department. It became a test facility for aircraft from 1915, and, after a brief period of disuse, expanded its operations between the wars. One of the most significant experiments took place between 1935 and 1937 when the facility was used to research radar.

During World War Two, the site was used for aircraft bombing trials, and parts of the site are inaccessible due to the possibility of encountering live ordnance.

Between 1953 and 1966, the site became a test site for Britain's top secret research into the atomic bomb, with several buildings built to carry out environmental tests such as vibration and extreme temperature on bomb casing. Large pagoda-like buildings were built so the site could contain a blast if such a test went wrong. That said, allegedly no nuclear material was used on the site.

The Atomic Weapons Research Establishment had fallen into disuse by 1987, having most recently been used by the RAF for bomb disposal. The National Trust took over in 1993, turning Europe's largest shingle spit into a nature reserve. It is only accessible by boat, and visiting the abandoned buildings and pagodas of the Atomic Weapons Research Establishment can only be done on a guided tour.

The Battle of Britain (1940) was the first battle fought primarily in the air, with the Royal Air Force (RAF) pitted against the German Luftwaffe. Both Britain and Germany had developed quite different innovations for aerial combat in 1939.

On 27 August 1939 Germany accomplished the first successful turbojet-powered flight. The Heinkel He 178 was potential a game changer. It was very fast, making it much harder to detect and intercept. However, it did not move out of prototype phase. Although the German Messerschmitt Me 262, the first operational jet-powered aircraft, debuted in 1942, it wasn't until later in the war that jet engines were used in numbers. Even then, there weren't enough to have an impact.

Britain, meanwhile, had developed an equally powerful if very different invention: radar. A chain of 29 radar stations were installed along Britain's coastline, part of an innovative early warning system which could see aircraft approaching up to 100 miles out and then instruct British fighters to intercept them. During the Battle of Britain, this technology gave the RAF early warning of the scale and bearing of German attacks.

The revolutionary radar system used a network of ground-based transmitters and receivers to detect the presence and location of incoming enemy aircraft from a distance, even in poor conditions. This enabled the RAF to delay deployment until the last moment. Once the value of radar towers was recognised, the Luftwaffe targeted them, yet they was nearly impossible to hit, and easily replaceable.

By September, Britain had gained the upper hand and was causing heavy losses on the German attackers. Attempts to destroy airfields and gain air superiority in southern England during August failed, and Hitler switched the Luftwaffe's attention to bombing British cities. On 15 September 1940, Germany embarked on its largest bombing attack, but was decisively defeated, with 58 aircraft destroyed. There wasn't a single German jet fighter in the skies that day, but radar played a key role in Britain's victory.

For something used so regularly, toilets perhaps don't get the historical column inches they deserve.

Oldest
The Neolithic settlement of Skara Brae (c.3000 BC) had drainage systems believed to be toilets attached to each interconnected dwelling. The Queen's Toilet at the Palace of Knossos in Crete (1700 BC) contained large earthenware pans connected to a flushing water supply.

Garderobes
The French word for 'wardrobe' also refers to the toilets of castles. Most were simple holes in castle walls that discharged into a cesspit. At the Siege of Château Gaillard in 1204, unfortunate French soldiers climbed up the garderobes to capture the castle.

First flushing toilet
Sir John Harington, poet and godson of Queen Elizabeth I, invented the first flushing toilet, named Ajax, with a pan and valve operated by handles and levers connected to a cistern. However, it took nearly 200 years and another inventor, Alexander Cumming, to patent the first flushing water closet in London in 1775.

Thomas Crapper's toilet
Contrary to popular belief, Thomas Crapper did not invent the flushing toilet, though his name is often associated with it. Crapper did play a significant role in popularising the flushing toilet and developed related inventions like the ball cock. However, the word 'crap' does not come from his name; it has Middle English origins and first appeared in the *Oxford English Dictionary* in 1846.

Death by toilet
Elvis Presley's death in 1977 was famously indecorous, with reports of him being found unresponsive near a toilet. England's George II also died after attending his close stool in 1760, from a possible aortic dissection.

THE TROSTON DEMON

St Mary's Church Troston, near Bury St Edmunds, in Suffolk, contains an intriguing collection of medieval murals and plenty of graffiti. On the bell tower arches there are dates and names inscribed. At the chancel end, there are many patterns and shapes engraved into the walls.

Among hundreds of other little scratches there's a more deeply drawn pentangle that sits on the ear of a cartoonish-looking 'demon'. The pentangle is now thought of as a 'Satanic Star' but had more positive connotations in the medieval period, as it was thought to represent the five wounds of Christ. The pentangle was probably inscribed to keep the 'demon' pinned down.

St Mary's Troston was built in the 12th century, with wall art dating from the 1350s. It is likely that the demon was inscribed around this time. It's a rare example of cartoonish medieval graffiti.

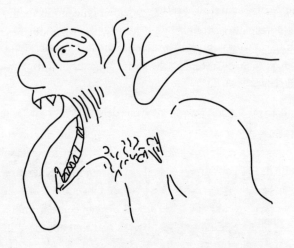

TOWER OF BUTTER

Rouen Cathedral's 77–metre-tall Tour de Beurre is so named because it was paid for by the taxes taken from peasants in the 15th century, in exchange for special dispensation to consume butter during Lent.

Magna Carta is one of the most famous documents in the world. First issued in 1215, it put into writing, for the first time, the principle that the English king was not above the law. The 'Great Charter' is about 3,500 words long with 63 clauses. Though most of it concerns medieval rights and customs, it's become a powerful symbol of liberty around the world thanks to some key clauses. Four of these remain part of English law today:

1. First, that we have granted to God, and by this present charter have confirmed for us and our heirs in perpetuity, the English Church shall be free, and shall have its right undiminished, and its liberties unimpaired.

13. The city of London shall enjoy all its ancient liberties and free customs, both by land and by water.

39. No free man shall be seized or imprisoned, or stripped of his rights of possessions, or outlawed or exiled, or deprived of his standing in any other way, nor will we proceed with force against him, or send others to do so, except by the lawful judgement of his equals or by the law of the land.

40. To no one will we sell, to no one deny or delay right or justice.

— BECOMING A KNIGHT WAS A SLAP IN THE FACE —

Becoming a knight was a major step forward for any ambitious medieval squire, or nobleman coming of age. It could happen fairly casually after a battle, but in peacetime there was a detailed ceremony to be followed. The night before the service would be spent taking a bath, to wash away sin, and then at a night-long vigil saying prayers.

In the morning, having given serious thought to the role he is about to take on, the service would begin with a sermon, reminding the knight-to-be of his duty to God. Next, an oath would be sworn to uphold the expectations of knightly behaviour; to fight wrong-doers, and defend widows, orphans and the poor. Following this, the candidate was girded with a sword – a belt with a scabbard attached was secured around his waist – and spurs were attached to the heels of his shoes.

The final stage was known as dubbing, or the accolade. Today, that involves being tapped on the shoulder with a sword. In medieval times, it was something a bit different. It is derived from the Old English word dubbian, meaning to beat, and the person conducting the ceremony would slap the candidate across the face. In some accounts, the flat of a sword is used to strike the cheek. This represented the last blow the newly made knight was expected to take without fighting back.

OLDEST PROSTHETIC

Disability has always been part of human experience. In 1997, an excavation near the ancient Egyptian city of Thebes revealed the oldest prosthesis ever discovered: an engraved wooden toe, fitted to the right foot of an Egyptian noblewoman who lived 3,000 years ago. The 'Cairo toe' was practical, modified over time to accommodate the woman's gait. But it was also designed with aesthetics in mind, intended to be worn in open-toe sandals, not concealed.

WORST PANDEMICS IN HISTORY

Disease	Death Toll	Date
Plague of Justinian	15–100 milion	541–549
Black Death	75–200 million	1346–1353
South American smallpox	c. 40 million	16th century
Spanish flu	17–100 million	1918–1920
HIV/AIDS	42 million	1981–present
COVID-19	c. 20 million	2019–2023

Estimates of death tolls from disease vary, but it is widely accepted that the 14th-century Black Death was the most devastating in history, killing anywhere up to half the population of Europe.

THE UNCERTAIN EPIDEMIC

Human Immunodeficiency Virus (HIV) may have jumped from chimpanzees to humans as far back as the turn of the 19th century, likely through contact from bushmeat. It spread slowly across Africa, reaching the USA around 1976.

In June 1981, doctors in the US became aware of rare forms of pneumonia in young homosexual men, which suggested weakened immune systems. Throughout the 1980s, reporting on the illness led to stigma towards gay men, but it was also identified between intravenous drug users and heterosexual contact later that decade. The links between HIV and AIDs (the late stage) were made in 1986.

By 1992, the virus had become the leading cause of death for men aged 25–44 in the US, with almost 34,000 people dying from AIDS that year. Antiretroviral drug therapy became much more effective in the mid-1990s, and had a downward effect on mortality, but it could not entirely cure HIV. Global AIDs deaths, the majority of which have been in Africa, peaked in the mid-2000s. A combination of widespread testing, antiretrovirals and better understanding of protection have made it a much more preventable and treatable disease.

THE BLACK DEATH'S EFFECT ON LABOUR

In the aftermath of a global pandemic, wage suppression and a cost-of-living crisis could lead to popular uprisings and riots. This was the combination of events that caused trouble more than 600 years ago. Known as the Black Death, a bubonic plague that may have coincided with a pneumonic plague devastated populations in Asia and Europe in the mid-14th century.

The Black Death reached England in the summer of 1348, probably at Weymouth (then called Melcombe Regis), and spread at a rate of around a mile and a half a day. Trade routes provided quick ways for the disease to be carried, but even remote rural communities were not spared. The initial waves were a shock, and the plague would revisit England in 1361–2, 1369, 1373–5 and frequently until 1665.

A reduced population in the mid-14th century led to the emergence of a wealthier and more ambitious class among the peasantry. Survivors may have inherited from several relatives and become comparatively wealthy. A small pool of labourers drove up wages, while a surplus of food saw prices fall sharply. As the initial plague outbreak saw wages spike, the Ordinance of Labourers in 1349 was followed by the Statute of Labourers in 1351. These fixed wages at pre-pandemic levels, with punishments for breaches including branding on the forehead with an 'F' for falsehood for anyone running away from their land to look for higher pay. When this wage suppression combined with tax demands to pay for foreign wars, trouble erupted.

The Peasants' Revolt of 1381 saw those described as rustics – often translated as peasants, but meaning all those living in the countryside, including craftsmen and landowners – gather near London, burning records of land ownership along the way. When the king failed to attend a meeting, they attacked London, burning palaces. They submitted demands to the 14–year-old Richard II when he did meet them, including the abolition of serfdom. That proved a step too far and the revolt collapsed, but the aftermath of the Black Death had begun to change how those at the bottom of the social ladder viewed their place in the world.

GREAT MEDICS

Edward Jenner (1749–1823)
Known as the 'Father of Immunology', Jenner pioneered the smallpox vaccine, the world's first vaccine. In 1796, he conducted a famous experiment using cowpox material to successfully immunise a young boy against smallpox. Prior to Jenner's discoveries, smallpox killed almost 10% of the world's population.

John Snow (1813–58)
Considered one of the founding fathers of modern epidemiology. He is best known for tracing the source of an 1854 cholera outbreak in London and establishing the link between contaminated water and disease transmission. His work had significant influence on public health policy and improvements in sanitation systems.

Elizabeth Blackwell (1821–1910)
British-born physician who became the first woman to receive a medical degree in the United States. After facing numerous challenges and discrimination, she graduated from Geneva Medical College in 1849. She went on to co-found the New York Infirmary for Indigent Women and Children, providing medical care and training opportunities for women.

Florence Nightingale (1820–1910)
Nurse, statistician and social reformer who played a pivotal role in nursing during the Crimean War. Nightingale was instrumental in establishing modern nursing practices, transforming the profession with her dedication to patient care, hygiene and systematic methods. She significantly improved sanitary conditions in hospitals, reducing infection rates and saving countless lives.

Alexander Fleming (1881–1955)
A Scottish biologist, pharmacologist and botanist. In 1928, Fleming observed that a mould called *Penicillium notatum* had contaminated one of his Petri dishes and was killing the bacteria growing in it. This observation led him to conduct further experiments and ultimately to isolate and purify the substance that would become penicillin – the first antibiotic.

The Spanish flu of 1918–19 was one of the worst pandemics in history, affecting some 500 million people globally, with an estimated 50–100 million deaths. It was unusual for affecting young people particularly badly, and, with no antibiotics available, pneumonia frequently ensued. Some people also experienced neurological symptoms including temporary psychotic delusions, caused by damage to the nervous system or brain inflammation.

The Paris Peace Conference in 1919 was convened to discuss the Treaty of Versailles, which would officially end the First World War. American President Woodrow Wilson brought his '14 Points' vision for achieving world peace, which called for transparent peace treaties, self-determination for all European nations, disarmament and the creation of the League of Nations to prevent future wars.

But Wilson faced strong opposition from Britain and France over Germany's economic punishment. The French leader, Clemenceau, demanded billions in reparations, while Wilson wanted to focus on building up a 'League of Nations' rather than humiliate Germany. By 3 April, negotiations were deadlocked – just as Wilson contracted the Spanish flu, leaving him bedridden for five days and battling a 103-degree fever.

Numerous sources indicate Wilson suffered influenza's more delusional effects, such as giving out unexpected orders, paranoia that he was surrounded by French spies and other signs of disorientation. After visiting Wilson, British Prime Minister David Lloyd George described his condition as a 'nervous and spiritual breakdown'.

When Wilson returned to negotiations, he no longer seemed to have the will or stamina to stand his ground, and conceded to the other world leaders' demands, caving in on all his 14 Points, except for the League of Nations.

Although the impact of Wilson's illness on the peace negotiations cannot be proven, his uncharacteristic conciliatory behaviour suggests influenza may have drained his stamina and impeded his concentration. Congress ultimately rejected American participation in the League of Nations, and six months later Wilson suffered a debilitating stroke. He died in early 1924, aged 67.

Did the Cold War really start after World War Two? Since its inception, the USSR had a frosty relationship with the West.

Having seized power in the October 1917 revolution, the Bolsheviks agreed to unfavourable peace terms with Germany in March 1918, through the Treaty of Brest-Litovsk. Fearful of German dominance in Eastern Europe, and the rise of international communism, Allied forces invaded Russia. Support for anti-communist forces failed, but it left a legacy of resentment and mistrust in the newly formed USSR.

Relations thawed somewhat during the 1920s and 1930s. Britain formally recognised the USSR in February 1924, although it temporarily broke off diplomatic relations in 1927 after Soviet espionage was exposed. America also gave formal recognition in November 1933. A year later, the USSR was admitted into the League of Nations.

But the Soviet Union maintained close trading ties to a rising Nazi Germany, culminating in the Nazi-Soviet Pact of August 1939. This included a non-aggression clause and an agreement to divide Poland. After invading Poland from the east on 17 September, the Soviets attacked Finland in November and were excluded from the League of Nations. Winston Churchill remarked that the Russian position was 'a riddle wrapped in a mystery inside an enigma'.

War between the Western Allies and the USSR then became a distinct possibility. Growing fearful of possible Soviet oil supply to Germany, Britain and France planned to bomb oil fields in the Russian Caucasus and ran reconnaissance missions. The plan was dropped after the Fall of France.

Germany declared war on the Soviet Union in June 1941. The Allies (later with direct American involvement) and the USSR were then united in their struggle against Nazi Germany. But the relationship has been described as 'Allies, not friends.'

Tensions remained. Stalin was suspicious at Britain and America not opening a major second front in Europe until June 1944, while the lack of Soviet support for Polish forces during the Warsaw Uprising in August-October 1944 damaged relations with Britain. The Cold War had been icing over long before 1945.

THE IRON CURTAIN SPEECH

'From Stettin in the Baltic to Trieste in the Adriatic an 'iron curtain' has descended across the continent. Behind that line lie all the capitals of the ancient states of Central and Eastern Europe. Warsaw, Berlin, Prague, Vienna, Budapest, Belgrade, Bucharest and Sofia; all these famous cities and the populations around them lie in what I must call the Soviet sphere, and all are subject, in one form or another, not only to Soviet influence but to a very high and in some cases increasing measure of control from Moscow.'

Winston Churchill, 5 March 1946

OPERATION UNTHINKABLE

'Operation Unthinkable' was a military plan ordered by British Prime Minister Winston Churchill and developed by the British Chiefs of Staff Committee in May 1945 against the USSR.

The plan called for a massive surprise attack by up to 47 British and American divisions on Soviet positions in Europe, with support from Polish and German troops (rearming up to 100,000 former German soldiers), to help 'impose upon Russia the will of the United States and the British Empire'. The plan aimed to pre-empt a potential Soviet attack and gain a 'square deal for Poland', as well as pushing the Soviet forces out of eastern Europe and take key cities, including Berlin and Prague.

The plan was initially approved by Churchill and scheduled for 1 July 1945, but was quickly deemed too risky by the British military leadership due the Soviets maintaining a vast superiority of manpower, and the possibility of a lengthy total war against the odds. American forces were also relocating to the Pacific for a possible invasion of Japan. After Clement Attlee won the General Election in July 1945, Operation Unthinkable was abandoned.

The plan was not made public by the Cabinet Office until 1998, seven years after the Cold War was over, and the maps and plans were never brought into the public domain. They were either destroyed or are still withheld.

Winston Churchill's inspirational leadership during World War Two has become a British legend. But it was by no means guaranteed that he would become Prime Minister. When war was declared, Neville Chamberlain was Prime Minister, but his government collapsed in Spring 1940 as Allied forces were defeated in Norway.

Up to this point, Churchill had a chequered political career with many high-profile mistakes. During the 1930s, he was largely in the political wilderness, and a persistent, if lonely, voice warning of a rearming, dangerous Germany.

When he took office as Prime Minister in May 1940, he mobilised the House of Commons and the nation via a series of speeches.

I would say to the House. . . 'I have nothing to offer but blood, toil, tears and sweat'. . . Victory at all costs, victory in spite of all terror, victory however long and hard the road may be; for without victory there is no survival.

13 May 1940

We shall go on to the end, we shall fight in France, we shall fight on the seas and oceans, we shall fight with growing confidence and growing strength in the air, we shall defend our island, whatever the cost may be, we shall fight on the beaches, we shall fight on the landing grounds, we shall fight on the fields and in the streets, we shall fight in the hills; we shall never surrender.

4 June 1940

Let us therefore brace ourselves to our duties and so bear ourselves that if the British Empire and its Commonwealth last for a thousand years men will still say, 'This was their finest hour.'

18 June 1940

CHURCHILL'S GREAT ESCAPE

Churchill's early career was as an army officer, but he also became a published war correspondent. In 1899 he resigned his commission and travelled to South Africa to report on the Boer War, on assignment from the *Morning Post*. He was captured but managed to escape, becoming a national celebrity on his return to Britain.

CHURCHILL'S LOVE OF DRINK

A smidgen of Johnnie Walker with water is how Churchill started many mornings, and a bottle of champagne for lunch was common even during the war years. Despite this, he was not an alcoholic, but somewhat 'alcohol dependent.'

During America's Prohibition era, Churchill referred publicly to the constitutional amendment prohibiting the production, importing and sale of alcohol as 'an affront to the whole history of mankind'.

After a collision with a car in 1931, he secured a doctor's note which read, 'This is to certify that post-accident convalescence of the Hon. Winston S. Churchill necessitates the use of alcoholic spirits especially at meal times. The quantity is naturally indefinite, but the minimum requirements would be 250 cubic centimetres.'

After being told he couldn't drink in front of the Saudi King due to the king's religious beliefs, Churchill said, 'My religion prescribed an absolute sacred rite smoking cigars and drinking alcohol before, after, and if need be during all meals and the intervals between them.'

One of his private secretaries noted that Churchill was never the worse for drink. Churchill said, 'I have taken more out of alcohol than alcohol has taken out of me.' He also noted that 'Hot baths, cold champagne, new peas and old brandy' were the four essentials of life.

Churchill's favourite brandy was Hine, his preferred champagne Pol Roger, and his top Scotch Johnnie Walker Red Label. His famous Churchill Martini consisted of a glass of chilled English gin supplemented with a nod toward France (vermouth was difficult to source).

Jeffrey Hudson – dubbed Lord Minimus – served Charles I's Queen Consort Henrietta Maria and fought alongside the Royalists in the English Civil War. He was captured by pirates and enslaved in Africa. It's a larger-than-life story for a man who was only 18 inches tall.

Hudson was born in 1619. A theory put forward to explain his smallness was that his pregnant mother had choked on a gherkin. While serving the Duchess of Buckingham, at a banquet for the king and queen, Hudson – dressed in armour – burst out of a pie. The delighted queen accepted him as a gift. Her household included a Welsh giant, William Evans. In one performance, Evans pulled Hudson out of his pocket along with a loaf of bread, and made a sandwich.

During the Civil War, Hudson was appointed a Captain of Horse. After fleeing to France with the queen, Hudson announced he would not suffer any more insults. An illegal duel with one taunter ended in disaster. Hudson's opponent had only a water pistol while Hudson fatally shot him in the forehead.

Returning to England, Hudson's ship was captured by pirates. He was taken to North Africa and enslaved. Over the next 25 years, he claimed to have grown to 45 inches, blaming it on the 'buggery' he had regularly received from his captors. Finally returning to London during a wave of religious unrest, he was imprisoned for being a Roman Catholic. Poor Lord Minimus died penniless – but with some amazing stories to tell.

THE TRAVELS OF DEAN MAHOMED

Sake Dean Mahomed was a remarkable man. After working for the army of the British East India Company, he broke convention by eloping to Cork in 1786 to marry Jane Daly. There, in 1794, he became the first Indian to write and publish in English. Having settled in England, the entrepreneurial Mahomed opened the country's first curry house: the Hindoostane Coffee House in Marylebone. He then established a bathhouse in the vogueish seaside spa of Brighton, where he popularised the Hindu word 'shampoo'.

It is hard to imagine a military career more jaw-dropping than that of Adrian Carton de Wiart, who served in the Boer War, First World War and Second World War and survived plane crashes, imprisonment and multiple wounds, receiving the Victoria Cross along the way.

After joining the British Army around 1899 under a fake name and using a fake age, he fought in the Boer War in South Africa until he was seriously wounded in the chest. He eventually returned to South Africa in 1901, where he served with the Second Imperial Light Horse and 4th Dragoon Guards.

Carton de Wiart next fought in World War One. First, he lost his left eye after being shot in the face during an attack on a fort in Somaliland in 1914, while serving with the Somaliland Camel Corps. He served on the Western Front from 1915, suffering gunshot wounds to his skull, an ankle, his hip, a leg and an ear. For years afterwards, his body would expel bits of shrapnel. He would also lose a hand, but not before tearing some damaged fingers off by himself when a doctor refused to amputate them. Even after suffering all of these horrendous wounds, Carton de Wiart commented in *Happy Odyssey*, his autobiography, 'Frankly, I had enjoyed the war.'

The 36-year-old lieutenant-colonel was awarded a Victoria Cross, the highest British military decoration, for his 'conspicuous bravery, coolness and determination' during fighting at La Boisselle in France on 2 and 3 July, 1916.

En route to a command in Yugoslavia during World War Two, Carton de Wiart's plane crashed into the sea. Then aged 61, and missing one eye and one hand, he managed to swim to shore, where he and others with him were captured by the Italians.

Carton de Wiart claimed to have made five escape attempts while a prisoner of war between 1941 and 1943, alongside four other inmates. During one attempt, Carton de Wiart avoided capture for about eight days even though he didn't speak Italian.

From October 1943 to his retirement in 1946, Carton de Wiart was appointed Prime Minister Winston Churchill's personal representative to China. He flew to Singapore to witness the Japanese surrender.

In the late summer of 1929, while getting his shoes shined on the street, Joseph Kennedy Sr (JFK's father) became alarmed when the shoe-shine boy gave him several investment tips on which stocks he should own. This unsolicited advice was a life-changing moment – being a wise investor, Kennedy thought, 'If shoe-shine boys are giving stock tips, then it's time to get out of the market.' His intuition told him that it was the end of the bull market.

Kennedy promptly went back to his office and started unloading his stock portfolio. He didn't just get out of the market but aggres-sively shorted it – a practice of selling stocks in advance of acquiring them, with the aim of making a profit when the price falls. When the Wall Street Crash came in 1929, he made a fortune. Money that would help his son JFK win the presidency in 1961.

Ever since, the shoe-shine boy has become a metaphor for 'time to get out'; for the end of the mania phase in investing where everyone, even the shoe-shine boy, wants in, believing the market is unstoppable.

Isaac Newton was one of the greatest minds Britain ever produced, particularly famous for formulating the laws of motion and gravity. This mathematical ingenuity did not, however, translate into investing.

In 1720 the South Sea Company significantly expanded its oper-ations in government debt, and its stock price rose dramatically.

One investor was Newton. He initially made significant gains on the stock, but cashed in before the real mania set in. With fear of missing out, he ploughed back in, but the bubble burst almost as soon as he did so. Even by conservative estimates, he lost £10 million in today's money, and possibly close to £20 million.

Speculative bubbles follow a similar pattern. From Bitcoin prices to the US stock market in the late 1920s, the white heat of demand leads to rapid increases in price before people take profits *en masse* and the market collapses. The Dutch 'Tulip Mania' of the 1630s is often seen as the first speculative bubble.

Tulips were first introduced to Europe in the 16th century from the Ottoman Empire, and they became a status symbol in the Dutch Republic, then at the height of its Golden Age. Trade in the flowers began to flourish in the 1630s, with some rare varieties of tulips fetching exorbitant sums, with single bulbs trading for the equivalent of an average worker's annual salary or more.

Sale of tulips could be made through a futures market, which was technically illegal, but this financial instrument allowed bulbs to be traded even before they were harvested.

By late 1636 the speculation had reached fever pitch. In January 1637, the common Witte Croonen bulb rose by about 26 times, but the market began to collapse in February, with this bulb falling to one-twentieth of its peak price a week later. While the episode is seen as the first example of a speculative bubble, its overall economic impact on the Dutch Republic is contested.

Adam Smith (1723–90)

The 'Father of Capitalism', Smith laid down the first rigorous, academic description of free-market economics. His analysis of the economy suggested that people are motivated by their own self-interest, and the collective effect of that activity is broad, benevolent economic growth.

Karl Marx (1818–83)

A revolutionary German socialist who co-authored *The Communist Manifesto* and wrote *Das Kapital*. Marx's analysis of capitalism and his theories on class struggle, historical materialism and the exploitation of workers have had a profound impact on political thought and continue to influence contemporary economic and social debates.

Vilfredo Pareto (1848–1923)

Italian economist whose most famous contribution is the concept of Pareto efficiency, which states that a resource allocation is efficient if no individual can be made better off without making someone else worse off. He also introduced the Pareto principle, or the 80/20 rule, which posits that 80% of effects often come from 20% of the causes.

John Maynard Keynes (1883–1946)

Keynesian ideas revolutionised macroeconomic theory and policy. He advocated for government intervention during economic downturns, arguing that deficit spending could stimulate demand and reduce unemployment. His work *The General Theory of Employment, Interest and Money* is a foundational text in modern economics.

Joan Robinson (1903–83)

Influential figure in the Cambridge School of economics, best known for her contributions to post-Keynesian economics. Her works include *The Economics of Imperfect Competition* (1933) and *The Accumulation of Capital* (1956). Although she never won the Nobel Prize for Economics, it was thought by many in the field that she deserved such recognition. Robinson grew increasingly left-wing, expressing admiration for Mao Zedong's China and Kim Il Sung's North Korea.

SNAIL MONEY

A cowrie is a type of sea snail with a glossy shell, most commonly found in the Indian Ocean. The small shells are highly durable, hard to counterfeit and have limited supply, and their use as currency became important for trading in Asia and Africa until quite recently.

In China, cowrie shells were used as currency as early as the Neolithic period, becoming common during Shang Dynasty (c. 1600–1046 BC). The classical Chinese alphabetic character for money is based on a cowrie shell.

The shells of the *Monetaria moneta* or 'money cowrie' are particularly common in the Maldives. The archipelago could act as a kind of mint, because the islanders worked out an efficient method of harvesting them. The snails would collect on coconut palm fronds laid out in shallow lagoons, then left to dry out in the hot sun and the shells collected.

The trade of cowries spread throughout the coasts of the Indian Ocean, and imported shells became an important medium of exchange throughout Africa well into the 19th century. They also made highly valued jewellery and ornaments. From the 16th century, European traders began importing tons of cowrie shells to trade for resources, with some 30 billion imported to the Bight of Benin. Cedi, the unit of currency of Ghana, is the Akan word for cowrie, and depictions of the shells have recently featured on the 20 cedi coin.

HOURS WORKED

The past was a time of backbreaking labour and few holidays. The weekend, for example, is a modern concept. Ancient Rome had an eight-day week with one of those days customarily for market or leisure. In the late 19th century British mill owners started giving the workers Saturday afternoon off. Hence the tradition of the Saturday afternoon football fixture. On 1 May 1926 Henry Ford went a step further and introduced a five-day week at his Ford Motor Company. The average working week has fallen from around 70 hours in 1870 to under 40 hours in the present day across Europe.

Burgundy, to the southeast of Paris, had been an independent kingdom in the 5th and 6th centuries before becoming part of the Frankish realm. King Robert II of France made Burgundy a duchy in 1004 and it passed to his younger son, another Robert, in 1032. Dukes of Burgundy were a junior, or cadet, branch of the French royal House of Capet.

In the mid-14th century, Burgundy was inherited by King John II of France, who gave it to his fourth son, Philip, who became known as Philip the Bold, Duke of Burgundy, ruling from 1363–1404. Philip married Margaret, Countess of Flanders, increasing Burgundian influence, and was succeeded by his son, John the Fearless, in 1404. John was involved in French government while his cousin Charles VI was incapacitated with mental illness. He was involved in the assassination of the Duke of Orleans, leading to civil war between the Burgundians and the French Armagnacs. He was in turn assassinated by Charles's son and heir in 1419. This caused John's heir, Philip the Good, to align with England in its war against France until the mid-1430s. Philip the Good ruled until his death in 1467, when his son, Charles the Bold, became duke. Charles was rash and impetuous, beginning a series of wars that led to his death at the Battle of Nancy in January 1477.

By his death, Charles controlled a large strip of territory from Burgundy to the Low Countries making him one of the most powerful and wealthiest men in Europe. Charles expanded his realm across swathes of France and the Netherlands. In the early 1470s he progressed plans to turn his territories into an independent kingdom, negotiating with the Holy Roman Emperor Frederick III to recognise and crown Charles. But that dream died with Charles' defeat and death. He was succeeded by his daughter Mary, who married Archduke Maximilian of Austria, a Habsburg. Burgundy was absorbed into France but its territories in the Low Countries became part of the Hapsburg Empire. A centre of trade and culture that embraced art in what was known as the Northern Renaissance, the Burgundian territories were broken apart, but had almost become a new royal powerhouse.

CONVICT TRAMWAY

Australia's first railway opened in 1836 in Tasmania. It ran for 5 miles on wooden rails and was powered by convicts who pushed the carriages. (On descending a hill, the runners were allowed to ride on the vehicle.)

PRESTER JOHN

During the reign of Pope Callixtus II (1119–24), a visitor arrived at the court of the Byzantine Emperor. Papal envoys there were so intrigued by the man that they invited him to visit Rome. Giving his name as Patriarch John of the Indians, he described a vast and wealthy kingdom at the farthest eastern edge of the world where the walls around the capital city were so wide, two chariots could ride side by side along them.

When the Muslims retook the Crusader State of Edessa in 1140 it prompted the Second Crusade, suddenly 'Prester John' was talked of as a powerful ally. Some thought he might have been succeeded by a son named David by now.

The myth of Prester John grew, in 1165 the Byzantine Emperor received a letter full of wild claims. Prester John was king of India and a descendant of one of the biblical Magi. The writer claimed Prester John's realm was filled with monsters, and that caves near his capital were filled with dragons tamed to fight for him.

During the Fifth Crusade which invaded Egypt in 1217, the Christian army paused for a year, partly due to intelligence that Prester John was marching to their aid. On that occasion, an army was on the move, but it turned out to be the Mongols. As exploration continued and Prester John's lands remained elusive, his kingdom moved and was believed to be in Africa, possibly in Ethiopia. The myths were a firm belief in many quarters until the late early modern period. Serious doubt was only cast on his existence in the late 17th century. Was Prester John wishful thinking, a misunderstanding, a prank, or simply storytelling run wild?

The Industrial Revolution is sometimes said to have begun in a small Shropshire town in the 1760s. Abraham Darby had been refining the process of smelting iron at the beginning of the century. His son, Abraham Darby II, continued his father's work and created wrought iron from coke pig iron at Coalbrookdale, using local, low-sulphur coal in 1755. In 1777, Abraham Darby III decided to publicise the family's work by building a new bridge, entirely from iron, across the River Severn. Completed in 1779 and opened on New Year's Day 1781, the Iron Bridge was a technical marvel.

Spanning 30 metres (100 feet), it required 378 tons of iron and cost £6,000 to build, almost double Darby's original estimate and equivalent to over £750,000 today. More than one-third of the cost was labour, and it also included £15 6s 8d, over £1,300 today, for ale to celebrate the completion of the project. Today, the Iron Bridge still stands in rural Shropshire and is a UNESCO World Heritage Site.

WORLD'S FIRST SKYSCRAPER

The story of skyscrapers often begins in New York and Chicago from around 1884 with increasingly tall buildings. However, what is technically the world's first skyscraper was built in Shropshire in 1796–7. Shrewsbury Flaxmill Maltings may not look like a skyscraper, but its Main Mill was the first building in the world to have an iron frame supporting the weight of the structure, the formula for every skyscraper ever built, so that it has been dubbed the 'Grandparent of Skyscrapers'.

On 2 August 1832, a 13-year-old girl, the future Queen Victoria, was travelling through the Midlands on her way to Wales. She wrote in her diary what she made of the industrial heartland of England.

'We just passed through a town where all coal mines are and you see the fire glimmer at a distance in the engines in many places. The men, women, children, country and houses are all black. But I can not by any description give an idea of its strange and extraordinary appearance. The country is very desolate every where; there are coals about, and the grass is quite blasted and black. I just now see an extraordinary building flaming with fire. The country continues black, engines flaming, coals, in abundance, every where, smoking and burning coal heaps, intermingled with wretched huts and carts and little ragged children'.

The term 'the Black Country' to describe the area around Dudley and Tipton that now includes parts of Wolverhampton doesn't appear for another 14 years, but the young princess may have inadvertently given the region its name with her vivid description of it.

THE ROAD TO WIGAN PIER

'A slag-heap is at best a hideous thing, because it is so planless and functionless. It is something just dumped on the earth, like the emptying of a giant's dust-bin. On the outskirts of the mining towns there are frightful landscapes where your horizon is ringed completely round by jagged grey mountains, and underfoot is mud and ashes and over-head the steel cables where tubs of dirt travel slowly across miles of country. Often the slag-heaps are on fire, and at night you can see the red rivulets of fire winding this way and that, and also the slow-moving blue flames of sulphur, which always seem on the point of expiring and always spring out again. Even when a slag-heap sinks, as it does ultimately, only an evil brown grass grows on it, and it retains its hummocky surface.'

George Orwell, *The Road to Wigan Pier* (1937)

Spouse	From	To	Months	Fate
Catherine of Aragon	Nov 1509	May 1533	287	Divorced
Anne Boleyn	Jan 1533	May 1536	40	Beheaded
Jane Seymour	May 1536	Oct 1537	16	Died
Single	Oct 1537	Jan 1540	26	
Anne of Cleves	Jan 1540	Jul 1540	6	Divorced
Catherine Howard	Jul 1540	Nov 1541	4	Beheaded
Single	Nov 1541	Jul 1543	20	
Catherine Parr	Jul 1543	Jan 1547	43	Survived

In April 1509, Henry VIII became the second Tudor King of England. He is famous for having six wives, and for the rhyme of their fates 'Divorced, Beheaded, Died, Divorced, Beheaded, Survived'. More accurately, two of Henry's marriages were annulled rather than ending in divorce. He spent the first 24 years of his reign married to Catherine of Aragon, mother to Mary I, but their failure to produce a son caused Henry to look elsewhere. His pursuit of Anne Boleyn led to the break with Rome and the creation of the Church of England when the Pope refused to annul his marriage to Catherine. When the marriage to Anne produced only a daughter, the future Elizabeth I, Henry's need for a son intensified. Anne was accused of treason for a string of alleged affairs, including with her brother, that were probably fabricated to create a justification for her execution.

Henry remarried within a fortnight to Jane Seymour and was soon the father to a longed-for son, the future Edward VI. Jane's death as a result of complications following the birth left Henry single for over two years. Aged 48, he married a Protestant princess, Anne of Cleves, in 1540 but ended the marriage almost immediately, claiming he found her too unattractive, when it was more likely his own growing health problems were causing him embarrassment in the bedroom. A swift marriage to the teenage Catherine Howard ended in disaster amid more claims of treasonous affairs that led to her execution. Henry's final wife, Catherine Parr, outlived the king.

ANNE BOLEYN MYTHS

There are many myths about Anne Boleyn. Several of them seem to have originated with Elizabeth I's adversaries, who sought to blacken her mother's reputation. Here are some of the most common:

Anne's was a rags-to-riches story – The Boleyns were a wealthy noble family of property owners and courtiers.

Anne's 'promiscuity' came from growing up in a lascivious French court – Anne served the devout and pious Queen Claude of France. Most of their days would have been spent sewing, embroidering and praying.

Anne was a homewrecker – Anne greatly admired Catherine of Aragon and served her devotedly. Henry was the one who did the pursuing and wooing.

Anne was a great beauty – Her exact appearance is difficult to pin down, as there are inconsistencies in her surviving portraits. Contemporaries also differed in their opinions of her attractiveness.

Anne was Henry VIII's own daughter – Henry categorically denied having an affair with Anne's mother. Besides, he may have only been ten years old when Anne was allegedly conceived.

Anne had six fingers – There's no evidence to suggest that Anne had any physical deformities, let alone six fingers. (Although she may have had a small, extra fingernail.)

Anne had an affair with her brother – Anne was very close to her brother George. They spent a lot of time together, but there's absolutely no evidence to suggest incest.

Anne was a witch – The charges against Anne were for treason, adultery and incest. There was an unsubstantiated report that Henry said he had been seduced into the marriage with Anne by being charmed – but that is hardly evidence of witchcraft.

In 1545, Catherine Parr published the first book to be written in England and in English by a woman under her own name. *Prayers or Meditations* was a collection of vernacular texts assembled for personal devotion. When Henry VIII died, she published a more Protestant-leaning pamphlet, *The Lamentation of a Sinner* (1547).

THE EXCHEQUER

The first reference to the Exchequer in England as the body that received royal income appears in a writ of 1110, during the reign of Henry I. It is unclear precisely when it actually came into existence. In its earliest form, the Exchequer was an event that took place twice a year, when sheriffs delivered the taxation they had collected to royal representatives. The name Exchequer referred to a cloth that was spread over a table to help reconcile the money submitted with what was expected. The cloth was 10 feet by 5 feet and chequered, like a chess board. The Old French word for a chess board is echiquier.

The Exchequer was overseen by the Justiciar, who served as President of the Board, supported by lords known as the Barons of the Exchequer. Sheriffs were expected to produce a fixed income from their county. Anything they raised above that was theirs to keep, hence their reputation for corruption and greed, and any shortfall was their responsibility. Tally sticks were used as receipts for income deposited at the Exchequer. A notch in the stick denoted the amount paid. As tally sticks accumulated, they were regularly destroyed to clear space. After they were abolished in 1826, the last remaining tally sticks were burned carelessly in October 1834, causing a fire that destroyed both Houses of Parliament and most other buildings on the site. Only Westminster Hall survived.

The records of the payments were entered onto pipe rolls, so-called because they were rolled up tight like pipes. The Pipe Rolls run from 1155 until 1832 and are the longest-running continual public record in Britain. The cloth would give its name to a government institution.

The Great Norway Serpent 'Sea Orm' (1539)

In 1539, Swedish cartographer Olaus Magnus published 'Carta Marina' – one of the earliest accurate cartographic depictions of the Scandinavian peninsula. It contained illustrations and descriptions of over 20 sea monsters including sea serpents, notably depictions of a sea orm. Rather than cartographical decoration, this allegedly represented a real creature, vividly described to Olaus on his travels by Nordic sailors and fishermen, said to be 200–300 feet long.

Gloucester's Sea Serpent (from 1639)

In 1639 the first American sea serpent was sighted off the coast of New England. As reported in *An Account of Two Voyages to New England* in 1641, sailors allegedly encountered a snake that 'lay quailed up like a cable upon the rock at Cape Ann', Massachusetts. Sightings occured again off the coast of Gloucester in the early 19th century. In August 1817, a group of seamen claimed to have fired a cannon at the creature, but it disappeared beneath the waves.

The Daedalus Sea Serpent (1848)

The Royal Navy's HMS *Daedalus* reported sighting a sea serpent while sailing to St Helena in the South Atlantic, with their account being published in *The Times*. Described as dark brown, with a 4-foot snake-like head and 60-foot-long body, it was later suggested to be a sei whale, which can reach a similar length.

Cadborosaurus (20th century)

There have been hundreds of sightings of sea serpent-like creatures in Cadboro Bay, near Vancouver, over the last two centuries. With a long neck, humps and a horse-like head. the creature (or creatures) has been nicknamed 'Caddy'. Two people have claimed to have caught a baby Caddy (in 1968 and 1991), only to return them to the water.

In Anglo-Saxon England, a body called the Witan, or Witenagemot, a counsel of the leading men, had the power to elect a king. The Norman invasion of 1066 ended that. Over the centuries, some nobles were inspired by this precedent to attempt to re-establish their influence over the crown.

Magna Carta established the principle in 1215 that the monarch was not above the law. The word Parliament first appears in England in 1236, in the reign of Henry III, to describe a gathering of the senior barons and clergy. The first elections to Parliament came in 1254. Simon de Montfort rebelled against Henry III (r. 1216–1272) and held him prisoner and in 1265 summoned the first meeting of Parliament not called by the king. Throughout Henry's reign, Parliament met to grant taxation in return for reform of what it identified as bad practice on the king's part.

Under Henry's son, Edward I (r. 1272–1307), Parliament began to codify and standardise law across England, which the king was explicitly not above. When Edward II was deposed in favour of his son Edward III (r. 1327–77), Parliament made the coup legal, and did the same in 1399 when Richard II (r. 1377–99) was deposed by Henry IV (r. 1399– 1413). By the time of the Wars of the Roses (1455–87), kings were submitting their claims to Parliament for adjudication or ratification and Parliamentary approval was viewed as an absolute requirement.

When Charles I (r. 1625–1649) tried to rule without reference to Parliament, the Civil War ensued and saw the monarchy temporarily abolished. The example of the Anglo-Saxon Witan influenced the debates and conflicts that have led today to United Kingdom's balanced constitution, a compromise between Crown and Parliament.

Tin mining had been an important industry in Devon and Cornwall since ancient times. During the reign of King John in 1201, tin mining became so important to the English Crown that a unique law code was set up in the West Country known as 'Stannary Law'.

This system acknowledged the rights of tin miners, which included exemption from certain taxes, the right to mine on public land and the establishment of stannary courts and parliaments. Sir Walter Raleigh served as Lord Warden of the Stannaries between 1584 and 1603.

The last stannary parliament sat in 1753. While stannary law no longer has practical relevance, it remains part of English law.

UNNATURAL ROYAL DEATHS

William II: Died in a hunting accident in the New Forest on 2 August 1100.

Richard: The older brother of William II, also died in a hunting accident in the New Forest, England, around 30 years before William II.

Henry I: Died after consuming a large quantity of lampreys, which resulted in food poisoning, on 1 December 1135.

Richard I: Died from a lingering injury caused by a crossbow bolt that turned gangrenous, 6 April 1199.

Edward II: Probably died in captivity, with later, unreliable accounts suggesting he was murdered by having a red-hot poker inserted into his rectum, September 1327.

Richard II: Imprisoned by a family rival and possibly murdered or he starved to death in captivity, February 1400.

Henry VI: Probably murdered on order by Edward IV, 21 May 1471.

Edward V: Possibly murdered by his uncle Richard III.

William III: Died after his horse tripped over a molehill, 8 March 1702.

THE WOODEN WONDER

Inexpensive and durable, plywood may seem rooted in modern manufacturing and contemporary design: today, after all, it is used for everything from structures to skateboards. But the history of plywood dates at least to the ancient Egyptians, who realised they could combine thin layers of wood to construct a robust board. In Third Dynasty Egypt (2686–13 BC), carpenters built a coffin made from six layers of wood, each ⅙ inch thick, held with pegs and dowels. A similar material was later used in ancient Egyptian furniture.

What made this material so special? As each veneer is set at a right angle to the grain of the layer beneath, plywood overcomes wood's weakness across the grain. It's very strong as a result, and an alternative to costlier timber – especially if good trees are in short supply.

English engineer Samuel Bentham filed the first modern patent for a plywood manufacturing process in 1797. Subsequent woodworkers steadily found new uses for plywood and ways of making it. Experimental designers in the 20th century turned plywood into an industrial material, pointing it to novel uses including forming the fuselage of the de Havilland Mosquito, a World War Two aircraft known as 'the wooden wonder' for its speed and agility.

THE COLOSSUS OF BLETCHLEY

Colossus was the world's first programmable electronic computer, built by British codebreakers at Bletchley during World War Two. The prototype was in use by February 1944, and by the war's end there were 10 'Colossi' that intercepted and processed a huge amount of German communications across Europe.

The computers were 7 feet high by 17 feet wide and 11 feet deep, weighing 5 tons. Rather than using a stored programme, Colossus used 2,500 valves and vacuum tubes to perform counting operations. By the war's end, 63 million characters of high-grade German intelligence had been decrypted by 550 people. The project was classified until 1975, and all but two of the original computers had been dismantled so that their use could not be deduced.

THE KING OF ENTERTAINMENT

While a much newer form of entertainment, the global video games industry is bigger than the music and film industries combined. Its roots were set in the 1950s, when computer scientists were first able to design simple games turning into a commercial industry in 1972 with the release of the first home gaming console and the legendary arcade game *Pong*.

From 1983–85, the overheated US market crashed with the loss of 97% of home gaming revenue. The fall led Japanese gaming brands Nintendo and Sega to enter the US market, and one of the biggest rivalries in entertainment was formed between their gaming consoles – initially the NES and the Master System – and their lead franchise characters Mario and Sonic.

The industry entered a new paradigm in 1994 with the introduction of the first 32-bit console, the Sony PlayStation. From here, Sega's position as a market leader faded away, particularly after the introduction of the Microsoft Xbox in 2001. Nintendo, Microsoft and Sony (the market leader) now dominate the home console market.

BEST SELLING VIDEO GAMES OF ALL TIME

Transport	Initial Release	Publisher	Sales
Minecraft	Nov 2011	Mojang	238m
Grand Theft Auto V	Sep 2013	Rockstar	180m
Tetris (EA)	Sep 2006	Electronic Arts	100m
PUBG: Battlegrounds	Dec 2017	Krafton	75m
Mario Kart 8 Deluxe	May 2014	Nintendo	62m
Super Mario Bros	Sep 1985	Nintendo	58m
Red Dead Redemption 2	Oct 2018	Rockstar	53m
Overwatch	May 2016	Blizzard	50m
The Witcher 3	May 2015	CD Projekt	50m
Tetris (1989)	June 1989	Nintendo	48m

THE FIRST BRITONS?

Our earliest current evidence for humans in Britain dates back some 900,000 years. In 2013, on a beach at Happisburgh in Norfolk, the waves exposed prehistoric sediment, hidden beneath a covering of deposits for hundreds of thousands of years. The sediment was filled with mysterious hollows.

A team of scientists were fortunately close at hand; they managed to record these hollows before the sea tides destroyed them within a fortnight. What they discovered was that these hollows weren't natural, but c. 900,000-year-old human footprints that belonged to both adults and children. An incredibly rare find – the oldest known footprints outside of Africa.

No human bones were discovered alongside the footprints, leaving some doubt as to which Homo species they belonged to. Considering their geographical location and human fossils dating to a similar time from elsewhere in the world, the scientists have suggested that these humans were either Homo antecessor or Homo erectus.

WONDERS OF ORKNEY

Situated just off Britain's north coast, the Orkney Islands have a rich concentration of prehistoric sites, dating back more than 5,000 years.

Knap of Howar
Built around 3700 BC, the Knap of Howar is a farmstead that lays claim to being the oldest building in Britain, and the oldest stone house in Northern Europe.

Skara Brae
The best preserved Stone Age settlement in Western Europe, consisting of several closely connected houses. The houses included furniture, and were occupied from roughly 3200 BC to 2200 BC.

The Ring of Brodgar
The largest stone circle in Scotland. The Ring originally consisted of 60 standing stones quarried from various sites across Orkney and transported to the Brodgar headland.

BROCHS

The pinnacle of Scotland's prehistoric architecture, brochs were massive, drystone round houses built largely during the latter half of the 1st millennium BC. Imposing circular towers could serve several purposes. Alongside being residential homes, they were also symbols of power and centres of larger communities – a bit like the Roman villa or the medieval manor.

There are now skeletal traces of more than a hundred of these structures today. Dun Beag broch on the Isle of Skye and Clachtoll broch in Assynt are examples with the original circular stone foundation structure still intact. The Broch of Mousa on the Shetland Islands is the best preserved broch, with much of its tower still remaining.

CLAPPER BRIDGES

A clapper bridge is an ancient form of bridge commonly found in the moorlands of Western England, and other upland areas of the UK. The name 'clapper' comes from the Latin 'claperius', which means 'pile of stones'.

Clapper bridges don't use any mortar, and are formed by placing large slabs together over a river, normally supported by another slab or pile of stones. The Tarr Steps, near Withypool in north Devon, is likely medieval in origin. It consists of 17 slabs, weighing up to 2 tons each, and crosses 50 metres of the River Barle.

1543: The Portuguese were the first Europeans to arrive in Japan, landing on the island of Tanegashima in the company of Southeast Asians, labelled *nanban* ('southern barbarian') by the Japanese.

1549: Following the arrival of Spanish Jesuits, including the influential Francis Xavier, Catholicism began to develop as a major religious force in Japan.

1580: Richly laden Portuguese ships arriving in Nagasaki helped the Jesuits fund their missionary work. In May 1580, the city's Christian *daimyo* gave it to the Jesuits. The result: a Christian domain in Japan with warlord allies.

1587: As Toyotomi Hideyoshi unified Japan, he grew concerned with Christianity's influence. He condemned it as a 'pernicious doctrine' and gave Jesuits 20 days to leave Japan. He relented, but seized Nagasaki the following year, curbing European – and Christian – influence.

1596 : When the Spanish galleon *San Felipe* was wrecked on Japan's coast and its cargo captured, its pilot alluded to the links between missionaries and the Spanish empire. In retaliation Hideyoshi ordered the crucifixion of 26 Christians.

1609: The Dutch East India Company was granted permission to establish itself at Hirado, near Nagasaki.

1614: The Tokugawa Shogunate, which came to power in 1603, firmly outlawed Christianity. The Tokugawa's isolationist foreign policy prioritised domestic unity and Japanese control over foreign relationships.

1635: The Sakoku Edict of 1635 forbade Japanese from leaving the country, banned Catholicism and restricted ports open to trade.

1639: The Portuguese were excluded from Japan definitively. This meant that for the next 220 years, the Dutch were the only westerners allowed to access Japan. They were admitted only at Dejima, an artificial island in Nagasaki Bay.

The term 'samurai' (meaning 'servant') initially referred to functionaries who served as clerks and administrators to ancient Japan's noble class. Japan's Heian Period (794–1185) saw campaigns to subdue native Emishi people, when samurai were first relied upon by nobles as warriors.

The transformation of samurai into a hereditary military nobility caste occurred after large numbers of imperial family members were downgraded to samurai status. The Minamoto and Taira families were among the earliest true samurai families, known for their participation in the Genpei War (1180–5), battling the central government, and each other. Minamoto Yoritomo emerged victorious, establishing a military government in 1192 under the Kamakura shogunate, resulting in samurai political rule for most of the next 700 years.

Originally, samurai were skilled mounted archers – their reputation as sword-wielding warriors developed in the Edo Period (1603–1868), with swords a symbol of prestige. Samurai also used other weapons like the naginata (polearm) and yari (spear). They adopted the 'bushido' moral code, similar to the European concept of chivalry. But much like medieval knights, the degree to which all samurai really followed this is debatable.

A ronin was a masterless samurai. Far from romanticised depictions as wandering warriors, the term historically encompassed individuals without purpose, including homeless people. During wartime, ronins sold their warrior services to the highest bidder. However, during the Edo Period, with no wars to fight or opportunities to regain samurai status, many fell into destitution and vagrancy, selling their swords or taking their own lives to avoid starvation.

In the prevailing peace, many samurai became courtiers and bureaucrats for their lords ('daimyōs') or teachers and administrators. Japan's feudal era ended in 1868 at the start of the Meiji Period (1868–1912) when the Emperor's imperial power was restored. Actual political power was transferred into the hands of a small group of nobles and former samurai, and the samurai class itself was abolished a few years afterwards.

The 16th to 19th centuries saw some of the most devastating natural disasters on record. Plague outbreaks and earthquakes were accompanied by the Little Ice Age. This brought extremes of weather, with rivers and even coastal seas freezing over. Some of the disasters are labelled 'great', but they can lay claim to being among 'the worst in history'.

Shaanxi Earthquake (1556)

Occuring in January 1556 in central China, the Shaanxi Earthquake was the deadliest earthquake in recorded history. The earthquake had a magnitude of 8.0, and the direct death toll is estimated at 100,000 people.

Great Plague (1665–67)

The last major epidemic of bubonic plague to strike England centred around London, but spread throughout the country. While less devastating than the Black Death, an estimated 100,000 people, or a quarter of London's population, died.

Great Famine (1695–97)

The 1690s was the lowest point of the Little Ice Age. The Swedish Empire was badly affected by cold and wetter weather. In Finland up to a third of the population perished due to lack of food and nutrition, making it the worst demographic disaster in Finnish history.

Great Frost (1709)

The European winter of 1709 was so severe that there were reports of frozen birds falling to the ground. The weather led to the collapse of the economy, and in Britain gross domestic product fell by 23%. The short but extremely sharp Coronavirus Recession (2020) was the most severe economic contraction since the Great Frost.

Great Hurricane (1780)

The most devastating hurricane on record hit the eastern Caribbean in October 1780, with windspeeds reaching a reported 200 mph. An estimated 22,000 people died as the storm passed through, and both the British and French navies (involved in the American Revolutionary War) suffered heavy losses.

THAMES FROST FAIRS

London's River Thames froze at least 23 times between around 1450 and 1850. Sometimes the ice was thick enough for carriages to cross it and for 'frost fairs' to be held. One of the earliest frost fairs was held in 1564, with Queen Elizabeth I in attendance, but the most celebrated fair occurred during the Great Frost of 1683–4, when the river was frozen for two months.

Diarist John Evelyn recorded the 1683–4 fair incorporating 'horse and coach races, puppet plays and interludes, cooks, tipling and other lewd places, so that it seemed to be a bacchanalian triumph, or carnival on the water'. 1813 saw the last frost fair, which was held for a month and featured stalls erected on the ice that sold food, drink and souvenirs.

GREAT FIRE OF LONDON

In 1666, the Great Fire of London broke out from the house of Thomas Farriner, a baker living in Pudding Lane. Over the next four days, much of medieval London was destroyed by the fire and thousands were left without homes.

Sir Thomas Bloodworth, Mayor of London, was woken up in the early hours of Sunday 2 September to be told that there was a fire. He rolled over and said 'a woman could piss it out.' He was wrong.

Over days it swept through the wooden city. It destroyed:

» 87 churches and St Paul's Cathedral
» More than 13,000 houses, 15% of the city's houses
» Three city gatehouses
» 44 Company Halls
» £10 million of property
» Fewer than ten human lives

Mansa Musa was ruler of the Mali Empire from around 1312 to 1337. He was the ninth Musa, or ruler, of the empire that had conquered the Ghana Empire, a territory rich with gold mines. In 1324, he went on hajj, a pilgrimage to Mecca, and left a great impression everywhere he passed through, including in Cairo, where his presence and lavish gift-giving saw the price of gold plummet.

Musa's rule was well documented and saw him foster closer links with other Muslim states, encourage scholars to come to Mali, and expand his borders. Musa is often held to be the richest man in history, though such claims are all but impossible to verify. One modern estimate suggests he was worth the equivalent of around $400 billion today, with others claiming he took over $950 million worth of gold on hajj.

— NZINGA MBANDE: WARRIOR QUEEN OF ANGOLA —

Nzinga Mbande was a 17th-century ruler of the Ndongo and Matamba Kingdoms, in present-day northern Angola. Born in 1583, Nzinga trained as a warrior, fighting alongside her father.

She is known for her diplomatic and military strategies in defending her kingdoms against Portuguese colonisers and the slave trade. When her brother, the new king, dispatched her to negotiate with the Portuguese, they refused her a chair. An attendant fell on their hands and knees, serving as her chair, enabling her to speak face to face and successfully convince them to sign a peace treaty.

Nzinga became queen in 1626 after her brother died and the Portuguese attempted to seize control. She fled, founding a new kingdom, Matamba. A skilled politician, Nzinga worked to strengthen her kingdoms through trade and alliances with neighbouring kingdoms and the Dutch. While making Matamba a commercial powerhouse, Nzinga continued fighting the Portuguese, leading troops into battle into her 60s. In 1657, the Portuguese signed a peace treaty, returning Ndongo. Nzinga died in 1663 aged 80, and remains revered as a symbol of anti-colonial resistance.

3 IMPORTANT AFRICAN KINGDOMS

Axum (c. 100–940 CE)
Situated in what is now Ethiopia and Eritrea, the Kingdom of Axum emerged around the 1st century AD. Axum's location along the Red Sea enabled it to control vital trade routes connecting the Roman Empire with India. It reached its peak between the 4th and 7th centuries under rulers who claimed descent from the biblical King Solomon and the Queen of Sheba.

Mali (c. 1235–1672)
The West African Kingdom of Mali thrived between the 13th and 16th centuries. Mali owed its prosperity to its command over trans-Saharan trade routes, which facilitated the exchange of gold, salt and other goods between West and North Africa. During the rule of Mansa Musa, Mali's capital of Timbuktu became a centre for Islamic scholarship and culture.

Zimbabwe (c. 1220–1450)
From its heart at the iconic stone city that gave the kingdom its name, the Kingdom of Zimbabwe was able to control parts of modern-day Zimbabwe, Mozambique and South Africa at its peak. It held an important position on the southeastern coast of Africa, controlling the trade of ivory and metals into the continental interior. The stone ruins of Great Zimbabwe are part of the largest stone structure in precolonial Africa.

OPERATION LEGACY

As British colonies approached independence in the mid-20th century, departing administrators went to great pains to obscure archives that, as a 1961 Colonial Office note described, might 'embarrass' the British or other governments. Blue smoke rose from government buildings in Palestine in 1948, while in 1957 British soldiers in Malaysia dispatched records for 'the Navy's splendid incinerator'. The governor of Trinidad was advised to dump files into the sea. In Uganda, officials dubbed the process 'Operation Legacy'.

Boudica's Revolt (60 AD)

The Queen of the Iceni tribe tapped into resistance to the Roman occupation of Britain and launched a rebellion that nearly swept away the Roman colony, destroying several settlements before her army was crushed.

Peasants' Revolt (1381)

Fury over high taxes, the dislocation caused by the Black Death and unpopular grandees led a group of rebels from Essex and Kent to storm into London. They breached the Tower of London, the only time it fell in its history, but their leader Wat Tyler was killed at Smithfield. The rebels dispersed, but trouble in the shires continued.

Jack Cade's Revolt (1450)

A force from southeast England marched on London protesting against corruption in government. They looted the capital and fought a pitched battle against Londoners on London Bridge.

Pilgrimage of Grace (1536)

Considered the most serious Tudor rebellion, it began in Yorkshire under the leadership of Robert Aske. It spread through the north in opposition to Henry VIII's break with Rome. It disbanded after handing a list of grievances to the king's officials but later connected violence saw the leaders rounded up and executed.

The Gunpowder Plot (1605)

Remember, remember the fifth of November. Guy Fawkes was caught in the undercroft of the Houses of Parliament after the authorities were tipped off about the plot. Some conspirators were killed in a shoot-out at Holbeche House in Staffordshire, others were executed in London.

The Newport Chartist Rising (1839)

The last armed uprising in British history took place in Newport, Wales in November 1839. Campaigns for electoral reform culminated in the Battle of Westgate and the death of a small number of Chartists. The leaders were convicted of treason and transported to Australia.

The highest confirmed number of casualties in the history of the British Army occurred on 1 July 1916, when 60,000 men were killed or wounded on the opening day of the Somme. British forces involved in the attack numbered around 200,000 men.

> Of the original thousand men (who served from the opening of the war), nearly 90% would become casualties during the war. A third would be killed. While recovered sick and wounded would be recycled through the Battalion, very few would serve (sic) to the end of the war unscathed.
>
> M. Gillott, editor of *Great War Diaries:*
> *1st Bn Grenadier Guards War Diary 1914–1919.*

5,400,000 men served on the Western Front in World War One, and 564,000 of them were killed, which is slightly over 10% of the total.

At the Battle of Bunker Hill in 1775 British general William Howe lost around 1,000 of his men killed and wounded, approximately 50% of his attacking force.

Out of the 89,000 officers and men who were sent to the West Indies between 1793 and 1801, a staggering 62,250, or 70%, became casualties. Among them, 45,250 lost their lives, with the majority succumbing to diseases rather than enemy action.

In the Peninsular War the chance of an officer being killed was 6.5%, and of being wounded 29%. For enlisted soldiers the percentages were 5.2 and 18 respectively.

> It occurred to me to count the number of officers who had served in the Battalion since D-Day. Up to March 27th, the end of the Rhine crossing [less than ten months] . . . I found that we had had 55 officers commanding the twelve rifle platoons, and that their average service with the Battalion was 38 days. . . Of these 53% were wounded, 24% killed or died of wounds, 15% invalided, and 5% survived.
>
> Col. M. Lindsay, 1st Gordon Highlanders.

Many US Presidents rose to high office on the back of military success and the resulting fame. Others served more anonymously in junior positions and others were given political appointments or served in roles away from the frontline. Here is a list of all the Presidents who have held military rank.

General of the Armies of the United States: George Washington

General of the Army: Dwight D. Eisenhower, Ulysses S. Grant

Major General: Andrew Jackson, Zachary Taylor, William Harrison, Rutherford B. Hayes, James A. Garfield, William Howard Taft

Brigadier General: Franklin Pierce, Chester A. Arthur, Andrew Johnson, Benjamin Harrison

Colonel: Thomas Jefferson, James Madison, James Monroe, James Polk, Theodore Roosevelt, Harry Truman

Commander: Lyndon B. Johnson, Richard Nixon

Lieutenant Commander: Gerald Ford

Major: Millard Fillmore, William McKinley

Captain: Abraham Lincoln, John Tyler, Ronald Reagan

Lieutenant: John F. Kennedy, George H.W. Bush, Jimmy Carter

First Lieutenant: George W. Bush

Private: James Buchanan

While some like Jackson, Grant, Eisenhower and Washington are some of the most celebrated soldiers in US history, Jefferson, Johnson, Fillmore, Polk and Tyler served in state militias and did not serve in combat theatres. Madison may have briefly seen action in his short militia career. Chester A. Arthur did not see action but was a superb logistician. Taft was Chairman of the Red Cross in the USA during World War One and was given military rank to facilitate his work. Reagan was barred from serving in a combat theatre because of poor eyesight. George W. Bush failed to meet the attendance and physical requirements for a F-102 pilot in the Air National Guard and was discharged early.

TIME TAKEN BETWEEN UK AND AUSTRALIA

Transport	Year	Time Taken
The First Fleet	1787–8	252 days
Sailing Steam Hybrid Ship	1850	100 days
Cutty Sark	1886	72 days
Cruise Liner	1909	45 days
First Flight	1919	28 days
First Commercial Flight	1935	12 days
First Avro Lancastrian	1945	4.5 days
First Jet	1953	40 hours 43 mins
One-stop hop	1984	20 hours
First commercial non-stop	2018	16 hours 45 mins

There are only a few destinations on Earth further away from the UK than Australia. New Zealand and Australia are known as the Antipodes because the antipode of anywhere on Earth is the place on the Earth's surface diametrically opposite it. Early voyages were perilous, with the First Fleet taking around eight months to reach Australia.

The advent of air travel revolutionised the journey between the two countries. In 1935, the first commercial air service between Britain and Australia was launched by Qantas and Imperial Airways, taking around 12 days with multiple stops. The introduction of jet airliners in the 1950s further shortened travel times, and the famous 'Kangaroo Route' was established. Today, with the availability of non-stop flights like Qantas's Perth to London route launched in 2018, travellers can complete the journey in around 17 hours, making the once-distant continent more accessible than ever before.

NOVELIST STATESMEN

Horace Walpole: *The Castle of Otranto* (1764) is considered the earliest Gothic novel, and was penned by the 4th Earl of Orford.

Johann Wolfgang von Goethe: *The Sorrows of Young Werther* (1774). Goethe's first novel was written before he became Chancellor of the Exchequer of the Duchy of Saxe-Weimar.

Napoleon Bonaparte: *Clisson et Eugénie* (1795). A romantic tale of a doomed romance between a soldier and his lover. Written before he became French Emperor, it went unpublished in his lifetime.

Benjamin Disraeli: *Vivian Grey* (1826). The later British Prime Minister's first novel was followed by 16 more.

Jimmy Carter: *The Hornet's Nest* (2003) was the first novel published by any President of the United States.

Bill Clinton: *The President is Missing* (2018) followed in Jimmy Carter's footsteps. Clinton has published two novels with author James Patterson.

EVERY LITTLE HELPS

The most valuable ship ever taken by pirates was the Mughal Empire's *Ganj-i-Sawai*, which was captured on its way to Mecca in 1695 by English pirate Henry Every. The loot totalled almost £100 million in today's money. Every became subject to the first ever worldwide manhunt, but he eluded capture and vanished in 1696.

A medieval manuscript has defied understanding for more than 500 years. In 1912, a Polish antiquary named Wilfrid Voynich purchased a collection of manuscripts. Among them was the mysterious book that now bears his name. The work had a documented history during the 17th century when academics had been trying to work out what it meant. Voynich spent years trying to raise interest in decoding the text, to no avail. After Voynich's death, a subsequent owner donated it in 1969 to Yale University, where it remains, catalogued as Beinecke MS 408.

The book comprises several sections of text and illustrations. The text is in an unknown code or language that no one has ever managed to translate. The images have proved similarly cryptic. A Herbal Section contains drawings of plants, some of which are recognisable, while others appear invented. An Astronomical Section has pictures of the sun, moon, stars and zodiac symbols. What is known as the Cosmological Section is a collection of circular drawings with no obvious meaning. A Biological Section appears to show mainly female anatomical drawings within a system of tubes and baths. A Recipe Section is made up of more than 300 brief paragraphs of undecipherable writings, each marked with a star.

Radiocarbon dating demonstrated in 2009 that the parchment of the manuscript dates from between 1404 and 1438. It remains under the care of Yale University today, with websites devoted to attempts to decipher its meaning. Some believe it was an elaborate hoax by a bookseller, while others believe it is a lost language that shows now-extinct species of plants. The truth remains elusive.

—————— GREAT MOLASSES FLOOD ——————

On 15 January 1919, a storage tank of molasses in Boston's North End collapsed. Two million gallons of molasses poured through the streets at speeds estimated at 35 miles per hour. The flood caused extensive building damage and killed 21 people, and dozens more were injured.

The Roman fort of Vindolanda was built near Hadrian's Wall from 85 AD. There have been more than 50 years of archaeological work at the site, with the most extraordinary objects uncovered being its famous, namesake writing tablets. These wooden tablets were Roman letters.

Birthday party

Sulpicia Lepidina was the wife of the fort prefect Flavius Cerialis in c. 100 AD. In one elegantly written tablet, the wife of another officer called Claudia Severa invites Lepidina to her birthday party on 11 September.

> Claudia Severa to her Lepidina greetings. On 11 September, sister, for the day of the celebration of my birthday, I give you a warm invitation to make sure that you come to us, to make the day more enjoyable for me by your arrival, if you are present. Give my greetings to your Cerialis. My Aelius and my little son send you their greetings. I shall expect you, sister. Farewell, sister, my dearest soul, as I hope to prosper, and hail.

The vet

Virilis was one of the vets stationed at Vindolanda. Vets were very important at Vindolanda, given that the fort was the home of Roman cavalry contingents. Several tablets mention Virilus, including one where he has promised to sell a man called Chrauttius his castration shears. . .

> Ask him (sc. Virilis) whether you may send through one of our friends the pair of shears which he promised me in exchange for money.

Another letter has Virilis complaining to one of his friends that he is yet to have his favourite castration shears returned.

Underpants on the double!

One letter mentions a list of vital supplies sent to one lucky individual. . .

> . . . I have sent you. . . pairs of socks from Sattua, two pairs of sandals and two pairs of underpants...

> *Translations reproduced courtesy of A.K. Bowman and J.D. Thomas.*

1066: Tostig Godwinson, exiled brother of King Harold, invades Yorkshire alongside Norwegian King Harald Hardrada. William of Normandy also invades and defeats Harold at the Battle of Hastings.

1138–1153: Multiple invasions from Normandy by forces loyal to Empress Matilda and her son Henry FitzEmpress (later Henry II) during The Anarchy.

1216: Louis VIII, heir to the French throne, invades England and conquers much of the south of the country.

1399: Henry Bolingbroke lands with a French army in Yorkshire to depose Richard II and has himself crowned king.

1405: A French army lands in Wales to assist Owain Glyndwr's Revolt and advances as far as Worcestershire.

1545: French troops invade the Isle of Wight. Henry VIII's ship *Mary Rose* sinks in a naval battle in the Solent between the Isle of Wight and the mainland.

1595: Spanish troops attack Cornwall, burning Newlyn, Mousehole and Penzance.

1667: Dutch forces seize Sheerness in Kent. They also sail up the Medway and destroy a good portion of the Royal Navy at anchor.

1745: Charles Edward Stuart, the 'Young Pretender', lands in the Western Highlands and goes on to invade England, reaching Derby.

1797: French forces invade Pembrokeshire, but get drunk and are rounded up fairly easily. News of the invasion triggered a financial panic in London.

1940: The Battle of Graveney Marsh in Kent sees a downed German bomber crew exchange fire with British troops. The last ground engagement with a foreign enemy on the island of Britain.

1940–45: German troops occupy the Channel Islands, which are only liberated the day after VE-Day.

WORLD WAR TWO TANK PRODUCTION

	1939	1940	1941	1942	1943	1944	1945
USSR	2,950	2,800	6,600	24,500	24,100	29,00	15,400
USA	-	400	4,000	25,000	29,500	17,600	12,000
UK	1,000	1,400	4,800	8,600	7,500	5,000	2,100
Germany	1,300	2,200	5,200	9,200	17,300	22,100	4,400
Japan	200	1,020	1,000	1,200	790	400	140

FIGHTERS AVAILABLE IN THE BATTLE OF BRITAIN

End of Month	RAF	Luftwaffe
July 1940	651	800
August 1940	764	750
September 1940	732	500

D-DAY BEACHES

Beach	Nation	Men Landed	Casualties
Utah	USA	23,000	300
Omaha	USA	34,000	2,400
Gold	UK	25,000	400
Juno	Canada	21,500	1,200
Sword	UK	30,000	630

Troops landed on the Normandy beaches and casualties for 6 June 1944 are rounded and approximate. An additional 23,500 Allied airborne troops landed.

THE HUMAN COST OF WORLD WAR TWO

Combatant Nation	Mobilised	Combat Deaths	Civilian Deaths
Australia	950k	40k	700
Canada	1.2m	42k	1.6k
China	14m	3.5m	8m
France	5m	210k	390k
Germany	19.7m	4.8m	2.5m
India	2.6m	90k	2.5m
Italy	9.1m	330k	153k
Japan	9.1m	2.2m	800k
Netherlands	500k	7k	187k
Poland	2m	240k	5.8m
Romania	2m	300k	200k
UK	7.6m	383k	67k
USA	16.3m	410k	12.1k
USSR	34.5m	10m	15m

World War Two was the largest conflict in history, with major theatres across Europe, Russia, North Africa, China and the Pacific. The above table gives an approximation of manpower and casualties for combatants, although many more nations were involved in the war.

Eastern Europe was devastated, with Poland losing around 17% of its population, while the USSR suffered both the most civilian and combat deaths. There were major famines in China, India and the USSR during the war years, adding to the toll on the civilian population. Aerial bombing also heightened civilian deaths for Germany and Japan, the latter experiencing the only nuclear attacks in history.

For different countries, World War Two started at very different times, with considerable differences between the European and specific theatres.

China and Japan, 7 July 1937: The conflict between these two large Asian powers had begun as early as 18 September 1931, when the Japanese invaded Manchuria. That war ended in February 1932, but Japanese and Chinese troops clashed outside Beijing in July 1937, leading to a full-scale war, although it was undeclared.

Germany and Poland, 1 September 1939: Having taken control of Czechoslovakia in March 1939 without a fight, Germany then invaded Poland.

France and the British Empire, 3 September 1939: The Western Allies had guaranteed Poland in the event of a German invasion. When Germany did not meet the Allied ultimatum to withdraw, they declared war.

USSR and Poland, 17 September 1939: As part of the August 1939 Nazi–Soviet pact, the USSR agreed to invade Poland from the east, and did so just over two weeks after Germany's western invasion.

USSR and Finland, 30 November 1939: The USSR invaded Finland without a formal declaration. The war ended with the Moscow Peace Treaty the following March, but Finland supported the invasion of the Soviet Union by Nazi Germany.

Italy, 10 June 1940: Italy declared war on Britain and France.

Germany and USSR, 22 June 1941: Having subjugated most of Europe, Germany launched a surprise attack on the USSR. The Soviet Union then became aligned to the Allies.

USA and Japan, 8 December 1941: America declared war on Japan, the day after Japan had launched a surprise attack on the US Pacific Fleet in Pearl Harbor. Germany (which was allied with Japan) then declared war on the USA on 11 December 1941. The USA sided with the Allies.

Conflict	Location	Century	Death Toll
World War Two	Global	20th	55 million
Mongol Conquests	Asia	12th	40 million
An Lushan Revolt	China	8th	36 million
Fall of the Ming Dynasty	China	17th	25 million
Taiping Revolt	China	19th	20 million
World War One	Global	20th	15 million
Russian Civil War	Russia	20th	9 million
Thirty Years' War	Central Europe	17th	5 million
Congo War	Central Africa	20th/21st	5 million
Napoleonic Wars	Global	18th/19th	4 million

REIGNS OF TERROR

The French Revolution began with the storming of the Bastille on 14 July 1789. It saw the rise of Maximilien Robespierre, who led the radical Jacobin faction and presided over the Reign of Terror, during which 16,549 aristocrats were executed, often by the infamous 'Madame La Guillotine'.

While the guillotine is commonly associated with the brutality of the French Revolution, the Nazis also used the guillotine during the 12 years they were in power.

In October 1936, Hitler secretly ordered 20 guillotines to be distributed to prisons in cities across Germany. According to Nazi records, they were used to execute approximately 16,500 people between 1933 and 1945, including resistance fighters and political protesters – a similar number to the French Reign of Terror.

ESCALATION OF NUCLEAR TESTS

The first nuclear test, codenamed Trinity, took place on 16 July 1945 near Alamogordo, New Mexico. Less than a month later, atomic bombs were dropped on the Japanese cities of Hiroshima and Nagasaki, leading to Japan's surrender and World War Two's end.

Trinity had a 20-kiloton yield – equivalent to 20,000 tons of TNT. Within less than 20 years, the US and USSR had both tested nuclear weapons with a yield much larger than 10 megatons, equivalent to 10 million tons of TNT – at least 500 times as strong as Trinity.

Test	Country	Date	Yield / Results
Ivy Mike	USA	1 Nov 1952	10.4 megatons
Castle Romeo	USA	26 Mar 1954	11 megatons
Test #123	USSR	23 Oct 1961	12.5 megatons
Castle Yankee	USA	4 May 1954	13.5 megatons
Castle Bravo	USA	1 Mar 1954	15 megatons
Test #147	USSR	7 Aug 1962	21.2 megatons
Test #219	USSR	24 Dec 1962	24.2 megatons
Tsar Bomba	USSR	30 Oct 1961	50–8 megatons

LARGEST CAVALRY CHARGE

At around 4 p.m. on 12 September, 1683, some 20,000 horsemen emerged from the forests onto the Kahlenberg hills north of Vienna, to cheers from allied German, Austrian, Polish and Lithuanian soldiers already on the field. Since early that morning, the combined infantry had been wearing down the huge Ottoman army attempting to breach Vienna's walls. Finally, the Polish-Lithuanian king John Sobieski gave the command. The largest cavalry charge in history stormed down the hills, headed by 3,000 Polish hussars distinguished by their daunting and ostentatious rear wings. The exhausted Ottomans collapsed immediately; they were subsequently pushed out of central Europe.

WORST TERROR ATTACK

On 11 September 2001, four coordinated terrorist attacks were carried out by 19 terrorists from al-Qaeda, an Islamist extremist group. Four commercial planes were hijacked, two of which deliberately crashed into the North and South Towers of the World Trade Center in New York, causing them to collapse. A third plane crashed into the Pentagon in Washington DC. After learning about the other attacks, passengers on the fourth hijacked plane, Flight 93, fought back, crashing it into a field about 20 minutes from Washington DC.

The attacks killed 2,977 people from 93 nations: 2,753 people were killed in New York, 184 people were killed at the Pentagon and 40 people were killed on Flight 93. Estimates of the cost of the damage and lost productivity range from $500 billion to over $1 trillion.

ENGLAND'S FIRST RECIPE BOOK

Richard II of England (r. 1377–99) was considered a bad king – bad enough to be deposed – but his court reached a new high point of culture. He is credited with inventing the napkin and his portrait in Westminster Abbey is the earliest surviving of any King of England. Richard also had the first recipe book in England compiled by the master cooks of his kitchen. It is named *The Forme of Cury* and contains 196 recipes. The first recipe is for ground beans, instructing:

> Take beans and dry them in a kiln or in an oven and dehull them well
> and winnow out the husk and wash them clean and let them steep in
> a good broth and eat them with Bacon.

This was a recipe for lower-status members of the court. At the higher end, the book contained details for preparing oysters, a variety of fish, pork and veal as well as goose, swan and lampreys. Pies were known as crustards and might contain meat or fish. Familiar dishes such as tarts appear with lost names such as flaumpens, a pork dish that sounds a lot like a pie. Some recipes sound familiar, but are not what we would expect now. A medieval blancmange included rice, capons and almonds.

SOUTH AMERICA'S GEORGE WASHINGTON

Simón Bolívar led several campaigns against Spanish rule in South America in the 19th century, ultimately contributing to the liberation of six countries and to him being honoured with the sobriquet 'The Liberator'. A Venezuelan soldier and statesman, Bolívar became famed as the George Washington of South America. Yet Bolívar fought for twice as long as Washington, across a much greater area.

Bolívar made tactical gambles that often paid off and one victory in particular has cemented his reputation. In 1819, he led an army over the freezing Andes to surprise the Spanish in New Granada. He lost a third of his troops to starvation and the cold, as well as most of his weapons and all of his horses. Yet hearing of his rapid descent from the mountains, perhaps recalling Bolívar's ruthless 1813 decree that permitted the killing of civilians, the Spanish abandoned their possessions in haste.

THE LUCKIEST MAN IN THE WORLD

Japanese engineer Tsutomu Yamaguchi survived the atomic bombings in both Hiroshima and Nagasaki during World War Two.

Yamaguchi was in Hiroshima on a business trip when the first atomic bomb was dropped on 6 August 1945. Despite being only three kilometres away from the blast, Yamaguchi survived, though was seriously burned and temporarily blinded. The following day, he began the journey back to his hometown of Nagasaki, arriving on 8 August. On 9 August, he was a little over a mile from the epicentre of the second atomic bomb when it dropped on Nagasaki. He survived, but was injured again, along with his wife and infant daughter.

In total, it is estimated that around 260,000 people died from the two bombings. Yamaguchi was one of the few survivors of both, earning him the nickname 'the luckiest man in the world'. Despite his incredible story, Yamaguchi was hesitant to speak publicly about his experiences for many years. It wasn't until the 2000s that he spoke openly, using his story to promote peace and nuclear disarmament. Yamaguchi died in 2009 aged 93.

. . . demand the right to vote in America?

Margaret Brent (c. 1601–71) was an English immigrant to the colony of Maryland who campaigned for women, advocating for her legal rights as an unmarried gentlewoman of property.

. . . write an opera?

Francesca Caccini (1587–c. 1641) was a composer, singer and instrumentalist in the Medici court from the age of 20, hobnobbing with such luminaries as Galileo. She created an opera – first performed in Florence in 1625 – that featured a ballet for 24 horses and riders.

. . . to be convicted for lesbian acts in America?

Sarah White Norman (c. 1623–54) was tried in 1648, alongside 15-year-old Mary Vincent Hammon (1633–1705), for 'lewd behavior with each other upon a bed.' The trial is the only known record of sex between women English colonists in North America in the 17th century. Only Sarah was convicted. She was ordered to acknowledge publicly her 'unchaste behavior' and warned against future offences.

. . . earn a living as a writer?

King Charles II employed Aphra Behn (1640–89) as a spy in Antwerp. Unsuccessful at espionage, she wrote plays, poems and prose about women's rights, colonial oppression and slavery.

——————— **LATRINE DISASTER** ———————

On 26 July 1184, Henry VI, King of the Germans, called a diet, a meeting of German nobles, to try to settle a feud between Landgrave (equivalent to a Duke) Louis III of Thuringia and Archbishop Conrad of Mainz. As they gathered in a room, many perhaps wearing mail armour, the floor collapsed beneath their weight. The problem was that directly below was a communal latrine. Many fell into the piles of excrement and were drowned or suffocated by the fumes as others were crushed by debris. Sources claim between 60 and 100 died. Henry VI and a few others were standing near a window and managed to hold on to the frame until they were saved with ladders.

Impressionism

Emerging in France in the 1870s, Impressionism aimed to capture the fleeting effects of light and colour. Impressionist art often depicted scenes of modern life, such as cafes, parks and boulevards. Key Impressionist artists include: Claude Monet, Pierre-Auguste Renoir and Edgar Degas.

Expressionism

Expressionism emerged in Northern Europe, particularly Germany, around the turn of the 20th century. Expressionists conveyed their inner emotions and subjective experiences through vivid colours, distorted forms and a heightened sense of emotion. Key Expressionist artists: Edvard Munch, Wassily Kandinsky and Franz Marc.

Fauvism

Fauvism lasted between 1905 and 1908 and had three exhibitions. It was a movement that ran in tandem with Expressionism, and rejected traditional painting styles through bold, vivid colours and expressive brushwork. 'Les Fauves' translates to 'the wild beasts', a term first used by critic Louis Vauxcelles. Key Fauvist artists: Henri Matisse, André Derain and Maurice de Vlaminck.

Cubism

Instead of a traditional representation of a single object, Cubist artists dismantled the subject into multiple planes and geometric forms, highlighting its various facets and perspectives. Cubism has been called the most influential art movement of the 20th century. Key Cubist artists: Pablo Picasso, Georges Braques (the founders of the movement) and Fernand Léger.

Futurism

Futurism was an Italian movement focusing on speed, technology and the modern world. Some of its most important works were created in the early 1910s, just before World War One. The movement had a strong influence on later art movements such as Constructivism and Surrealism. Key Futurist artists: Umberto Boccioni, Giacomo Balla and Gino Severini.

Constructivism

Constructivism was founded in 1915 in Russia, with a focus on industrial production and functional design, with influence from Cubism. Constructivist artwork often featured geometric shapes and bold colours more akin to graphic design than traditional art. Key Constructivist artists: Vladimir Tatlin, Alexander Rodchenko and El Lissitzky.

Dadaism

Dadaism was an international anti-art movement developed in reaction to World War One, with left-wing political overtones. Dada art often involved collages, readymades and other unconventional techniques. Marcel Duchamp's famous *Fountain* (1917), a urinal, is seen as an icon of 20th-century Dada art. Key Dada artists: Marcel Duchamp, Tristan Tzara and Francis Picabia.

Surrealism

Surrealism emerged from France in the 1920s, and explored the subconscious mind and dreams. Surrealist art often depicted strange and irrational scenes, and sought to challenge traditional notions of reality and perception, such as Salvador Dali's sculpture *Lobster Telephone* (1938). Key Surrealist artists: Salvador Dali, Max Ernst and René Magritte.

Abstract Expressionism

Abstract Expressionism emerged in the 1940s in the United States. It was characterised by spontaneous gestural mark-making and splatter painting over large canvases, and explored the relationship between the artist and the canvas. Key Abstract Expressionist artists: Jackson Pollock, Willem de Kooning and Mark Rothko.

Minimalism

A reaction against the perceived excesses of Abstract Expressionism, Minimalism emerged in the United States in the 1960s. It emphasised the use of simple geometric forms, industrial materials and the reduction of visual elements to their basic essence. Key Minimalist artists: Donald Judd, Dan Flavin and Sol LeWitt.

The *Mona Lisa*

Italian patriot Vincenzo Peruggia believed Leonardo da Vinci's the *Mona Lisa* should be returned to Italy. Working as an odd-job man at the Louvre, on 21 August 1911 Peruggia removed the painting from its frame, hiding it under his clothes, and managed to sneak out.

The theft was only noticed 26 hours later. The Louvre closed immediately and a large reward was offered, becoming a media sensation. Two years later Peruggia attempted to sell the painting to the Uffizi Gallery, Florence. He was persuaded to leave it for examination, then arrested later that day.

The Scream

Edvard Munch's *The Scream* has four versions, two of which have recently been stolen.

The first theft took place on 12 February 1994 (the opening date of the Lillehammer Winter Olympics) from the National Gallery in Oslo. The thieves left a note reading, 'Thanks for the poor security,' but the painting was recovered three months later after a sting operation. Four men were convicted of the theft in 1996, although they were released on appeal.

Another version was taken in 2004 from the Munch Museum in Oslo. As tourists admired the various masterpieces, masked thieves held guards at gunpoint and grabbed the painting. While the thieves were arrested a year later, the painting remained missing until 2006.

The Isabella Stewart Gardner Museum heist

Just after 1 a.m. on 18 March 1990, two men posing as police conned their way into the Isabella Stewart Gardner Museum in Boston, pretending they were responding to a disturbance call.

After declaring, 'Gentleman, this is a robbery,' the thieves tied up the security guards and looted the museum. An hour later, they made off with 13 works of art, with an estimated value of half a billion dollars – the most valuable theft of private property ever. Among the pieces were a Rembrandt, Manet, several Degas drawings and one of the 34 known Vermeers. None of them have been recovered.

Napoleon Bonaparte was one of eight children of Carlo Buonaparte and Letizia Ramolino who survived infancy. And when he reached the pinnacle of power, he took most of his siblings with him.

Joseph: An older brother, he was made King of Naples in 1806 and King of Spain in 1808; after Napoleon's fall he retired to New Jersey.

Lucien: A younger brother, he disagreed with Napoleon crowning himself Emperor and went into exile. He was cheered when he landed in Britain.

Louis: Napoleon's younger brother married his wife's daughter. Napoleon made him King of Holland in 1806 but they fell out, Napoleon annexed Holland to France, and Louis went into exile.

Pauline: A younger sister, she was made Princess of Guastalla in 1806.

Caroline: A younger sister, she married Napoleon's dashing cavalry commander, Joachim Murat, who Napoleon then made King of Naples. So Caroline became Queen of Naples. She was the driving force behind the excavation of Pompeii.

Jérôme: The youngest brother, he became King of Westphalia in 1807.

Elisa: A younger sister, she was made Grand Duchess of Tuscany in 1809.

THE BATTLE OF GAUGAMELA IN PHASES

On 1 October 331 BC, Alexander the Great came face to face with the Persian King Darius III for a final showdown. Darius had assembled a massive army from all corners of his empire, consisting of between 50,000 and 100,000 soldiers. The Persians greatly outnumbered Alexander and his c. 40,000 troops. Yet Alexander was able to pull off an extraordinary victory.

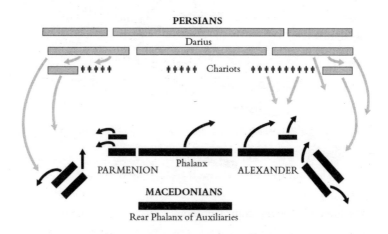

After assembling his forces in a trapezoidal shape formation, Alexander ordered his army to advance and march to the right. He had noticed that the Persian left wing stretched much further than his own right.

The Persians responded by sending cavalry to outflank and envelop Alexander. They wanted to prevent Alexander from moving too far to the right, away from ground that they had deliberately flattened for their chariots.

Alexander sent cavalry and light infantry to counter this attempted Persian envelopment and a vicious clash erupted on the right wing of the battlefield. More and more soldiers were dragged into this melee.

The Persian scythed chariots then charged the Macedonian lines, but were repulsed.

On the other side of Alexander's line, the Persians began to outflank and envelop the Macedonian left wing, commanded by Parmenion.

As the fighting continued, a gap in the Macedonian line emerged between the central infantry phalanx and the left wing. Seeing the gap, some Persian cavalry charged through and proceeded to attack Alexander's baggage train in the rear. Alexander's reserve infantry line moved in to plug this gap in the line.

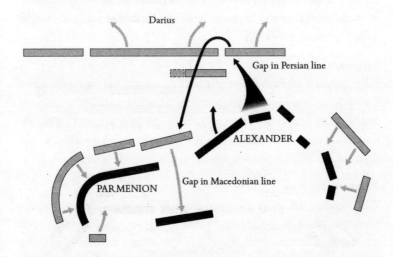

Alexander's left wing, commanded by Parmenion, desperately fended off a huge number of enemy troops attacking them from all sides. Despite being heavily outnumbered, Parmenion and his soldiers stood their ground.

A gap in the Persian line then also emerged, after more and more troops had been drawn into the clash on the far right-hand side of the battlefield.

Alexander spotted this gap in the enemy line, close to where King Darius had positioned himself. Gathering contingents of his elite Companion Cavalry, he made a beeline for Darius and the troops around the Persian King. Alexander and his heavy horsemen charged through the gap; Darius was forced to flee the field.

As news filtered through Persian ranks that their king had fled, the army crumbled. Rather than pursue Darius, Alexander turned his men around to defeat the last contingents of Persian resistance on the battlefield. Alexander won the Battle of Gaugamela and was heralded as the Lord of Asia.

Homer (c .800 BC)

Homer is said to have authored the epic poems *The Iliad* and *The Odyssey*, which chronicle the legendary Trojan War and Odysseus's journey home to Ithaca and have greatly influenced Western literature. Homer's historical existence is debated: it is possible his works were written by a collective from a long-lasting oral tradition.

Sappho (c. 600 BC)

Hailing from Lesbos, Sappho is regarded as one of the greatest ancient lyric poets. While only a small proportion of her poetry remains in fragmentary form, she is the first surviving female author in Western tradition. Desire between women is a trait of her work, and the words sapphic and lesbian derive from her name and home island.

Pythagoras (c. 570–495 BC)

Remembered today as an influential philosopher and mathematician from Samos, Pythagoras was the founder of a way of life that championed transmigration, religious ritual and self-discipline. His Pythagorean theorem remains a fundamental principle in geometry. His discoveries impacted mathematics, music and astronomy.

Herodotus (484–25 BC)

A historian from Halicarnassus, Herodotus penned *The Histories*, an extensive collection of tales gathered during his travels around the Mediterranean and beyond. His accounts offer a diverse view of ancient civilisations, with the Persian Wars forming the central narrative. He's often referred to as the 'Father of History'.

Socrates (469– 399 BC)

An Athenian philosopher, Socrates's wisdom is known through the dialogues of his pupil, Plato. His Socratic method, a form of inquiry to stimulate critical thinking, profoundly influenced Western philosophy. Accused of corrupting youth and disregarding Athenian gods, Socrates was sentenced to death, then required to carry out his own execution through drinking hemlock.

Euripides (c.480–06 BC)

A tragedian from Athens, Euripides authored over 90 plays, establishing himself alongside Aeschylus and Sophocles as one of three great ancient Greek tragedians. His tragedies often focused on women and their experiences, as exemplified in famous works like *Medea* and *The Trojan Women*. His plays explored morality and psychological depth.

Hippocrates (c. 460–370 BC)

Hippocrates, from the island of Kos, is revered as the 'Father of Medicine'. Establishing the Hippocratic School, he focused on the rational understanding of diseases and their treatment over superstition. His Hippocratic Oath, an ethical guideline for medical professionals, is still in use in various forms today. Although the oath is named after him, it is unclear whether Hippocrates actually wrote it.

Aristotle (384–22 BC)

A philosopher and scientist from Stagira, Aristotle studied under Plato and later tutored Alexander the Great. His extensive writings on a variety of subjects formed a comprehensive system of Western philosophy, encompassing morality, aesthetics, logic, science, politics and metaphysics.

Pytheas (c. 350 BC)

A daring explorer from Massalia, Pytheas embarked on an ambitious sea voyage around 320 BC. He covered the uncharted northern lands, from the Breton Peninsula and Irish Sea to the Scottish mainland. He even reached the far-flung Orkney and Shetland Islands. His exploration expanded geographical understanding during his time.

Archimedes (287–12 BC)

An inventor and mathematician from Syracuse, Archimedes developed the buoyancy principle, laying the groundwork for understanding physics. He also created an array of war machines to defend Syracuse against the Roman siege. He is credited with designing an enormous warship, the *Syracusia*.

THE SLAVE TRADE TRIANGLE

The Atlantic slave trade began in the 1500s. European slavers sailed to West Africa to forcibly transport enslaved Africans to the Americas. Britain began large-scale slaving in the 1640s, and by 1670 English merchants had probably overtaken Portuguese and Dutch as the leading European carriers of slaves from Africa to America. The trade generally followed a triangular route:

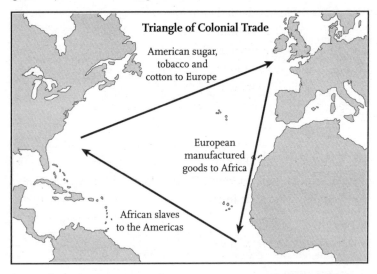

Triangle of Colonial Trade

American sugar, tobacco and cotton to Europe

European manufactured goods to Africa

African slaves to the Americas

West Africa: Traders set out from European ports for West Africa. They bought captives in exchange for goods. Alongside the Dutch and Portuguese, the British built around 40 slave-trading outposts along the West African coast from the 17th century onwards.

Middle Passage: Enslaved Africans were transported across the Atlantic to colonies in the Americas, a voyage that took 6–8 weeks. Slaves were shackled to prevent mutiny while many died from disease, suicide, dehydration and murder.

Enslaved labour: In the Americas, slaves were sold and put to work as labour on plantations. Ships returned to Europe with goods produced by enslaved labour, including sugar, coffee, tobacco, rice and cotton. As the trade expanded, Africans also settled in Europe as slaves and free people.

On 18 August 1781, the British slave ship *Zong* left Accra, bound for Jamaica, with 442 enslaved Africans on board – twice as many as the ship was designed to hold. Poor seamanship and navigational errors meant that with ten days left until their arrival in Jamaica, the ship had only four days' supply of water.

If the enslaved people died ashore, or of 'natural' causes afloat, the owners could not claim their value on insurance. So they decided to throw many of them into the sea. On 29 November, 54 women and children were thrown overboard. On 1 December, 42 men were thrown in, followed by another 36. Ten men, in a final act of defiance, chose to take their own lives by jumping.

Upon reaching Jamaica, *Zong's* owners attempted to claim for the 'jettisoned cargo'. The courts initially ruled for the owners but it was overturned on appeal. Anti-slave-trade activists Olaudah Equiano and Granville Sharp used the horrifying details of the massacre to raise awareness of the evils of the trade, an important step on the road to the abolition of the trade in 1807.

EMANCIPATION AND THE AMERICAN CIVIL WAR

When Abraham Lincoln issued the Emancipation Proclomation on 1 January 1863, the United States was approaching its third year of bloody civil war. The Southern States had seceded and formed the Confederate States of America in 1861, convinced that Lincoln's election threatened white supremacy, on which their economy depended.

The proclamation declared that all slaves held in states that were in rebellion were to be set free. This proclamation marked a turning point in the American Civil War, transforming the struggle from a fight to preserve the Union into a fight to end slavery.

Although the Emancipation Proclamation did not actually free all slaves, it set in motion a process that ultimately led to the end of slavery in the United States. The 13th Amendment to the Constitution, which officially abolished slavery, was passed in 1865, shortly after the Civil War's end.

GREAT ABOLITIONISTS

Olaudah Equiano (c. 1745–97)
An African writer and abolitionist who was enslaved as a child and later bought his own freedom. He wrote an autobiography, *The Interesting Narrative of the Life of Olaudah Equiano*, which provided a firsthand account of the brutalities of enslavement and the Middle Passage, significantly influencing the British abolitionist movement.

William Wilberforce (1759–1833)
Politician and abolitionist who led the parliamentary campaign to end the British slave trade. His efforts culminated in the passage of the Slave Trade Act of 1807, which prohibited the transportation of enslaved people within the British Empire, and the Slavery Abolition Act of 1833, which granted emancipation to most enslaved people in British territories.

John Brown (1800–59)
Best known for his raid on the federal armoury at Harpers Ferry, Virginia in 1859, which was aimed at starting a slave rebellion. Brown and his followers were captured and Brown was tried and executed for treason. His raid and subsequent execution helped to polarise the United States over the issue of slavery and is often cited as a key event leading up to the American Civil War.

Frederick Douglass (1818–95)
African American who escaped slavery and became a prominent leader in the fight against slavery in the United States. His powerful speeches and autobiographical works, such as *Narrative of the Life of Frederick Douglass*, brought attention to the horrors of slavery and influenced public opinion.

Harriet Tubman (1822–1913)
African American abolitionist and conductor of the Underground Railroad who escaped slavery and helped hundreds of enslaved people find freedom in the North. During the Civil War, she served as a nurse, scout, and spy for the Union Army. Her bravery and dedication to the abolitionist cause made her a symbol of resistance against slavery.

Name	Known as	Relation to predecessor	From	To
Æthelstan			927	939
Edmund I		Half-brother	939	946
Eadred		Brother	946	955
Eadwig	All-Fair	Nephew	955	959
Edgar	the Peaceful	Brother	959	975
Edward	the Martyr	Son	975	978
Æthelred	the Unready	Half-brother	978	1013
Sweyn	Forkbeard	Conqueror	1013	1014
Æthelred	the Unready	Returning king	1014	1016
Edmund II	Ironside	Son	1016	1016
Cnut	the Great	Son of Sweyn	1016	1035
Harold I	Harefoot	Son	1035	1040
Harthacnut		Half-brother	1040	1042
Edward	the Confessor	Half-brother	1042	1066
Harold II	Godwinson	Brother-in-law	Jan 1066	Oct 1066

Æthelstan was the first ruler to call himself King of the English, or *Rex Anglorum* in Latin, from 927. Previous rulers of the single realm had been known as King of the Anglo-Saxons, a title first used by Alfred the Great from around 886. In Anglo-Saxon England, succession was confirmed by a council known as the Witenagemot, or Witan for short, who elected the next ruler from a pool of candidates.

Sweyn Forkbeard, King of Denmark conquered England in 1013 but died the following year, leading to the return of the deposed Æthelred the Unready. Sweyn's son Cnut took back the throne in 1016. He was followed by two of his sons before Æthelred's son, Edward the Confessor, became king in 1042. In 1066, the Norman Conquest put a stop to Anglo-Saxon rule in England for good.

After the Last Ice Age, the glacial coverage of Europe retreated north-ward, revealing a new land in what is now the North Sea. Sea levels would have been around 35 metres shallower than today, and what is now the Dogger Bank (you may have heard about it on the shipping forecast) was a landmass connecting East Anglia with the coast of the north European mainland.

Neanderthal peoples would have been able to move freely, without the use of boats, between where London now sits over to Amsterdam. The land bridge itself was very flat and marshy, possibly like the Norfolk broads today.

As the temperature increased and ice further receded in the early Neolithic period, the sea rose, flooding this ancient landscape around 6500 BC. It now lies under nearly 32 metres of water.

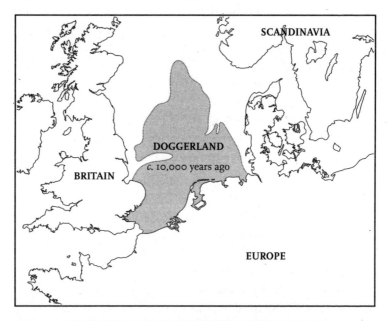

———— THE HUMAN LIGHTNING CONDUCTOR ————

Shenandoah National Park ranger Roy Sullivan was struck by light-ning and survived seven times, in 1942, 1969, 1970, 1972, 1973, 1974 and 1977. He holds the world record for human lightning strikes.

On 31 October 1517, Martin Luther nailed his Ninety-Five Theses to the door of All Saints' Church in Wittenberg, Germany. Luther was a priest and theologian who campaigned for reform of the Roman Catholic Church, particularly opposing indulgences, the practice of buying forgiveness of sin. He was arrested and tried before the Diet of Worms in 1521. Although excommunicated, he was not executed and lived until 1546. Luther is considered the prime mover in the Protestant Reformation that swept through parts of Europe, breaking the monopoly of the Roman Church.

However, Luther was not the beginning of the story. John Wycliffe was born in England around 1328. He became a priest and a professor at Oxford University and began criticising the Roman Church, particularly its veneration of saints and the belief in transubstanti-ation. He helped translate the Bible into English, which was considered heretical at the time. Wycliffe initially had powerful support, particularly from Edward III's son John of Gaunt..

On 21 May 1382, a synod of the Church sat to address Wycliffe's teachings. An earthquake occurred as they debated. The Archbishop of Canterbury declared it was the Earth wishing to shake off heretical doctrine. The Earthquake Synod declared Wycliffe's views heretical, though political support meant he was not excommunicated. He died on 31 December 1384 after suffering a stroke. Wycliffe's followers were called Lollards, which may derive from the Middle Dutch word for someone who mumbles or mutters because of their tendency to pray out loud to themselves. It became a derogatory term and in the early 15th century Lollards were persecuted as heretics.

John Wycliffe's beliefs also influenced others on the Continent, most notably Jan Hus. A Czech religious reformer whose ideas fore-shadowed Protestantism, Hus was burned at the stake as a heretic in 1415. His death sparked the Hussite Wars that lasted from 1419 to 1434 and which saw the rise of Jan Žižka, a Czech national hero who followed Hus. As he died, Hus was heard to call out that God would send another whose reforms would not be suppressed. Martin Luther was seen by many as the fulfilment of Hus's prophesy.

The idealised role of the medieval knight is difficult to reconcile with their actions in the real world. Several manuals exist to tell knights how they should behave. Sir Thomas Malory's *Le Morte d'Arthur* is considered the pinnacle of the medieval Arthurian legend and describes the conduct King Arthur required of his Knights of the Round Table:

> He charged them never to commit outrage or murder, always to flee treason, and to give mercy to those who asked for mercy, upon pain of the forfeiture of their honour and status as a knight of King Arthur's forever more. He charged them always to help ladies, damsels, gentlewomen, and widows, and never to commit rape, upon pain of death. Also, he commanded that no man should take up a battle in a wrongful quarrel – not for love, nor for any worldly goods.

This expectation proved hard to live up to. A favoured medieval military tactic was the chevauchée, a raiding tactic used to devastating effect during the Hundred Years' War. It saw mounted knights ride into enemy territory to destroy crops, burn homes and steal supplies. These hit-and-run assaults were meant to weaken an enemy, but also to demonstrate to those loyal to a lord that he was unable to protect them. The question it really asked was whether the people would be better off transferring allegiance. It achieved this, though, by targeting the poor, bringing battle to those who were not knights or combatants – breaking the code of chivalry by which knights were meant to live.

———————— **ALL WARFARE IS BASED ON DECEPTION** ————————

In late 1917, engineer Fernand Jacopozzi was commissioned by the French War Office to build a fake Paris, with the aim of fooling German air raids. Building work began at Villepinte in 1918, where a replica of the Gare de l'Est railway station was constructed, complete with the illusion of a moving train. He then set about creating a fake industrial zone 10 miles east of the capital. The last German bombing raid on Paris came in September 1918, and the war was over two months later. However, Jacoppozzi's creation had a major influence on deception techniques used by the Allies in World War Two.

- WILLIAM 'THE' MARSHAL - THE GREATEST KNIGHT -

Born around 1146, William Marshal was a younger son of a minor nobleman, John FitzGilbert. After his death, his family commissioned a biography entitled *The History of William the Marshal* to tell the incredible story of his life. Although it may be exaggerated in parts, its framing of William as the greatest knight who ever lived doesn't feel unreasonable.

William's first adventure is recounted as a siege of his father's Newbury Castle by King Stephen when William was a young child and a hostage for his father's good behaviour. Stephen supposedly threatened to catapult William over the walls. John replied to the threat to his son that 'he still had the anvils and hammers to produce even finer ones'.

In 1168, when Eleanor of Aquitaine was attacked near Poitou, Patrick, Earl of Salisbury was killed protecting her. William, one of Patrick's knights, fought a rearguard action to allow Eleanor to escape. He was captured and Eleanor paid his ransom in gratitude, taking William into her service. He moved into the household of Eleanor and Henry II's oldest son, Henry the Young King. The two toured the European tournament circuit, growing rich and famous. After Henry the Young King's death, Marshal went to Jerusalem carrying his master's cloak in fulfilment of the young man's crusading vow.

In 1189, as Henry II was pursued by his son, the future Richard I, Marshal again fought a rearguard action. He charged at Richard, who shouted, 'God's legs, Marshal! Don't kill me.' Lowering his lance, Marshal struck Richard's horse, bellowing, 'Indeed I won't. Let the Devil kill you!' He would serve Richard as king, and remain loyal to his younger brother and successor John.

When John died in 1216, Marshal became regent to the 9-year-old Henry III. He pacified the barons by reissuing Magna Carta and the Charter of the Forest and drove out the French forces that had almost conquered England. At the Battle of Lincoln on 20 May 1217, aged around 70, William rode into battle so enthusiastically that a squire had to catch his reins and remind him to put his helmet on. William died on 14 May 1219 and was buried in the Temple Church, London, having joined the Templars on his deathbed.

Spinning Jenny (1764)

James Hargreaves's spinning jenny improved on John Kay's 1733 flying shuttle, and allowed unskilled workers to spin multiple textile threads simultaneously. This significantly increased efficiency and shifted cloth production from small-scale, home-based cottage industries to large-scale industrial manufacturing.

Watt Steam Engine (1769)

The first steam engine, introduced by Thomas Newcomen in 1712, filled a chamber with steam, then cooled it. James Watt introduced his improved design in 1776, using a separate condensing cylinder. Along with other refinements, Watt was able to produce the same amount of power from half the quantity of coal.

Water Frame (1769)

Richard Arkwright's invention, the water frame, harnessed water power to drive spinning machines that produced stronger, finer threads, making improvements on Hargreaves's spinning jenny. Arkwright first installed a water frame in his cotton mill at Cromford, Derbyshire in 1771. The factory was one of the first to be built specifically to house machinery.

Power Loom (1785)

Edmund Cartwright's power loom automated the weaving process through steam or water power, considerably increasing the speed and output of cloth manufacturing. The loom was initially slow to catch on, but improvements made it increasingly common in textile mills. By 1850 there were around 260,000 power looms in England.

Cotton Gin (1793)

Eli Whitney's cotton gin streamlined the separation of cotton fibres from seeds, which otherwise relied on manual labour. This reduced the time and cost of processing cotton, contributing to the cotton industry's growth, but also increased the demand for slave labour in the American South.

— INDUSTRIAL INVENTIONS OF THE 19TH CENTURY —

Telegraph (1837)
Samuel Morse's invention of the telegraph allowed for the rapid transmission of messages over long distances using Morse code. Information could now travel quickly through electrical wires, which was faster than existing signalling techniques such as semaphore. The telegraph enabled faster decision-making and coordination in business, government and military operations.

Bessemer Process (1855)
Henry Bessemer's method for producing steel removed impurities from molten pig iron. The process could also create steel with precise amounts of carbon and other elements, allowing it to be used in a wider variety of industrial applications. The process played a crucial role in the expansion of railways, construction and shipbuilding industries.

Sewing Machine (1851)
Isaac Singer's sewing machine made it possible to produce clothing at a much faster rate than by hand. It opened up new employment opportunities for women, who could now work as seamstresses in clothing factories. It also helped to standardise clothing sizes and styles, making it easier for clothing manufacturers to produce garments that would fit a wider range of people.

Dynamite (1867)
Alfred Nobel's invention of dynamite provided a powerful and relatively safe explosive, which had its uses across construction, mining and warfare. Prior to the invention of dynamite, industrial explosives were unstable and difficult to transport.

Internal Combustion Engine (1876)
Nicolaus Otto's internal combustion engine provided a more compact and powerful source of power than the steam engine. This invention laid the foundation for the development of the car industry and aeroplanes, reducing the reliance on animals such as horses as a means of transport and in agriculture.

James Watt (1736–1819)

Best known for his improvements to the steam engine, making it more practical for industrial use. Watt's innovations, including the separate condenser and rotary motion, contributed to the growth of factories and manufacturing. He invented the idea of horsepower, and the unit of power – the watt – is named after him.

George Stephenson (1781–1848)

Known as the 'Father of Railways', Stephenson designed the world's first public intercity railroad, the Liverpool and Manchester Railway, and built the famous locomotive the *Rocket*. The rail gauge selected by Stephenson, occasionally referred to as the 'Stephenson gauge', became the foundation for the 4 feet 8½ inches (1.435 metres) standard gauge adopted by the majority of the world's railways.

Isambard Kingdom Brunel (1806–59)

A stunningly versatile engineer who designed railways, ships, tunnels and bridges. Among the most well-known constructions are the Clifton Suspension Bridge, the SS *Great Britain* and Box Tunnel. In their time, these were the world's longest single-span bridge, biggest passenger ship and longest tunnel respectively.

Gustave Eiffel (1832–1923)

Known for his innovative designs and construction of iron structures, Eiffel made his name through building bridges for the French railway network. His most famous work, the Eiffel Tower, was completed in 1889 as the centrepiece of the Paris World's Fair. Eiffel also designed the internal framework of the Statue of Liberty and numerous bridges and railway stations.

Thomas Edison (1847-1931)

American inventor who held over 1,000 patents. His most notable inventions include the phonograph, the motion picture camera, and a practical, long-lasting electric light bulb. Edison also developed electrical power distribution systems and established the world's first industrial research laboratory.

WORLD POPULATION

Following the gigantic volcanic eruption of Toba, Sumatra in Indonesia just over 70,000 years ago, Homo sapiens almost went extinct. A thick layer of ash across our East African homeland and an atmosphere full of ash pushed numbers down to perhaps only 1,000 breeding pairs. This is how it grew from that nadir:

Year	Population	Year	Population
70,000 BC	5,000	1800	1 billion
10,000 BC	4 million	1930	2 billion
500 BC	100 million	1960	3 billion
500 AD	190 million	2000	6 billion
1100 AD	320 million	2022	8 billion

LIFE IMPROVEMENTS OVER 200 YEARS

	1800	2000
Literacy of world population	12%	87%
Women dying for every 100,000 pregnancies	900	342
Children out of 1,000 dying before aged 5	430	77

It wasn't all bad. While the world population has exploded since the beginning of the Industrial Revolution, healthcare, life expectancy and education have all dramatically improved.

And I tell you that Wellington is a bad general, that the English are bad troops, and that this affair is nothing more serious than eating breakfast.

Napoleon, 18 June 1815

The advancement of the arts, from year to year, taxes our credulity and seems to presage the arrival of that period when human improvement must end.

Henry Ellsworth, United States Patent Office Commissioner, 1843

Louis Pasteur's theory of germs is ridiculous fiction.

Pierre Pachet, Professor of Physiology at Toulouse, 1872

This 'telephone' has too many shortcomings to be seriously considered as a means of communication. The device is inherently of no value to us.

Western Union internal memo, rejecting an offer to purchase Alexander Graham Bell's telephone patents, 1876

Mr Carter is a good-natured lad whose interest is entirely in painting and natural history. It is of no use to me to work him up as an excavator.

Flinders Petrie, Egyptologist, dismissing Howard Carter, 1891

Flight by machines heavier than air is unpractical and insignificant, if not utterly impossible.

Simon Newcomb, Professor of Mathematics and Astronomy at Johns Hopkins University, 1902

Aeroplanes are interesting toys but of no military value.

General Ferdinand Foch, 1911

The tank was a freak. The circumstances which called it into existence were exceptional and not likely to recur. If they do, they can be dealt with by other means.

Major General Sir Louis Jackson, 1919

Who the hell wants to hear actors talk?

H.M. Warner, Warner Brothers, 1927

Stocks have reached what looks like a permanently high plateau.

Irving Fisher, Professor of Economics, Yale University, 1929

We only have to kick in the door and the whole rotten structure will come crashing down.

Adolf Hitler on Germany's prospects in the USSR, 1941

As yet there is no immediate prospect of the invasion.

Assessment by German forces on the eve of D-Day, June 1944

I think there is a world market for maybe five computers.

Thomas Watson, Chairman of IBM, 1941

Not to mince words, Mr Epstein, we don't like your boys' sound. Groups of four guitarists are on the way out.

Decca Records executive Dick Rowe, rejecting The Beatles, 1962

Internet 'may be just a passing fad as millions give up on it'

Headline in the *Daily Mail*, 2000

CASUALTIES IN WELLINGTON'S ARMY 1811–1814

	General	Officer	Soldier
Wounded	40%	29%	18%
Killed or died of wounds	10%	6.5%	5.2%
Disease or accident	6%	3.6%	11.3%

Being a general in the Duke of Wellington's army in the late Peninsular War was extremely dangerous. Generals had around a 50% chance of being killed or wounded in battle. The only category in which the enlisted men were more likely to die was from disease or accident; they were twice as likely to die from this as their senior commanders. This suggests that generals, while not sparing themselves on the battlefield, made sure they had access to the best food and accommodation away from it.

ODD JOBS OF MODERN LEADERS

Leader	Odd Job	Later Title
Ho Chi Minh	Pastry Chef	President of Vietnam
Heinrich Himmler	Pig Farmer	Reichsführer SS
Herbert Hoover	Gold Miner	President of the USA
Idi Amin	Doughnut Vendor	President of Uganda
Jorge Bergoglio	Nightclub Bouncer	Pope Francis

DAY OF FATE

Important events in German history have frequently occured on 9 November, dubbed *Schicksalstag*, 'Day of Fate'. In 1918, Kaiser Wilhelm II abdicated. In 1923, Adolf Hitler's Nazis attempted the Munich Putsch, and in 1938 they attacked Jews on *Kristallnacht*. In 1989, the Berlin Wall fell.

Saint-Domingue (modern Haiti) was a valuable French colony in the Caribbean that produced vast amounts of sugar on plantations worked by enslaved Africans. It was one of the world's most profitable colonies, the value of the exports to France almost equalling the value of all exports from the 13 American colonies to Britain.

In 1791, inspired by revolution in France, the enslaved population rose up. It was the start of more than a decade of astonishingly brutal fighting that saw hundreds of thousands killed. In 1804, France grudgingly accepted Haitian independence, making it the only successful slave revolt in history. Toussaint L'Ouverture, aka the 'Black Spartacus', and Jean-Jacques Dessalines won towering reputations as leaders of the revolt but there are a notable number of women who held senior positions, and we have listed a few of them here:

Victoria Montou

Believed to be a member of the all-female elite unit of the Dahomey Empire (which inspired the recent movie *The Woman King*) before Montou was abducted from West Africa, she was enslaved alongside Jean-Jacques Dessalines. She trained him to fight and served alongside him in battle.

Marie-Jeanne Lamartinière

Lamartinière wore a uniform and served alongside the men defending the Crête-à-Pierrot fort from a French assault. She used her sword to great effect in the press of battle and was a good shot with a musket, sniping at French troops at longer range.

Sanité Bélair

Bélair seems to have joined as a soldier and was rapidly promoted, becoming a lieutenant in the revolutionary army. When captured by French forces, Bélair's husband handed himself over too because he couldn't bear to be separated from her. Both were sentenced to death. She watched her husband's execution, having told him to die bravely. Then she refused a blindfold for her own execution and shouted just before the firing squad did its work, 'Viv libète! A ba esclavaj!' ('Long live freedom! Down with slavery!')

MONASTIC ORDERS FOUNDING

Order	Founded	Founded By	Type
Benedictines	c. 529	St Benedict	Monastic
Cluniacs	910	William I	Monastic
Carthusians	1084	Bruno of Cologne	Monastic
Cistercians	1098	Robert of Molesme	Monastic
Knights Hospitaller	1113	Crusaders	Military
Knights Templar	1119	Hugues de Payens	Military
Premonstratensians	1120	Norbert of Xanten	Monastic
Teutonic Knights	1190	German merchants	Military
Trinitarians	1198	St John of Matha	Monastic
Franciscans	1209	St Francis of Assisi	Mendicant
Dominicans	1216	St Dominic	Mendicant

Monks and monasteries are a familiar feature of Christianity, and their way of life emerged from the region around Syria and Egypt early in Christianity's history, as small groups came together to live in prayer and service to God. Monastic devotion emphasises greater dedication to worship through the rejection of worldly pursuits, though Christian monasticism is itself divided into several groups, each with a particular focus. Mendicant friars, who roamed without a monastery as a base living off the generosity of others, sought to

imitate the work of Jesus more closely. Military orders also grew up as a result of crusading, primarily in the Near East, but also on the Iberian Peninsula (now Spain and Portugal), and the Teutonic Knights eventually forged a kingdom in central Europe on the south coast of the Baltic Sea.

LITURGY OF HOURS – A MEDIEVAL CLOCK

Within monasteries, the daily routine of prayer was broken into eight defined sessions that structured the day. The Liturgy of Hours was designed in the 6th century by St Benedict and changed little over the following millennium.

Matins: The service held at sunrise.

Prime: Held within the first hour after sunrise.

Terce: Held three hours after sunrise.

Sext: Celebrated six hours after sunrise.

None: The service that came nine hours after sunrise.

Vespers: Said at sunset (the forerunner of Evensong).

Compline: Marked bedtime in the monastery.

Vigils: A service held in the middle of the night.

All daily work, whether in the fields, preaching, writing or illustrating, had to be made to fit around these services that provided the structure for every day in a monastery.

AN ORDER TO KILL?

The murder of Thomas Becket, Archbishop of Canterbury on 29 December 1170, inside Canterbury Cathedral, sent shockwaves across Europe. Henry II was long credited with roaring the words, 'Will no one rid me of this turbulent priest?'

Edward Grim, a monk at Canterbury who was with Thomas, wrote an account of it all later. The words he discovered Henry said translate from Latin as 'What miserable drones and traitors have I nurtured and promoted in my household who let their lord be treated with such shameful contempt by a low-born cleric!'

Did Henry, who had once been very close to Becket, mean to order the Archbishop's death? Four knights loyal to the king rode away to Canterbury believing they were following his instructions. Henry insisted he never intended for Becket to be murdered. In 1174, as he faced rebellion to his rule, he prayed for forgiveness at Becket's tomb.

European castle building began in the 9th and 10th centuries to secure local areas from lawlessness. Castles vary greatly in size and layout, but many features are common.

Keep: The large, usually rectangular building that is the defensive core of the castle, the place to make a last stand. Keeps were originally called donjons, a French term that is the root of the word dungeon as a place for storing things you want to keep secure.

Baileys: Areas that surround the castle, sometimes in circles, sometimes as a series of spaces. In peacetime, they might house tradesmen. When under attack, they provide defensive areas.

Walls: Encircling a castle with walls helped to project dominance over the surrounding area, but also made it hard to assault, offering a vital first line of defence. Crenellations or ramparts are the series of alternating high and low areas around a wall or tower that offer cover for defenders.

Towers: Rectangular towers offered the most internal space, but flat outer walls were vulnerable to bombardment and corners could be undermined. Circular towers deflected missiles more effectively, but they sacrificed internal space.

Moat: Some castles had moats, sometimes filled with water and sometimes dry moats. They served as another layer of defence that made it harder for an attacker to get close to the walls.

Gatehouse: If a castle has a moat, it will need a drawbridge, which can be raised when under attack. The gatehouse may also have features like a portcullis, a large metal gate that could be dropped to block the entrance, and murder holes above to allow defenders to drop things on attackers.

Ishiyama Hongan-ji (1570–80)

Once considered an impenetrable fortress in what is now Osaka, Japan, Ishiyama Honga-ji was held by a faction of Buddhist monks and peasants opposed to the samurai class. The warlord Oda Nobunaga laid siege to it with 30,000 soldiers. The siege dragged on for close to 11 years before the defenders surrendered.

The Fall of Philadelphia (1378 – 1390)

When the Byzantine Emperor gave the city of Philadelphia (Asia Minor) to the Ottoman Turks, the residents refused to accept it and held out for 12 years. In a strange twist the Ottomans forced the Byzantines, who were by now a vassal state, to the siege. The defenders surrendered upon seeing the imperial banner.

Siege of Candia (1648–1669)

The Ottomans landed 60,000 troops on Venetian Crete in June 1645, occupying the island and then laying siege on the Duchy's capital of Candia. In 1669, an allied French force moved to lift the siege, but the expedition failed with the loss of its flagship. Having held out for 21 years, the Venetian garrison finally surrendered.

Siege of Ceuta (1694–1720)

Also known as 'the thirty-year siege', Moroccan forces blockaded the Spanish-held city of Ceuta on the north coast of Africa. It is the longest siege in history, and was lifted by Spanish forces after 26 years. The relief forces left the city and the Moroccans besieged the city again from 1721 to 1726, when they finally left.

THE ROMAN PHAROS

The Roman Pharos (lighthouse), which sits in the grounds of Dover Castle, is the most complete standing Roman structure in Britain. The pharos was built around 50 AD and was originally six storeys high, although it now stands at four storeys. It is one of only three surviving Roman lighthouses in the world.

Lake Titicaca: (Notable city / Civilisation): Tiwanaku / Andean
Situated almost 4,000 metres above sea level on the border of Peru and Bolivia, Lake Titicaca is the highest navigable lake in the world.

Oxus River: Bactra (Balkh) / Oxus
Starting in the Pamir Mountains and flowing down into the Aral Sea, the Oxus River is today the Amu Darya.

Indus River: Harappa / Indus Valley
Situated in modern Pakistan, beginning in the Himalayas and flowing out into the Indian Ocean.

River Nile: Thebes / Egypt
The Nile River and its fertile soils were vital to the ancient Egyptians and their agricultural-based civilisation. It was also a vital ancient motorway, critical for trade and connecting the lands of the Pharaoh.

Euphrates: Babylon / Mesopotamia
Situated in modern-day Iraq. Ancient civilisation after civilisation wrestled for control of this wealthy area of the world, from the Assyrians to the Romans.

Yellow River: Luoyang / Chinese
Farming communities were cultivating rice along the Yellow River more than 5,000 years ago. It was here that the first Chinese dynasty, the Xia Dynasty, emerged in the late 3rd millennium BC.

Red River: Cổ Loa / Vietnamese
Farming communities emerged along this valley from the 3rd millenium BC onwards, cultivating wet rice.

SHORTEST WAR IN HISTORY

The shortest war in history is the Anglo-Zanzibar War, which lasted 38 minutes on 27 August 1896. It followed the refusal of the Zanzibari Sultan to step down after the British issued an ultimatum. British warships then fired on his position and the Sultan surrendered.

Witchcraft was not a common charge in the medieval world. There are examples of it being deployed for political aims against powerful women. Henry V had his stepmother Joan of Navarre imprisoned as a witch so that he could seize her property. Eleanor Cobham was forced to divorce Humphrey, Duke of Gloucester, whose nephew Henry VI was convinced the couple were plotting against him. Such charges were used during the Wars of the Roses (1455–87) to destabilise enemies.

There is little evidence of a genuine belief in witchcraft until the early modern period. Perhaps the most influential text was *Malleus Maleficarum* (*The Hammer of the Witches*), written by Heinrich Kramer in 1486. As fear rose, witch trials in Europe reached their peak from around 1560–1630, with estimates suggesting 40–60,000 people may have been executed, around 80% of them women. As the 17th century progressed, the scepticism around witchcraft that had always existed began to win through.

As fear of witches waned in Europe, it broke out in the New World. In 1692, the Salem witch trials in Massachusetts saw more than 200 accused, 30 found guilty, and 19 of them hanged – 14 women and 5 men. Witch trials seem to frequently be a mix of local community and political issues as much as religious concern or genuine fear. There have been theories that ergotism might be behind the hysteria. Ergot is a fungus that grows on rye and other cereals. It can cause confusion, headaches, hallucinations and other symptoms often associated with outbreaks of witchcraft accusations.

Sire ~ it is the misfortune of your life that you should never have been acquainted with the language of truth, until you heard it in the complaints of your people. It is not, however, too late to correct the error.

'Junius' writes to George III, 1770

They are really the shabbiest set of dirty politicians that was ever seen.

Former Prime Minister Lord Grenville said of the Tories who replaced his government, 1807

I will engage that there is not, even amongst the lowest of the people, a single man now to be found in England, who would not laugh to scorn any attempt to make him believe that one of the parties is better than the other.

William Cobbett, 1816

Never surely was there a man at the head of affairs so weak, undecided and utterly useless.

William Huskisson, a former cabinet colleague of Prime Minister Viscount Goderich, 1828

Many of us . . . have a feeling that we are living in a country where fanatics, hooligans and eccentrics have got the upper hand.

British Ambassador to Berlin, 1933

Politics is more difficult than physics.

Albert Einstein, 1946

It has been said that democracy is the worst form of government except for all those other forms that have been tried from time to time.

Winston Churchill, 1947

The *Diamond Sutra*

Printed in 868 AD in China, it is considered the oldest surviving printed book in the world, using woodblock printing.

Nag Hammadi Library

In 1945, an Egyptian farmer discovered the Nag Hammadi library buried in a jar near Nag Hammadi. It consists of 12 papyrus codices written in Coptic Egyptian and dates back to the 3rd–4th centuries.

Codex Sinaiticus

Written in the 4th century in Greek, it is one of the oldest surviving complete Christian Bibles.

Gärima Gospels

These two Ge'ez-language illuminated books date back to 390–570 AD. The first book has its front cover attached, making it the oldest book with this feature.

Pseudo-Apuleius Herbarius

Compiled in the 4th century, this was the most influential herbal books in Europe during the medieval period, containing descriptions and illustrations of plants and their medicinal properties.

St Cuthbert Gospel

Written in the 7th century in Latin, this Gospel is the oldest surviving European book with an original intact binding. It was discovered in 1104 when the coffin of St Cuthbert was opened at Durham Cathedral.

Codex Parisino-Petropolitanus

A 7th–8th-century manuscript that contains some of the oldest extant copies of the Quran. Originally kept in Egypt, it came to Europe after the Napoleonic expedition of 1798, when a few folios were brought to Paris.

Rule of St Benedict

This 8th-century manuscript is the earliest surviving copy of the guide to the principles of monastic life, which was enumerated by St. Benedict of Nursia around 540.

EXPENSIVE COLLECTIBLES SOLD AT AUCTION

Item	Artist/Creator	($m)	Year
Salvator Mundi	Leonardo da Vinci	450.3	2017
Shot Sage Blue Marilyn	Andy Warhol	195.0	2022
Les Femmes d'Alger	Pablo Picasso	179.4	2015
The Gigayacht	Frank Mulder	168.0	–
Pointing Man sculpture	Alberto Giacometti	141.3	2015
Rabbit	Jeff Koons	91.1	2019
Pool with Two Figures	David Hockney	90.3	2018
Oppenheimer Diamond	–	57.5	2016
1962 Ferrari 250 GTO	–	48.4	2018
White Flower No 1	Georgia O'Keeffe	44.4	2014

EMU WAR

In 1932 the government of Western Australia declared war on emus, a native bird species that was damaging crops in the region. The government sent soldiers armed with machine guns to hunt the emus, who proved elusive. Despite firing thousands of rounds of ammunition, the soldiers were able to kill 'only a few' emus before the government declared peace after less than a week.

BEYOND THE PALE?

A 'pale' refers to a wooden stake or palisade, which makes a boundary. The phrase 'beyond the pale' refers to anything being outside an authority's boundary being uncivilised.

In the late Middle Ages, English power in Ireland had waned to a strip of land around Dublin, surrounded by a fortified boundary ditch (The Pale). Thus it is commonly thought that 'beyond the pale' refers specifically to this boundary. However, the *Oxford English Dictionary* states there is insufficient evidence to support the term's exact origins.

Often seen as the preserve of men like Blackbeard and Captain Kidd during the Golden Age of Piracy (1690–1730), there have also been several significant female pirates. From Dido, who, according to legend, founded Carthage before 800 BC and operated as a pirate, women have long been involved in piratical activities.

Jeanne de Clisson (1300–59) was known as the Lioness of Brittany. After her husband was executed by the King of France during the War of the Breton Succession, Jeanne became captain of a fleet of three ships, all painted black with red sails. She would kill entire crews of French merchant vessels, leaving only one alive to deliver a message to the King of France that Jeanne was still seeking vengeance. She was eventually employed by Edward III of England to support his efforts in the Hundred Years' War.

During the Golden Age of Piracy, women were frequently found among pirate crews. Perhaps the most famous were Anne Bonny and Mary Read, who were recorded in Captain Charles Johnson's *A General History of the Pyrates* in 1724. Much of the detail of their lives is speculation, but he reports that Anne married the pirate James Bonny and had an affair with another, 'Calico Jack' Rackham. Mary joined Rackham's crew after her ship was captured.

Both were disguised as men for a time and fought alongside the crew. One of their victims wrote that they 'wore men's jackets, and long trousers, and handkerchiefs tied about their heads: and . . . each of them had a machete and pistol in their hands and they cursed and swore', with some sources claiming they fought bare-chested. After their capture and conviction for piracy, both pleaded pregnancy to escape hanging. Mary died soon afterward, perhaps as a result of childbirth, and Anne's final fate is unknown.

As recently as the 1990s, a Chinese woman known as 'Sister Ping' owned and financed pirate ships in the South China Sea as a 'Snakehead' (human smuggler), running the world's largest people smuggling network for 20 years. She was convicted in the United States for smuggling Chinese immigrants to the US and Europe and sentenced to 35 years in prison, where she died in 2014.

This is the chapter of naval history they don't teach or celebrate in England. In June 1667, just two years after the country was ravaged by plague, a year after the capital city had been decimated in a Great Fire, the Dutch sailed into the HQ of the Royal Navy and sank, burned or stole the larger part of King Charles II's fleet while it sat helpless at its moorings.

By the summer of 1667 King Charles was broke and there was no money to pay for the fleet. Charles was in Breda, suing for peace with the Dutch, trying to end the Second Anglo-Dutch War. The biggest, most powerful ships were 'laid up', stripped of their crews and many of their more perishable fittings, and kept at anchor in the River Medway in Kent. Complacent about the possibility of attack, they were largely unmanned and unprotected. The naval base at Chatham was the kingdom's primary installation, the best place to deploy from to meet England's most potent adversary at the time, the Dutch. But the sea is a two-way street.

In early June the Dutch sailed into the Thames Estuary. They bombarded, captured and demolished Sheerness Castle and sailed up the Medway towards Chatham. The English desperately tried to block the river. They sank ships, ran a chain from one side to the other and reinforced Upnor Castle. None of that stopped the Dutch, who brushed aside the chain, and blasted any ships or land-based artillery that attempted to engage them. They set fire to ships and captured a few of the biggest and best. The pinnacle of humiliation was the capture of the *Royal Charles*, the pride of Charles's fleet, bearing his own name. It was deemed so important that the Dutch towed it back to Holland.

English losses were over a dozen, including three of the four biggest battleships in the navy. On top of this the English sank 30 of their own ships to avoid their capture. The only glimmer of good news was that the Dutch did not press their advantage and attack the defenceless capital city, instead choosing to head home with their loot. The *Royal Charles* became a tourist attraction in Holland, and its stern still sits in Amsterdam's Rijksmuseum.

THE QUEEN OF DIPLOMACY

Overseas tours, hostings and visits by Queen Elizabeth II 1952–2022.

Occasion	Number
Official overseas royal tours	285
State visits hosted by Elizabeth II	116
State visits made by Elizabeth II	97*
Countries visited on official occasions	106

*97 as Queen of the United Kingdom. Two as Queen of Canada.

During her reign, Queen Elizabeth II also met 13 US Presidents (her reign spanned 14) and oversaw 15 British Prime Ministers. She also met with hundreds of Commonwealth leaders.

BIRTH OF PHOTOGRAPHY

In 1826, Joseph Nicéphore Niépce produced the first permanent photograph, a 'heliograph', using a camera obscura to capture an image of the view from his window onto a polished pewter plate coated with bitumen – which hardened in the areas exposed to light, creating a permanent image. Niépce continued to refine his process with Louis Daguerre's help. After Niépce's death, Daguerre developed the daguerreotype, which produced highly detailed, one-of-a-kind images on a polished silver plate.

James Clerk Maxwell took the 'first durable colour photograph' in 1861 by taking three separate photos of the same subject through red, green and blue filters and projecting them onto a screen with matching filters. The Lumière brothers developed a commercially successful colour photo in 1907 using a simpler 'Autochrome' process. George Eastman pioneered the use of photographic film, starting with paper film in 1885, then celluloid in 1888, creating rollable photographic film made from nitrocellulose that allowed for multiple exposures. His 'Kodak' camera (introduced in 1888) made photography more accessible.

On 20 October 1803, the United States purchased one-third of modern America from Napoleon's France. And it only cost them $15 million. Extending from parts of Canada to the city of New Orleans, the territory of Louisiana had been claimed by France since 1699. It switched hands to the Spanish in 1762, but Napoleon made a bid to reclaim the territory by transferring French troops to New Orleans in 1801.

Yet a disastrous French expedition to prevent rebellion in Haiti convinced Napoleon that his destiny lay instead in Europe. In 1803, negotiations for the purchase of New Orleans began, with the American party prepared to pay $10 million for the city alone. The Americans did not anticipate the French Treasury Minister Barbé-Marbois' offer of the entire Louisiana Territory for $15 million – an offer made at Napoleon's insistence. The Americans wasted no time in signing it, effectively doubling the size of the United States of America.

With Louisiana, President Thomas Jefferson secured a vast tract of land to furnish his vision of small, independent landowners expanding westwards over the continent. Expeditions were instructed to explore its wilderness; the military was authorised to take possession.

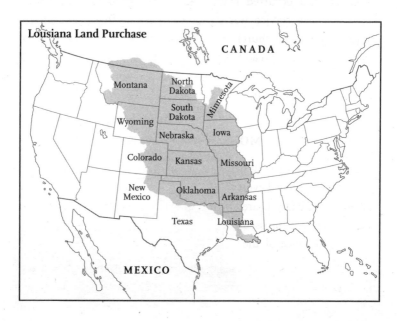

The West was seen as open territory to be occupied. In truth it was already occupied by a native population – now alarmed by a wave of migrants backed by the US army, which would inflict military defeats upon a Shawnee-led defensive alliance at the battles of Tippecanoe (1811) and the Thames (1813).

The acquisition of land that stretched from the Mississippi River to the Rocky Mountains was Jefferson's greatest contribution to the nascent Union. It was, however, also the prelude for subsequent decades' policy of 'Indian removal' that, between 1810 and 1850, resulted in more than 100,000 Native Americans of 30 tribes voluntarily or forcibly relocating westward into newly designated 'Indian Territory'.

DANCING MANIA

In July, 1518, Frau Troffea began dancing in chaotic fervour on the streets of Strasbourg. She danced for a week straight, and soon others joined her. Within a month, the Dancing Plague of 1518 claimed between 50 and 400 victims. Historical sources make it clear the victims danced, but why they did remains unexplained. Mysterious outbreaks had occurred before: in 1020s Bernburg, Germany, a Christmas Eve service was disturbed when revellers inexplicably danced around the church. In Aachen, 1374, a large-scale outbreak was recorded that spread to Cologne, Flanders, Hainaut, Strasbourg, Utrecht and other towns. In 1428 in Schaffhausen, a monk even danced himself to death.

MORBID OBSESSION

For the last five years of his life, Holy Roman Emperor Maximilian I (r. 1508–19) travelled everywhere with his coffin. In 1501 he fell from his horse and badly injured his leg. Some historians have suggested he was 'morbidly' depressed as a consequence of the accident.

──────────────── THE WINDRUSH ────────────────

The Windrush generation refers to people who migrated to the United Kingdom between 1948 and 1971 from Caribbean countries (mainly Jamaica, Trinidad and Tobago, and Barbados) to help fill post-war labour shortages in Britain.

The term 'Windrush' comes from the name of the first ship, the *Empire Windrush*, which brought the first group of Caribbean migrants to the UK, arriving at Tilbury Docks, Essex, on 22 June 1948, carrying 492 passengers.

The Windrush generation includes those who came to the UK as British subjects and citizens to help rebuild post-war Britain, as well as their children and grandchildren who were born or grew up in the UK. The Windrush generation and their descendants are now estimated to make up around 3% of the UK population.

When the Immigration Act 1971 came into force on 1 January 1973, the position of these Commonwealth citizens was preserved. The Act also preserved the right to come and go for those who had already arrived, and recognised the right of their wives (not husbands) and children to join them.

The Windrush migrants were British citizens and had the right to live and work in the UK indefinitely, but many did not have documents to prove their status. In 2018, it was revealed that the UK government had wrongly classified some Windrush migrants as illegal immigrants and had subjected them to deportation, detention and denial of rights to healthcare, housing and employment, prompting a public apology and a commitment to reform the UK immigration system.

──────────────── CAN'T STOP LAUGHING ────────────────

In 1962, a mysterious epidemic of laughter broke out in a girls' school in Tanganyika (now Tanzania). The laughter quickly spread to other schools and eventually to the surrounding villages, affecting thousands of people. The epidemic lasted for several months and was so severe that many schools were forced to close.

India's most famous structure is a monument to romantic love. The Taj Mahal is a mausoleum some 350 years old, commissioned by Shah Jahan, the Mughal Emperor between 1628 and 1658. It is dedicated to the memory of his favourite wife, Mumtaz Mahal, who died in childbirth in 1631.

Overlooking the Yamuna River, the Taj Mahal is located in Agra, once the capital of the Mughal Empire that covered much of South Asia. Distinguished by its white marble, elegant minarets, elaborately crafted facades and soaring central dome, the Taj Mahal is also the zenith of Mughal architecture, described by Bengali poet Rabindranath Tagore as 'a teardrop on the face of eternity'.

The Taj Mahal incorporates much of what ultimately defined Mughal architecture's blend of Indian, Persian and Islamic styles. It stands to the north of a vast walled garden in Islamic style, with long pools in which the Taj Mahal is reflected. Decorating the complex – and balancing the mausoleum's extensive white marble, which reflects different colours as daylight changes – are verses from the Quran inscribed in Arabic calligraphy, and inlaid gemstones, including jade, lapis lazuli and crystal turquoise. It took 22 years and 20,000 people to construct the entire complex, which also includes a mosque and gateway. The mausoleum itself was finished around 1638–39.

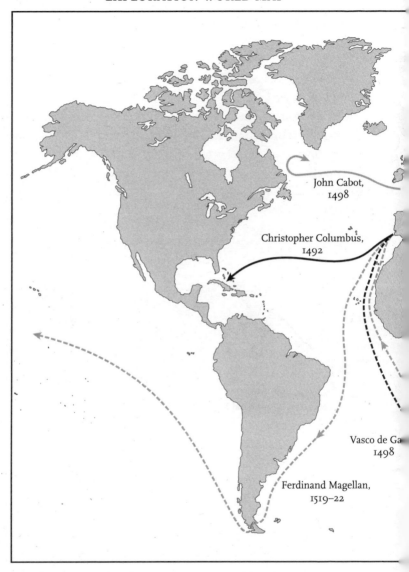

John Cabot,
1498

Christopher Columbus,
1492

Vasco de Ga
1498

Ferdinand Magellan,
1519–22

In the early modern era, improvements in ship design and navigational techniques enabled explorers to pioneer new shipping routes
across the seas and link up far flung regions around the world. At the
turn of the 16th century, European navigators not only established

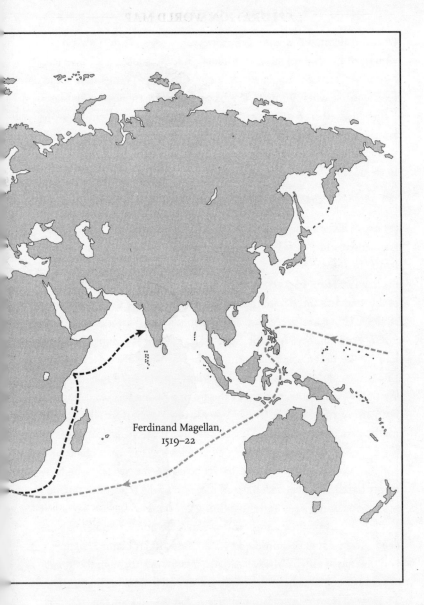

Ferdinand Magellan,
1519–22

routes to the Americas and back, but forged a new route between Asia and Europe. Suddenly it was possible to sail directly between the Americas, Europe, Asia and Africa. This would have world-changing consequences.

Otto von Bismarck is among European history's greatest statesmen, who used his diplomatic and military guile to mastermind the unification of Germany for Kaiser Wilhelm I in 1871. Things took a turn for the worse when Wilhelm II took over in 1888. An ageing Bismarck found himself in regular contention with the new Kaiser. After one argument too many, he was replaced as Chancellor. His tomb reads 'Loyal Subject of Kaiser Wilhelm I', a not so subtle dig at Wilhelm II.

OXFORD'S TOWN AND GOWN DIVIDE

Oxford University is known as the oldest university in the English-speaking world. There is evidence of teaching in the town from at least 1096. In 1209, an Oxford student accidentally killed a woman from the town and fled. In revenge, the mayor oversaw the arrest and hanging of the student's three roommates. Outraged, many of the teachers and students left Oxford and set up a new institution at Cambridge.

On 10 February 1355, St Scholastica's Day, a group of Oxford University students were drinking in the town's Swindlestock Tavern. The innkeeper, John Barford, also happened to be the mayor. When the students complained about the quality of his ale, an argument erupted during which a tankard was thrown at Barford's head. The mayor ran to St Martin's Church and rang the bells to rouse the town. The students rang the bells of St Mary's to call out all their own support. A riot broke out and by the evening the students had the upper hand. The next day, Barford rode out of the town and returned with 2,000 more men and the fighting continued.

By the end of the rioting 30 townspeople and 63 students were dead. An investigation ordered by King Edward III blamed the town, and the mayor and bailiffs were instructed to walk through the streets of Oxford each St Scholastica's Day and attend a Mass for those killed. They were then required to publicly recognise the university's privileges and pay a fine of 63 pence, one for each student killed. The parade was repeated every year, with the officials jeered by students, until 1825, when the mayor refused to take part. With the university's agreement, it was abandoned after more than 450 years.

THE END OF HISTORY?

By 1989 the Soviet Union was beginning to dissolve. The American political scientist Francis Fukuyama published his essay *The End of History?* that summer. The essay argued that Western liberal democracy had triumphed against other forms of government, such as communism and fascism, and that it was the final form of government for all nations.

> *That is, the end-point of mankind's ideological evolution and the universalization of Western liberal democracy as the final form of human government.*
>
> **Francis Fukuyama, 1989**

The Soviet flag was lowered from the Kremlin on Christmas Day 1991, by which time all of the Soviet states had declared their independence. Fukuyama expanded his thesis in his 1992 book *The End of History and the Last Man*, which gained mainstream popularity.

However, it was not without its critics. Fukuyama's former Harvard professor Samuel P. Hungton published *The Clash of Civilizations and the Remaking of the World Order* in 1996, which contested that cultural and religious identity would be the main source of conflict in the post-Cold War world.

The strength of autocratic regimes such as Russia and China, the 2008 Financial Crisis, along with growing populist movements across Europe, further challenged the notion that liberal democracy was unnassailable or the last form of human government. Despite Fukuyama's claim, history, it seems, will keep on going.

THE EVOLUTION OF GOODBYE

The first use of 'goodbye' was recorded in a letter by Gabriel Harvey in 1573, which reads: 'To requite your gallonde of godbwyes, I regive you a pottle of howdyes.' 'Goodbwye' is a diminution of the phrase 'God be with ye'. Phrases such as 'good day' or 'good evening' grew in usage around the same period, and 'God' in 'God be with ye' was substituted with 'Good' and the phrase shortened.

SOME HISTORICAL MYTHS, CORRECTED

Napoleon wasn't short. Napoleon was 1.7 metres or 5 feet 7 inches tall – average for the time period. There was a difference between the French and British inch at the time.

At the Battle of Hastings, King Harold was probably hacked to pieces by a Norman hit squad rather than shot in the eye by an arrow.

Viking helmets did not have horns on them. That was a 19th-century German opera invention.

Adolf Hitler didn't snub Jesse Owens at the Berlin 1936 Olympics. Owens said that they greeted each other and that it was his own American politicians who snubbed him.

There is no evidence that Shah Jahan mutilated or blinded anyone after the construction of the Taj Mahal.

Emperor Nero didn't play the fiddle while Rome burned. The fiddle didn't exist in 64 AD and there is no strong evidence he played an instrument during the fire.

George Washington didn't have wooden teeth. The most likely explanation is that he had some ivory teeth, which were easily stained.

Thomas Edison didn't invent the light bulb. He just improved it.

Tomorrow, at sunrise, I shall no longer be here.

**Michel de Nostredame, better known
as Nostradamus**

Pardon me, sir, I didn't mean to.

**Marie Antoinette, after accidentally stepping on her
executioner's foot before being beheaded**

I must go in, the fog is rising.

Emily Dickinson

*I have offended God and mankind because my work
did not reach the quality it should have.*

Leonardo da Vinci

Pity, pity, too late!

**Ludwig van Beethoven, as he was told of a gift
of 12 bottles of wine from his publisher**

They couldn't hit an elephant at this distance.

**General John Sedgwick, Union Army commander killed
in action during the American Civil War**

*This wallpaper and I are fighting a duel to
the death. Either it goes or I do.*

Oscar Wilde

I'm bored with it all.

Sir Winston Churchill

ACKNOWLEDGEMENTS

The original idea from this book came from twenty years' worth of notes that Dan Snow kept on his Evernote. There were a thousand or so historical gems to inspire us, but then we embellished with the rest of the History Hit team's own historical truffle hunting and knowledge, particularly the stories shared from thousands of guests on our podcasts over the years. So a thank you to Dan for his extensive record keeping, thanks to our editing team for bringing it all together and a huge thanks to the many, many interviewees who have furthered history for millions of listeners to History Hit.

Another thank you to the publishing team at Hodder: Rupert Lancaster, Ciara Mongey and Christian Duck for first being so excited about the idea, and then spending the time to refine it into what it is now. It was a pleasure to work with you all. Also our page designer, Briony Hartley, who did a fantastic job arranging the giant historical word salad we created into a tasty dish.

To our agents, who got us all sorts of interesting meetings and first helped to shape our initial proposal: Caspian Dennis at Abner Stein, and David Larabelle at CAA.

Lastly, to all the History Hit team who continue to work tirelessly across our audio network, online TV channel and website. Finding and telling amazing historical stories is what this book is all about.

CONTRIBUTORS

Editor: James Carson
Assistant Editor: Kyle Hoekstra
Contributors: Dan Snow, Matthew Lewis, Tristan Hughes,
Amy Irvine, Celeste Neill, Rob Weinberg
Additional Contributions from: Mariana Des Forges, Luke Tomes,
Lily Johnson

Publisher: Rupert Lancaster
Managing Editor: Christian Duck
Assistant Editor: Ciara Mongey

Page Design: Briony Hartley
Maps: Jeff Edwards
Picture Research: Lesley Hodgson
Battle of Gaugamela Drawings: Barking Dog Art
Copyeditor: Ross Jamieson
Proofreader: Jacqui Lewis

PICTURE CREDITS

HISTORY HIT

History Hit is an online channel of hundreds of exclusive history documentaries and thousands of podcasts that subscribers can access. You can watch and listen on web, mobile app and on your smart TV.

With this book, you can get a special offer of 50% off your first three months to History Hit on a monthly subscription. Or, if you want to sign up for an annual subscription, you can get 25% off the standard annual price.

All you need to do to claim this offer is head to **historyhit.com/subscribe**, enter your details and use one of the following codes:

Monthly: MISCELLANY3

Annual: MISCELLANY12

Sign up today, and you'll get access to more history than you can ever finish.

First published in Great Britain in 2023
by Hodder & Stoughton
An Hachette UK company

3

Copyright © Hit Networks Ltd 2023

The right of Hit Networks Ltd to be identified as the
Author of the Work has been asserted by them in accordance
with the Copyright, Designs and Patents Act 1988.

A CIP catalogue record for this title is available
from the British Library

Hardback ISBN 9781399726009
Trade Paperback ISBN 9781399727341
ebook ISBN 9781399726023

Typeset in Scala Pro by Goldust Design

Printed and bound in Great Britain by
Clays Ltd, Elcograf S.p.A.

Hodder & Stoughton policy is to use papers that
are natural, renewable and recyclable products and made
from wood grown in sustainable forests. The logging and
manufacturing processes are expected to conform to the
environmental regulations of the country of origin.

Hodder & Stoughton Ltd
Carmelite House
50 Victoria Embankment
London EC4Y 0DZ

www.hodder.co.uk